SATAN'S ARENA

by

Christopher Chance

Strand Non Fiction

Copyright © 2022 Strand Publishing UK Ltd

The right of Christopher Chance to be identified as the author of this work has been asserted in accordance with the Copyright, Designs and Patents Act 1988.

All rights reserved. No reproduction, copy or transmission of this publication may be made without written permission. No paragraph of this publication may be reproduced, copied or transmitted save with the written permission or in accordance with the provisions of the Copyright Act 1956 (as amended.) Any person who does any unauthorised act in relation to this publication may be liable to criminal prosecution and civil claims for damage.

First published 2022 by Strand Publishing UK Ltd
Registered in England & Wales Company Number 07034246
Registered address: 11 St Michael Street,
Malton, North Yorkshire, YO17 7LJ

info@strandpublishing.co.uk
www.strandpublishing.co.uk

Paperback edition
ISBN 978-1-907340-26-0

*This book is dedicated to
the love of my life, my wife, Susan*

Psalms 23 – The King James Bible

A Psalm of David

The Lord is my shepherd; I shall not want.
He maketh me to lie down in green pastures: he leadeth me beside the still waters.
He restoreth my soul: he leadeth me in the paths of righteousness for his name's sake.
Yea, though I walk through the valley of the shadow of death, I will fear no evil: for thou art with me; thy rod and thy staff they comfort me.
Thou preparest a table before me in the presence of mine enemies: thou anointest my head with oil; my cup runneth over.
Surely goodness and mercy shall follow me all the days of my life: and I will dwell in the house of the LORD forever.

Acknowledgements

To the men of the Mezclado who were strong, tough characters who, just like the Musketeers with their *all for one and one for all* attitude, rose above the stress of the animal life that existed in the infamous Carabanchel prison in Madrid and made my survival in prison successful:

Ali Saff, Iranian hit man and Hapkido Black Belt,
Vito, Sicilian Mafioso assassin (the real thing),
Jake, the Belgian bouncer (fearless tough guy),
Abdulla Habibullah (Afghani mujahidin War Lord),
Lucky Johnstone, black guy sporting facial tribal scars (skilled RIB jockey),
Kennedy, black guy (highly skilled mariner),
Chinky, Bruce Lee lookalike (skilled Chinese martial artist).

Mike Sherman, Californian (skilled mariner with a positive, sensitive nature and my best cellmate).

Mark Wingett (actor and all round great guy) for his friendship and support for my writing and especially for his performance in THE DAREDEVIL DRUG RUNNER series 6, episode 6, for *National Geographic* (currently screening worldwide).

Last but not least, for her professional integrity, support, encouragement and friendship my editor Jane Lee.

From the bottom of my heart I thank you all

Christopher Chance

SATAN'S ARENA

Out Of The Frying Pan

Blood contrasted starkly with the whiteness of the shirt as it sprayed from the torn jugular vein of the Spanish prison officer's neck, across the front of the fresh white shirt of the jefe del servicio[1] who was standing next to him, on the day the Carabanchel closed its gates for the last time.

That vision returned in vivid detail, sleep was denied, and the memory haunted me yet again as I lay on my prison bed, the shrouds of time peeled back to reveal the day I left the infamous Carabanchel prison in Madrid. The projector in my mind flickered onto the screen of imagination as my history unfurled.

The scream of the injured screw jolted his compadres[2] into action as the giant black inmate bit savagely into his scrawny neck. Shouts and screams pierced the morning sunshine and all eyes were drawn to the goose-fleshing scene before us. Even the buzzing, irritating flies seemed to disappear in the drama of the moment. The mighty black hands encased the screaming head while the great thick neck bulged with the effort of pulling the mouthful of flesh, caught in big, white teeth, away from the spindly neck of the hatchet-faced screw. Fresh blood spurted as the huge black head released its bite momentarily in order to get another scarlet mouthful, eliciting a louder scream in the moment of disengagement. That scream was squeezed to a gurgle as the great white teeth clamped into the ragged tangle of veins and sinews, giving the neck an hourglass appearance, as the screw mercifully fainted into shock.

The stomach-churning spectacle escalated into a thrashing melee as the revenge-incensed Spanish prison officers belaboured the bald, black head with polished hardwood truncheons. The cursing, grunting, scuffling, blue serge uniforms kicked up the dust of the yard and the sunlight glinted off the shiny batons as they thudded into the

---

[1] jefe del servicio - senior officer, chief screw
[2] compadres – workmates, friends

black head, eventually silencing the growling Negro - the crimson mouth was still gnashing its teeth as consciousness departed under the onslaught of flashing truncheons. The blanch-faced screw was hauled away with the flapping wound pulsing blood across the shoulder of the screw helping him to the enfermeria[3], and his compadres became breathless with the effort of beating the body of the inert Negro.

A Guardia Civil[4] officer unholstered his pistol and stooped over the Negro, aiming at point-blank range between the eyes, when the jefe del servicio pulled the aiming arm out of alignment, assuring the green uniformed policeman that it really was not worth all the paperwork and, besides, there were too many witnesses. The Guardia Civil officer purposefully gazed at the dozens of on-looking inmates and then deliberately applied the safety-catch on his pistol. In the fascinating silence of the moment he stood astride the unconscious Negro then, feeling satisfied that he had everyone's attention, repeatedly crashed the butt of the pistol into the ear, mashing it and the surrounding facial tissue into lifelong scars.

A wheelbarrow appeared and the black man was unceremoniously dumped into it face up with his bleeding head hanging over the front, his arms out at the sides and his legs dangled over the handles. A large oafish prison officer grabbed the handles and stumbled away, with three screws alongside extending the wooden lullaby with their discordant batons, as they all scurried out of earshot. Everyone noticed the satisfied crimson smile on the black face before it disappeared into the bowels of the Carabanchel.

Suddenly the spell broke and we were again part of the exodus from this dreadful prison. The prison screws and the escorting Guardia Civil officers quickly forgot about the vengeful Negro and hurriedly pushed and prodded us onto the waiting prison buses, which were to take us away from this ungodly place. That was the Carabanchel, Europe's most sinister prison, in the city of Madrid, Franco's favourite torture chamber, where a multitude of barbaric sins and brutal killings happened with the condoning and licentious

---

[3] enfermeria – infirmary, hospital
[4] Guardia Civil – police officer

grace of the ruling classes, government and the alta burguesia[5]. Those walls were the backdrop to executions and unspeakable cruelty and suffering perpetrated by Spanish prison officers and inmates alike; the training grounds that produced those racist, depraved martinets who strutted around Spanish prisons seeking amusement.

At last Satan's feculent sump was about to close forever. Well, that was what they told us. I personally would not believe it until I saw the dust of the bulldozers settle on that disgraceful pit. But for that moment I was the last Englishman to be shackled and pushed out of there, shoved, prodded and kicked into a stinking prison bus for the six hour journey north to a newly built La Moraleja prison in the Palencia region. The closing days of the Carabanchel were fraught with danger with an intense feeling of vengeance in the air. Due to the closure the inmates and prison officers were to be dispersed to other prisons, so debts had to be paid and long-standing scores settled.

The giant Negro with the big white teeth was from the Caribbean and was married to a girl from Amsterdam. The feud between him and the near headless screw had started several months earlier when the Negro had a vis-à-vis (conjugal rights) visit with his wife. He was taken from his cell to the visiting block where he would meet his wife, who had come all the way from Amsterdam just for a two-hour visit. When they met and hugged deliriously the supervising screw, Scrawny Neck, became so incensed because she was a beautiful white woman, he immediately separated them and quickly threw her out and had the black man escorted screaming and raving back to his cell. The Dutch girl was led out of the prison and rudely told to fuck off back to Holland - white trash! Such was the poisonous mind of this xenophobic administration manned by witless racists.

That last day was payback time for Scrawny Neck who unwittingly placed himself in the path of the outgoing Negro, who could not believe his luck as he was leaving Satan's lavatory. 'Vengeance is mine, sayeth the Lord' – that was Jack Lord, a man I knew years ago that used to fight in the fairground booths. The demise of Scrawny Neck

---

[5] alta burguesia - bourgeoisie

was a wonderful farewell gift for all who witnessed it. I hoped he had nightmares for the rest of his insane life. The furore was soon forgotten as the skittish prison officers continued to process us out of the dying Spanish beast called Carabanchel.

When I boarded the bus I was punched and kicked into it along with the man I was shackled to. We were poked and prodded with truncheons along the aisle of the bus, then cuffed and kicked into a metal cubicle, where we had to sit on a metal bench that took up half of the square metre of space into which we were squeezed. We each had a bag of bread rolls and a plastic bottle of water. The floor was awash with stinking piss and floating phlegm, put there by the previous batch of Spanish prisoners who really did not care where they squirted their bodily fluids. Thank God there were very few Spanish prisoners in La Moraleja, it would be cleaner there.

And so the journey began.

Six hours earlier we were processed out of Europe's most infamous prison, the Carabanchel in Madrid, where I spent the previous six months as a preventivo[6] awaiting my trial for drug trafficking hashish.

We were in transit to Spain's new international prison, La Moraleja. My travelling companion was an American, a man of few words. Maybe that was because he did not know many. He was a big chap about the size of a refrigerator, which made matters worse in our stinking square metre of space, especially because my left wrist was shackled to his right wrist. As the prison bus lurched around the bend, the centrifugal force and the weight of my travelling companion squeezed me into the rusty metal side of the stinking Spanish charabanc. I elbowed him back into an upright position and shoved him back onto his half of the metal seat, just as the bus careened in the opposite direction redirecting the centrifugal flow and assisting me to shove the big fat bastard onto his own side.

Our bus quivered and shook its way northwards to Segovia where a noisy, screaming Spaniard was ejected and pushed into what looked

---

[6] preventivo - remand prisoner

like an old prison. I looked through a slit in the metal grating which served as a means of circulating the foul air within the bus. The slit was not wide enough to be effective, but wide enough for me to see that the prisoner was a Spanish gypsy whose arse was kicked through the big gates, followed by a lot of friendly banter between the guards outside, as the bus idled and vibrated noisily waiting for them to get back on board. Then it pitched forward and jerkily found its gears to get us to Salamanca prison, where upon another gypsy was jettisoned with the aid of a size twelve boot and a welcoming drag through the big gates.

Apart from the rattle and wheeze of the bus there were no other noises. No shouting, no funny remarks, no banter, just the vibrating metal pulsing, along with the intermittent pangs of foreboding as each passenger thought about what lay ahead. What could possibly be worse than the Carabanchel? I knew that nothing could be more unpleasant or ungodly than Satan's lavatory, so I looked forward to getting off that stinking mobile latrine and having a shower, followed by something edible and a sip of hot coffee. I wanted more than anything to get out of that claustrophobic mantrap.

The prison bus rattled out of Salamanca and on through Valladolid, which looked like a busy little town through my slit in the window grating. We were south of the Cantabrian Mountains in the north of Spain, rolling along the crinkum crankum roads to Centro Penitenciario La Moraleja near the town of Duenas in the Palencia region. We then reached the little hamlet of Duenas where we lurched into a country lane leading out to a remote area where lay the isolated prison called La Moraleja. After a couple of miles of open country we arrived at the grey concrete scar on the landscape. At last the end of our ordeal drew near and we approached the final reeling curve before crunching to a halt outside the prison gates.

The bus waited while the electronic gates opened then rumbled into a high walled enclosure where a reception committee of sourpuss prison officers congregated around the bus door. The inhuman metal lockers were opened and the Guardia Civil officers, who removed the shackles at gunpoint, dragged us out two at a time. We were shouted and screamed at to stand spread-eagled with our hands against the wall in order to be frisked. I sensed immediately that the shakedown screw was inexperienced because he failed to fondle my bollocks and try to finger my hole like the Carabanchel cacheros[7] loved to do. Cacheros were usually psychotic with a bent for fingering hairy arseholes and rolling back foreskins.

As the blue serge clad screw finished frisking me a green uniformed Guardia Civil officer screamed at me to retrieve my baggage from the bay at the rear of the bus and join the line of prisoners silently waiting to be processed into our new kennel. We stood there, the loud sullenness of our abjection seeming to hum around the high walls. We were then herded through a metal gate into a reception yard manned by more prison officers. When we were all corralled in the inner yard the Guardia Civil officers holstered their weapons and made their way back to their stinking transports in readiness to drive back to Madrid for yet more human cargo.

May you spend the rest of your hapless lives riding on those grunting turds on wheels, you shower of bastards!

I was relieved to be detached from the Yank. No doubt he was relieved to be rid of me. I had just spent six hours manacled to a bloke who uttered barely six words. My attempts at conversation early on had died a death, simply because I might as well have been talking to a fucking polar bear. I knew he was a nutcase having met him six months earlier when first I was put in galeria cinco[8] in the Carabanchel. He was an avid chess player. Not good, just avid. I beat him every time I played him and I am truly not a good player. Anyway we were separated and luckily I never laid eyes on him again. After a few days a very different American would enter my life, but first I had to get through ingreso[9] and be shoved into a cell somewhere amongst the bricks and concrete of that piss-pot administration.

Processing in was very different in La Moraleja in comparison with the Carabanchel. This was a brand spanking new prison so there was toilet roll with which to wipe off the ink after my fingerprints were

---

[7] cacheros - specially trained prison officers, experts at body and cell searching
[8] galeria cinco – wing 5
[9] ingreso - reception

taken. Good grief, such extravagance and technology! There were metal-detector frames, handheld detectors, baggage x-ray machines, and brand new mop buckets on ball-bearing castors. Only the latter was in use because nobody on the shift knew how to operate the other stuff. Anyway, you could not beat the good old-fashioned methods, so we all stripped off to be searched again as our baggage was rummaged.

My kit was being rifled by a cretin with a withered arm, just one dirty little paw burrowed through my bag as our eyes held each other. His gaze was defiant, while mine was pure hatred. I must have touched a nerve because he withdrew his grubby fingers and plunged his five-clawed ferret into my neighbour's bag. A brief perusal of my armpits and scrotum by a limp-wristed screw wearing Cosmo Smallpiece spectacles had me dressed and waiting for yet another search within a few minutes.

The European Union had paid for this prison along with all its sophisticated technology so, me being a taxpayer, I was delighted to see the high-tech really expensive kit all highly polished and definitely not being abused by overuse. There were many high-tech items that did not come into use until European prisoners from the north breathed life into them. Much of this machinery was too complicated to be understood by the indigenous primitives clad in blue serge, who were now herding us into small holding cells in order to then again extract us and process us singularly.

The shouting and screaming died as the sound of female voices filtered through the din calming the obstreperous prison officers. The atmosphere changed instantly with the intrusion of female prison officers. Some of the older screws gave each other pained expressions as though the female intruders were not welcome. The fun and joy of gaping up arseholes and ogling male genitalia was denied them. Fucking spoilsport women! The female screws went to their various desks and tables to take part in the processing-in rigmarole, as we were brought out of the holding cells singly and sent to whichever table was empty.

I was unlucky. I did not get one of the girls. I got a barrel-chested moron by the name of Don Adolfus; a man I would never forget because he was the blustering bully who, I am certain, killed a young Colombian with his truncheon, but more of that later. He yelled at me to empty my bags on the table in front of him. Some species of human being who amble around this planet are deemed never to progress mentally beyond the age of eight years. Here was one such creature, right in my face. A fifty-year-old infant who sported a short back and sides haircut, which looked as though he had just removed his school cap, because the crown was all tufted while the rest was plastered flat with the aid of the ubiquitous olive oil. He clutched his genitals as his glittering eyes feasted upon my glossy magazines, but his enthusiasm quickly waned as he realised they were martial-arts magazines, so there was nothing for him to bash his pudding with. All the letters I had received during the previous six months in prison were bundled together and secured with elastic bands. This moron handled the bundle then tossed it to one side because it did not interest him.

This was a trait I had discovered amongst all Spanish screws; they could not read English so did not bother scanning through the pages. It was a gamble for me because all my street money was hidden between the pages of my loved ones' letters. During all of the many shakedowns I had in the Carabanchel, La Moraleja, Valdemoro and Malaga prisons, my loved ones' letters successfully concealed my money and other bits and pieces that could have got me into hot water. I concealed my passport for years using this method.

At last the low-browed lubber waved me away from his table. So I hurriedly stowed my kit in my sports bags and was escorted up several flights of stairs to the top floor of the ingreso building. There I was shoved into a cell and told to dump my kit and report to the bedding store, where I was issued with a foam rubber mattress, sheets, blanket and pillows. After signing for the bedding I was rushed back to my cell by two lunatic screws and locked in. I quickly threw my mattress on the bottom bunk and made my bed. I then stowed my kit underneath my bunk, lay on my bed and waited to see who my new cellmate would be.

I had a habit of gazing back on my past life and mentally kicking the shit out of myself for being so stupid. So I lay on my bunk thinking 'what if, what if' but immediately dismissed the stupid questions building up in my mind. Remorse and self-reproach was the kiss of death if dwelt upon constantly. Prison was my penance and all the powers in the universe could not unspill the milk. I picked up the bundle of letters I had received over the last six months of my life while locked in Satan's lavatory, Madrid's Carabanchel prison. In this bundle of love were all the words that helped me through Hades; words I had read over and over again, words that painted the pictures of the writer's face, heartbroken. But in my mind I saw the paintbrush of time applying the finishing touches to her portrait, painting over the heartache when I would join her in freedom. When would that be I wondered, as I lay on the bunk trying to guess when my trial would happen.

In May 1998 I was caught by the Spanish secret police driving my VW Caravelle mini-bus with half a ton of hashish on board. I was taking the hashish from the Costa del Sol in the south of Spain to Burgos in the north, where it was to be transferred from my VW onto a truck en-route to Rotterdam, from where it would be sold to the legal dope cafes of Amsterdam. Unfortunately, I had got myself roped in with a gang of spicks[10] who were already earmarked for a stint in prison. The secret police had been monitoring this lot for months and the bloke who should have driven the hashish to Burgos disappeared just a few days before the rendezvous up north. In desperation, Paco, an English-speaking Spaniard, came to me because he knew I had a vehicle capable of lugging half a ton of Morocco's best up to Burgos. His driver had let him down, his life and that of his family were threatened and yours truly fell for the sob story, thus setting into motion the downward spiral of my love for all things Spanish. The treatment I received at the hands of the Spanish secret police is recorded in previous journals, as is my time spent in the ungodly Carabanchel. So please dear reader, bear with me when I say I want to piss in every Spanish reservoir.

I drifted into sleep and my recurring nightmare attacked me yet again with the clubbing pistols and flailing boots of the Spanish secret

---

[10] spicks - the Spanish (slang)

police as they arrested me back in May 1998. It always starts with the metallic, whirring clicks of the handcuffs as they shackled my hands behind my back. My nightmare somehow distorts itself with all the horrible bits doing a cameo performance with an amplified version of the sounds and a magnification of impacting pistols and blood flow. My face was bashed into the wall and during the flattening process, my nose appeared under my left eye accompanied by the crackling sound of breaking gristle as my nose broke and my cheekbones and forehead crunched into the unyielding glossy wall tiles. A strange lumpy feeling occurred in my nose as a deluge of hot blood cascaded from my nostrils. Flashing lights danced behind my eyes and sparkled, like I was gazing into a twinkling kaleidoscope. I was now stunned and helpless with my hands secured painfully behind my back, stooping forward so the blood missed my clothes. I was bleeding cats and dogs! My eyes started to close with the rapid swelling as the impact tested my pain threshold and five armed men surrounded me menacingly. I felt like a wounded dolphin being circled by five Great Whites. It was over quickly, but my nightmare dragged it out as the first gun barrel struck my head, sending a river of blood flowing down my face. Then a second and third pistol dug into my skull, but my nightmare was not clever enough to segregate the following blows, as my kidneys exploded with starbursts of pain as the pistols sought my inner organs. The five policemen were merciless as they crashed their weapons into my defenceless body. Like the poor dolphin the Great Whites were in frenzy as they tore into my flesh. Suddenly my legs were yanked from under me and I crashed face down onto the ceramic tiled floor. With my hands fastened behind my back I could not break my fall so my face whip-lashed into the shiny tiles. Slowly the floor approached my face as the nightmare provided a slow-motion sequence of my descending body, enabling me to squint through closing eyes at the colour and shine of the tiles as they met my mouth, breaking and splintering my teeth and lacerating my lips and gums, unkindly leaving me conscious. I could feel hands grabbing my ankles and pulling my legs apart as someone clouted my head. My testicles detonated into my guts as boots crashed into my groin, tearing the flesh of my rectum and massively swelling my bollocks.

The nightmare could not differentiate the blows as the five brave Spanish policemen rained them into my numb, nerveless body, but it did amplify the loud crack as a rib fractured. When they had worn themselves out, they bundled me into a vehicle and took me to their police barracks in order to clean me up before taking me to hospital, but the nightmare always ended before I got there. I awoke clutching my bollocks.

That beating left an indelible scar of hatred of the Spanish police that would live with me forever. The recurring nightmare ensured that I would never forget those scums of the earth and the subsequent experiences I had in the Spanish prison system compounded my dislike of all things Spanish.

The twinge in my bollocks left me as a whirring, grinding sound accompanied the electronic opening of my cell door as it rolled along its steel runners on the outside of my cell. Later I would use the back of the cell door as a pug[11] because if I stuck anything to the back of the door it was hidden in the one-inch gap behind the wall as it slid open. Screws never locked themselves in while doing a shakedown, so they never saw what was on my side of the door.

The door clunked to a halt on its mountings and standing there was a screw screaming at someone I could not yet see. The screw disappeared momentarily and I could hear him cuffing someone and shouting his stupid head off. A foam mattress appeared first, followed by a military style kitbag, then a bundle of sheets, pillows and a blanket all piled up in the doorway. A body came hurtling through the door propelled by two screaming screws who then kicked the kit and bedding through the door just in time before it closed with a loud clunk. A sneer of hatred dressed my new cellmate's face as he glanced at the closing cell door and the now vanished screws.

"Cabrones![12]" shouted the new bloke at the closed door, then turning to me with a big grin he said, "Ola, Eengleesh!"

I grinned back at him as I recognised Hugo, a Portuguese bloke whom I knew from the Carabanchel.

---

[11] pug - hiding place
[12] Cabrones! – bastard, son of a bitch, ponce, pimp, cuckolder (slang, profanity)

"Hi Hugo," I chuckled, "I see you've been pissing the screws off again."

"Yeah, da bastardos kick my arse up da fuckin' escalera 'cos I wanna fuck da bitch screw."

"Oh yes mate, that's definitely an arse kicking job. If they are Carabanchel screws you'll be getting a visit tonight from spicks with big sticks," I said, chuckling.

"Nah, fuck dat! I only says jigajig to 'er, I didn' pull my chimbo out."

"I hope you're right, I don't want your fucking blood all over me tonight."

We both laughed as he heaved his mattress onto the bunk overhead and started to make his bed.

"It's not worth unpacking," I said, "we'll be out of here tomorrow."

"Yeah, dat bitch tol' me I'm goin' to modulo 9 in da mornin' so fuck it, I'm leavin' everythin' in da bag."

I lay back on my bunk and started to check the cell out. Everything was new and looked as though the building contractors had recently finished. As well as our two bunks there was a wash hand basin fixed to a pedestal, a lavatory pan and a shower stall, all in stainless steel. There was also a mirror made of polished stainless steel riveted to the wall. Just above that was an interior light that was recessed into the wall. There was no light switch in the cell, so the screws controlled the light. On the wall next to the light was a console and speaker, which was the intercom between cell and screws' office. So the screws or anyone who had an interest were earwigging us. Hugo had finished stowing his kit and making his bed and was now lying on it singing a French song. His voice sounded like a cinder caught under a door but strangely suited the frog lyrics.

"Where did you learn that song?" I asked, when he finished singing and started to hum.

"Foreign Legion!" he snapped.

"The French Foreign Legion?" I asked, incredulously.

"Yeah man, I done five fuckin' years wid dat fuckin' lot, an' I got fuck all to show ferrit."

Hugo did not look the type to forego his freedom to serve five years with the frog legion and he had no military bearing about him whatsoever.

"Where did you serve?" I asked, half guessing the reply would be a lie.

"Algeria and France."

"Did you have any rank?"

"Yeah man, I was Chief Corporal."

I know that Chief Corporal is equivalent to Lance Sergeant in the Brigade of Guards and, besides the chevrons indicating the rank Chief Corporals, wear a black kepi instead of a white one that the lower ranks wear.

"What colour was your cap?" I asked.

"Red, I was a paratrooper."

"Oh right, but what about your kepi, what colour was that?"

Silence for a moment then, "White of course, all kepis are white in the Legion."

"This place should be like a kindergarten after five years with that fucking lot." I said.

"Yeah man, it was fuckin' 'ard, but I 'ad loadsa buddies an' we fucked our way all over Africa."

I chose to give Hugo the benefit of the doubt and decided that he had been in the frog legion for at least twenty minutes before he deserted. I dropped the subject and feigned sleep in the hope that I would sleep and forget about the lying bastard in the bunk above me. He nattered on about something for a minute and when I did not respond I felt him move to peer down at me. Seeing that I was asleep, or so he thought, he grunted and turned over.

Silence reigned for ten minutes or so, and then I felt him move as he stealthily checked that I was sleeping. Then, very slowly like a python, he silently writhed his way down the far end of the bunk to crouch noiselessly at the bottom of my bed. He held his breath as he pulled out one of my bags from under the bed. He caught his breath again as he gently pulled open the zip, I could feel him staring at my supposed inert form as he deftly rummaged my bag. I gave him his first heart attack by turning over so I could see him through my closed eyelashes. Though my vision was impaired I could see exactly what he was doing. His second heart attack happened as he stashed my new trainers into his kitbag. I was off my bunk like shit off a shovel and drove my rigid knife hand under his floating rib, snatching a handful of spleen and crushing it between my fingers and his ribs. My other hand grabbed his ear with my thumb squelched into his eye socket as my knee crashed into his testicles with tremendous force. His body became limp for a moment, but not before he cracked my eardrum with a magnificent scream.

Clunk went my cell door as it slid open on its runners and two wild-eyed prison officers wielding truncheons started screaming for me to release him, or else! I threw him at their feet and immediately grabbed his kitbag and produced my trainers, shouting, "Ladron! Thief!" while shaking my trainers at the writhing Hugo. I threw my trainers on my bed. Then grabbing Hugo's bedding and kitbag, threw it on top of him, yelling, "Cambio! Yo no queri ladron in mi celda!"

My Spanish is shite but the screws twigged immediately what had happened, so here was the excuse to even things up for the insulted female prison officer. Crash, bang, wallop, went the truncheons as the thieving Hugo wished he had never deserted the frog Legion. My cell door slowly glided back into its closed position, blocking out the scene as the happy wallopers battered the shit out of the Portuguese Legionnaire. Had he still been in the frog Legion he would be nursing broken fingers, wrists and arms right now; thieves get a hard time in the FFL. I heard the orderlies removing Hugo's inert body from outside my cell and I never laid eyes on him nor heard about him ever again. I sometimes wondered what happened to him but I really did not care a flying bollock about lying thieves. I dozed on my bunk for a while then clunk went the door as it reached the stopper on its runner.

"Comida! Food!" someone shouted.

There was a rush of bodies as everyone dashed to the stairs end of the wing where stainless steel trolleys laden with steaming food awaited us. A noisy queue had formed and was fairly orderly apart from the pushing in at the front by the Moroccans. Suddenly a loud crack rang out, followed by another, as two Moroccans hit the deck with lumps on their heads. Don Adolfus the retard screw was supervising the food trolleys with his colleague Don Umberto, a swarthy giant who, like Adolfus, I would later learn, was a swaggering bully capable of doling out monstrous beatings.

The two unconscious Rockies had barged in at the front jostling a couple of blokes into the food trolleys, sending a wave of soup to splash out and onto Umberto's shoes. His response was the instant swish of polished hardwood swiped across the temple of the first impatient Rocky, while Adolfus clouted the other one across the back of the head sending him to dreamland. Two younger screws ordered a couple of blokes at the front to pull the two stunned men out of the way where they could be attended to by concerned countrymen. The urgency to get to the front of the queue died instantly. Had they known what would be dished out there would have been no sense of urgency, and besides, the North Africans were told to fuck off because the Moslem food had not yet arrived on the wing, and they would have to wait for theirs.

When it was my turn I picked up a bandeja[13] and offered it to the server who ladled some bean soup into one of the four indentations in the tray. The next food orderly dropped a boiled egg and three slices of ham next to the soup. With a flimsy gloved hand the third server dropped a dripping handful of oily salad next to the ham as his other hand dropped a brown banana into the soup. I returned to my cell to place my bandeja on my bunk then went back to the trolleys to help myself to coffee from the steaming urn.

I acknowledged many familiar faces but I had no friends there. I would have to wait until I got out of ingreso before I saw any of my pals. I enjoyed the coffee but the egg was of dubious age and was somewhat odious. I wondered why the Spanish managed to fuck everything up in the cookhouse, I was sure the egg was fine when it left the chicken. As for the rest of the food it was fetid and practically putrescent. Now I know why the bandeja is made of stainless steel!

The Spanish were arrogantly proud, but I had no idea why, as everything they touched turned into rat shit! Here was a brand new

---

[13] bandeja - stainless steel tray

prison, supposedly reserved for foreign prisoners, which should have been a showcase example for the rest of Europe, especially as a replacement for the evil Carabanchel, but although the bricks and mortar were brand new and the fixtures and fittings brought unexpected comfort to the ex-Carabanchel inmates, the prison officers had brought their old habits with them. Satan's henchmen were not impressed nor influenced by the newness of the place and their inability to organise was apparent by the standard of the food. It would be some time before the food improved and only then due to the skills of the north European prisoners who eventually got jobs in the cookhouse. I had never to forget that a screw's aim in life was to inflict pain and misery on all who fell under their spiteful shadow behind the high walls of their Spanish prisons. It mattered not to them whether the bricks were new or ancient, just as long as they hid the goings on from the outside world.

I lay on my bunk with the cell door still open, watching inmates interacting and searching for pals. Lots of blokes popped their heads in just to say hello in various tongues. Some of them were familiar, but most of them were complete strangers cadging ciggies. A friendly Moroccan face beamed at me and politely asked if he could enter my cell, so I beckoned him in.

"Ola Francois, how do you like our new home?" he chuckled.

"Ola Kader, I'll tell you next week when I've seen more of it," I said, smiling.

I was normally called Chris or Chancer, but Moroccans who hailed from the Nador region knew me as Francois because I was a well known yacht skipper and RIB[14] jockey over there and Francois was my chosen name for that part of the world.

I respected men like Kader because he started life in the Rif[15] hills and grew up without a formal education but that did not prevent him from becoming fluent in English, French, Dutch, Spanish, Turkish and of course Arabic - a useful ally in a place like this. He was dressed in Arab garb befitting an oil millionaire, which was what he was, a cannabis-oil millionaire - a bearded handsome man of about forty

---

[14] RIB – Rigid Inflatable Boat
[15] Rif hills - Mediterranean mountain region of Morocco

years, not unlike the film actor Omar Sharif. Surprisingly he was wearing a gold Patek Philippe wristwatch and on each beautifully manicured hand was a diamond ring worth a fortune. He was looking outside through the barred window of my cell.

"I hope to be in your modulo when we move out of ingreso. We have much to talk about Francois."

I kept silent, as he seemed to focus on something in the distant hills. Then he slowly turned to face me.

"You do not know me very well, but you do know of my business and you have many friends in my country. We can also be good friends and do good business with my merchandise."

Kader was talking about the many tonnes of top grade hashish that his family grew and processed in Morocco. A family business that had blossomed and was renowned for its production of the sought after Mercedes Star brand of hashish, from the apilado[16] bars normally sent to the UK, to the ten times more expensive burbuja[17], normally destined for royal tables and wealthy Dutchmen. My skills as a RIB jockey[18] were always in demand by blokes like Kader.

I could tell you all about that trade but I would feel uneasy about that because the temptation may outweigh the foolhardiness and I would not want you to lose your life after reading my book. Smuggling at sea is most dangerous and life threatening in more ways than one. Unless you have nerves of steel and exceptional seamanship skills you will most certainly die at sea. If you lose the cargo in heavy seas, or dump it overboard to escape capture by the pursuing law enforcement cutters, the North Africans could perceive you as a slippery infidel and, unless you had a Moroccan witness to corroborate your story, you would surely die. Also, unless you are known and respected by the Moroccan overlords, your approach to offer your services may well end with your body lying on the seabed strapped to a concrete post. This is because many police interlopers

---

[16] apilado - lowest grade hashish
[17] burbuja - highest grade
[18] RIB jockey - Rigid Inflatable Boat skipper

attempt to enter the smuggling world, thereby creating much suspicion around any unsolicited appearance. The kiss of Judas was, and is, prevalent in the smuggling world.

I knew of a Frenchman who was recommended to Kader by the Miffer brothers, Brian and Roy from Gibraltar. The frog stole two tonnes from Kader by sailing the cargo to a different rendezvous, a cove where his frog mates were waiting to load it onto a truck to take it north. The Moroccan youth who travelled with the cargo was found dying on the beach. The hashish world was not such a big world that you could hide yourself easily, especially if you were lugging two tonnes of Mercedes Star shit. It did not take Kader and his cohorts long to put a few bullets into the frog and redirect the shit to Holland. Roy and Brian were no longer welcome on the Tetuan beaches, so they made a living running the gauntlet of the Gibraltar Straits. I was to meet Brian four years later in Malaga prison. He was doing a three stretch for getting caught on La Linea beach with a tonne of happy herb he had just shipped over from Tangiers, a kamikaze trip if ever there was one.

"We can talk 'til the cows come home," I said, "but I don't know when I'll be getting out, my friend."

Kader's face wore a serene smile.

"It matters not when you get out, it matters only that you come to my house after you have seen your family. I will give you a villa and servants. You can live by the sea or in the hills, the choice is yours," he said.

This may seem strange to people but wealthy Arab drug barons were exceedingly generous with proven skippers, especially reliable ones who had never lost a cargo. Kader, like most serious villains, was making use of his downtime. Instead of languishing in prison, he would make contact with serious international dealers and traficantes[19] from every country in Europe, and guess where they were? Right there in Spain's international prison La Moraleja. Not

---

[19] traficantes - smugglers

only was prison the university of crime it was also the marketplace where one's expertise was the main commodity, the villains' jobcentre.

Kader and I chewed the fat about various personalities we both knew and I recall thinking about how small the traficante world really was. The movers and shakers in North Africa appeared to all know each other, no matter their rank or social standing. Kader had only nice things to say about each Moroccan villain I mentioned, from senior government officials and naval and military officers, to farmers and wealthy landowners whose main livelihood was growing and selling hashish by the tonne. I had only to mention a name and he would give me a biographical rundown better than any rap sheet could disclose. I asked him if he knew Mustafa Hamza Daal, a big noise Moroccan on the Costa del Sol in southern Spain. Kader told me they were great pals. So knowing that Mustafa had a limp I asked if there was anything peculiar about him.

"Yes, he limps badly because I shot him two times in his right leg," he said, disarmingly. "He's a very nice man, but we had a slight misunderstanding five years ago because he enticed one of my sea captains away from me. We are good friends Francois, I assure you."

Christ almighty! What a condensed world I lived in! Here I was in a Spanish prison talking to a Moroccan I hardly knew, yet he knew each and every person I knew in his homeland. Kader's case was quite complicated, but its conception was created by his refusal to increase the layer of grease on the palms of certain senior Guardia Civil officers who looked the other way when consignments of hashish entered their coastal areas. Kader's revenge was sweet. Shortly after his release, several Guardia Civil officers hit the headlines because they were living way beyond their means and were sacked - tout court[20].

The duty screws came bustling in to lock us up for the night at 9:00 pm, so Kader had to go back to his own cell to spend his first night in La Moraleja with one of his countrymen. We did not share the same wing until months later when he joined me on the workers

---

[20] tout court – (French) simply; and nothing else

wing, modulo cinco[21]. I enjoyed my few hours with Kader, which was the birth of a lasting friendship initiated in the villains' jobcentre.

I prepared my bed and stripped naked in readiness for a shower. The hot-water tap was one of those press-in button types that had to be pushed hard to keep a steady flow of water, so I had to tolerate a cold dowsing before the hot water arrived. The tap was on the back wall of the shower cubicle, too far away to operate without getting wet. I solved the problem the next day by wedging the broom handle between the press button and the opposing wall until I saw the steam and then I entered the shower cubicle. I dried myself then shaved before I got into bed. I had a feeling that the morning would be hectic and ablution time might be short, so I organised my kit and fresh clothes ready for a snappy exit. I climbed into bed feeling cool and clean tucked up between new bed sheets. I mentally turned back the pages of the day and made a few notes in my journal. Then it dawned on me that I had slipped out of Satan's grasp and I would never again see the innards of the beast called Carabanchel. Thus ended my first day in La Moraleja prison.

As the projector in my mind fades out my thoughts return to contemplate my present situation. How the hell did I get here? It is January 2007 and I am in another Spanish prison, Daroca – Satan's arena.

---

[21] modulo cinco - wing 5

Caught Again

My mind took me back to my capture in France just a few weeks before. I awoke from a fitful sleep, cold and hungry and with an aching back. It was the early hours of Thursday 4th January 2007 and I had spent the night in a holding cell near the French port of Calais. The cell was four metres high by four metres long by two metres wide with no bed, just the concrete floor on which I lay wrapped in a filthy blanket.

I was arrested the previous day at 8:00 pm as I drove off the car ferry from Dover to Calais. The resulting arrest was due to a European Arrest Warrant issued by the Spanish authorities because I had absconded from Spain during a Libertad-Condicional[22] order in 2002. The French police had clocked my passport during the voyage across the English Channel, so a welcoming committee of armed police greeted me on arrival.

I had good reason to believe an arrest warrant would never be issued because of the circumstances surrounding the method of my release in 2002, which must remain secret because I cannot betray the influential people involved. I was driving our Mitsubishi Pajero loaded with Christmas shopping en-route to the newly rented house in the south of France at Lezignan Corbieres, accompanied by my lovely wife Susan who was now distressed because we were being separated for an unknown period of time. She was instructed to continue her journey because I was to be extradited to Spain to complete a sentence that had begun in 2001. Susan waited outside then followed the police car that took me to the holding cells somewhere on the road to Boulogne-Sur-Mer. Fortunately there was a hotel nearby so she stayed the night and in the early hours she dug out suitcases to find clothes to give me later in the morning. She is a diamond, a Koh-i-Noor[23] no less!

---

[22] Libertad-Condicional - parole
[23] Koh-i-Noor, also spelt Kohinoor and Koh-i-Nur - one of the largest cut diamonds in the world, weighing 105.6 carats. It is part of the British Crown Jewels, currently set in the crown of The Queen

During the night I was given a plastic packet of food, two hundred and eighty grams of pasta, which I could not eat. I asked for a hot drink but was laughed at by the female officer and the guard that accompanied her. She was tall with ginger hair and smudged bright red lipstick. Her lipstick was all across her front teeth and her uniform fitted like a *Dad's Army* uniform dyed navy blue. She thought she was the bee's knees but looked more like Kermit the frog in drag. I will never forget her ugliness.

"Please give me a drink... anything... water?" I asked.

The guard found an empty plastic bottle lying in the nearby lavatory and filled it from the tap. Knowing that the Islamic detainees used this bottle to clean their arses after defecating I could not take a drink from it. They locked me in my cell and went away laughing. I imagined the bright red gash in her ugly painted face smearing more lipstick across her teeth as her big boots echoed up the filthy corridor along with her cackling laughter.

At 9:00 am I was taken from the cell by a policeman who told me my wife was there to see me. I was walked along corridors and up stairs and told to sit on a plastic chair outside his office and to keep my handcuffs in view by resting my elbows on my knees. After twenty minutes or so the policeman returned to tell me he had taken a bag of clothes from my wife and ordered her away from the premises. This was heartbreaking for me, and particularly distressing for Susan as she later told me in a letter. I was then taken back to my cell passing several smirking policemen.

I spent thirty-six hours on the floor of that filthy French cell then escorted to the town of Douai where I was frog-marched up the stairs of 1, place de Pollinchove to face a magistrate, who sent me to Maison d'Arret de Douai, 505 rue de Cuincy, the Douai Dungeon - that infamous old French prison where human civil rights have yet to reach. As I was being processed in I asked the duty screw if I could telephone my wife to inform her what was happening to me - the magistrate had informed me that this was one of my rights. The screw replied in English.

"In France we shit on your English rights so bend over so I can look up your arsehole."

I was naked at the time so I dutifully bent over so he could inspect my rectum for hidden weapons: drugs, bolt-cutters, ropes, grappling-hooks or maybe he thought there could be an extending ladder up there. I am not saying my arsehole is bigger than anyone else's, but it is somewhat disfigured due to a heavy beasting by the boots of the Spanish secret police in 1998. After first pistol-whipping me, they gave me a kicking and battering so severe I had to be taken to hospital. My little cornflake (anus) had been kicked into a three-inch gash and this dopey frog was trying to figure out the difference between his and mine.

"I have never seen one like that before," he said, in his frog accent, making that sound like zat.

"Oh really! You don't get about much in your job; arseholes like mine were all the rage in Madrid in '98," I said, as I stood upright.

Just then another screw entered the stripping cubicle to escort me to a cell. He was not happy with the speed I was getting dressed so he became abusive and started to shove me around the tiny cubicle. I could see he was winding himself up to give me a clouting. He could not understand my English, but he did heed the warning from his colleague who called from his desk to 'beware because he is a Black Belt martial artist'. Well I guessed that was what he said because I recognised the words judo and ceinture noir and the frog bully hurriedly stepped backwards out of the cubicle shouting, "Allez!" a frog word I would hear a million times over the next couple of weeks.

This incident warned me that they had a copy of my rap sheet from Madrid and were aware of my martial arts and possibly my military background. This was not good because it made me a target for antagonistic prison officers. I soon discovered that the prison arena in France is just the same as in Spain, with hostile screws around every corner. I quickly assumed they were all martinets by the way they constantly screamed at inmates and how they swaggered about in uniform, trousers tucked into boot tops military style. Most of their heads were shaven and their attitude was always aggressive. This gave me the impression they all thought they were in the French Foreign Legion. You wish, I thought.

My escort screw seemed quite unhinged. His behaviour was that of a Jack Russell terrier waiting for his master to throw a stick. He was excited and cautious as he shoved me to his front, and then, after just a few paces, repeatedly pushed me face first into the walls of the corridor while he opened one of the many iron-barred gates, until we arrived at the centre of the prison.

The Douai Dungeon resembled a wheel in design with all of the wings converging on the central hub, the hive of activity from where everything was controlled. Belligerent prison officers shouted at inmates busy mopping the floors; all conversation was shouted or screamed. A madhouse manned by madmen. The dividing sections of iron-barred enceinte[24] were set at oblique angles in a facetious attempt at art, a design that Picasso would have split his sides laughing at; an abstract metallic sculpture I instantly deciphered as merde[25] and I was in it up to my neck.

On entering the central control area we were then accompanied by two more screws who immediately started shouting at me. One of them was the dead spit of Quasimodo but without the hump. He thrust his big ugly mug into mine then screamed abuse, as he stressed himself out needlessly with an unwarranted tirade of distorted French. This blustering bullfrog nearly burst a blood vessel in his attempt to intimidate me. He stepped back quickly when his colleague said something about martial arts and Black Belt.

Gates were hastily opened and I was escorted meaningfully to a cell. All the way there these three screws goaded and shouted at me, hoping I would respond in a way that would justify them beating me senseless. By the time we reached the cell they realised I had been down this road before and I detected a glint of respect in their eyes. As the key was being turned in the lock, one of them asked me in English if I really was a Black Belt martial artist and which art did I practise. I asked him if it was on my documents. He said it was, but written in Spanish with the word peligroso[26] stamped in red across the top of the pages. He then told me he was Shodan (1st dan) in

---

[24] enceinte - enclosed end of wings
[25] merde – (vulgar) turd
[26] peligroso - dangerous

Kyokushinkai Karate. I glanced at his neck to see that it was two shirt sizes thicker than his colleagues and was impressively muscled. I stiffened my back to bring myself up to my full height and bowed respectfully.

"Yondan Ju-Jitsu[27]," I said.

He immediately stood to attention and bowed deeply.

"I will talk with you later," he said curtly and strode away alone whence he came.

The heavy iron cell door was pulled open by my escort screw and the other shoved me into the darkness. As the big iron door clanged shut behind me the stink overwhelmed me. My nasal hair and some of my eyebrow hair fell to the ground as I breathed in the fetid air of the dark cell. In the darkness I saw a movement. I stood motionless as my eyes became accustomed to the poor light from the barred window, which had a bed sheet draped across it to keep out the light.

As my night vision adjusted I could see a body turning over on the lower bunk of the two-bunk cell. I strode over to the window and yanked away the bed sheet to let in some light. The body on the bed suddenly scrambled and lurched at me with its hands outstretched as though to strangle me. I drove my right fist between the outstretched hands to smash hard between the eyes. My fist stung for a moment as the body collapsed at my feet. The stunned man let out a groan and started to pick himself up. Grabbing a chair I placed it across his shoulders and neck, pinning him to the floor. I knelt on the chair with my right knee as my left foot pressed into the small of his back.

"Keep fucking still, arsehole," I grunted. "Do you parlez English?"

"Oui, a little," he cried hoarsely, "my name is Mark, let me up. I thought you woz zer guard. Let me up. Let me up!"

"You are a fucking liar. No guard would set foot in here. It's a health hazard."

"Zey do!" he cried. "Zey drag me out to let in ze cleaning prisoners to clean ze place up."

"It's been a few years since you were last dragged out then?" He did not quite catch that so I gave up and lifted the chair from him.

---

[27] Yondan - 4th dan Ju-Jitsu

"Okay Mark, you can get up now and climb back into your nest," I growled.

He did just that and was snoring like a pig in less than a minute. I thought the screws' practical joke had gone on long enough so I started banging the iron door. The one good thing about iron doors is the noise they make when thumped or battered with a chair, it brings the screws running tout de suite. The door swung open slowly on its creaking hinges revealing two screws with their noses twitching.

"Move me to another cell!" I demanded.

They argued, but they knew I was right, so they slammed the door in my face and stomped off. Two minutes later they returned, but not to change cells. They took me to the doctor who promptly pronounced me fit for prison.

When I arrived back at the cell, Mark had reinstated the bed sheet across the window and had attempted a clean up. His bedding had been removed and fresh clean bed linen was folded on the top bunk - mine. I quickly divided the bedding into two piles, one for Mark and one for me. I then set about making my bed just like I did when I was a professional soldier, which seems like a century ago. Satisfied with my bed, I arranged my prison issue washing and shaving kit. My own kit had been confiscated, which was annoying when I thought of the trouble Susan had gone through to retrieve it from our car. The razors were new and plastic wrapped so I felt pleased about that. However, when I came to use them, it was like having a skin graft. Why on earth did they manufacture such shite and wrap it so well? My father's wartime razor, which was sixty years old, was superior to this new French crap.

Mark unfolded his bedding and simply threw it at the bed, then clambered into it fully clothed and with his shoes on! This cretin was a King Kong turd with arms and legs pulling and kicking the corners of the blankets and sheets in an effort to cover his dirty body. His pillow resembled disrupted pattern material (camouflage) because the pillowslip was not on the pillow, it was tucked beneath the mattress at the head end of the bed where he could grab it easily to wipe his nose. He then has a clean rag to blow his nose on.

Feeding time came around 5:00 pm. Food was brought to the cell and dished out from a trolley by a surly prisoner who looked as though he was dying on his feet. I wondered what he was dying of and if it was contagious. A lot of blokes had AIDS[28] and TB[29] and nobody cared a toss in that place.

My appetite deserted me just then because the scran was truly very bad. I was served with a lump of meat that I had never tasted the likes of before, so after tasting it I pushed it away to the centre of the dilapidated table in disgust. Mark pounced on it and devoured it like a starving hyena. He then wolfed the few green beans that accompanied it and mopped up the greasy gravy with a piece of stale bread. He then continued to eat his own portion as though I was not there. His whole attention was taken up by the shite on his plate, making me worry about how often we were fed and would it be consistently as bad as this? I can tell you now that never once did I eat anything good in French prisons. God forbid I overhear a frog bragging about French cooking. As he was gulping the last scraps from his plate Mark commented that the meat was tender. So that horse could not have won many races.

"Maybe the screws can find you a nosebag, you eat like a horse," I replied.

Mark was fifty-five years old and was doing time for fighting in the street. Seemingly he is well known locally for pissing in shop doorways and generally being a shit to all and sundry. He was no more than a down and out gypsy, bereft of conscience and self-respect, who told me his family tree was a long line of bastards right down past the roots. I had the gross misfortune to be in that cell when he had a bowel movement. That event will live with me until I die. The smell in the cell was already akin to a badger's sett so I should have been prepared for what was to come.

In the night he started farting and guess who was in the top bunk above him? Yep, yours truly, so I opened the glass partition in the iron-barred window. It was the early hours of a Saturday in January 2007 and it was freezing cold. Whether it was the cold that got to him

---

[28] AIDS – Acquired Immunodeficiency Syndrome
[29] TB - Tuberculosis

or the green beans and horsemeat I will never know but he moved fast, with the bed linen hanging from him, as he struggled to drop his trousers. I wondered why he bothered to drop them anyway because they were already stiff with shit and piss stains. In just a moment I knew why he had dropped his rotten trousers. It was like a ready-mixed cement lorry discharging its load of concrete onto a new highway. I feared that at any moment his head would disappear down through his chest cavity to fall out of his arse and the rest of him would follow to vanish down the pan. It did not. He simply squatted there and thundered and rumbled like a rock crusher. This was truly the monster of all shits and I hope never to experience any such thing ever again. I survived by fully opening the window to dissipate the fumes regardless the icy wind.

With the bed linen covering my head I tried to sleep, but thoughts of my wife driving alone to the south of France kept me awake. The heartache was overwhelming as I visualised her loneliness, navigating her way south to set up home single-handedly in Lezignan Corbieres. Her problems were much greater than mine. I was simply in prison. Susan had an empty house to go to, then to arrange the unloading of the shipping container of furniture, get the water and electricity switched on, all without knowing anyone and unable to speak French. These thoughts crushed my resolve as tears of frustration drenched my pillow and I prayed for her safety and wellbeing.

After not much sleep the dawn and the cutting wind awoke me, prompting me to close the window. The filthy cell was freezing cold and the stink was now neutralised. I was ravenous and breakfast was being served from the trolley. I was handed bread and water. I did not expect bacon and eggs, but bread and water in the year 2007 was something you might expect in a banana republic, not a senior European Community member like France. Both here in Douai and in Fresnes prisons I had bread and water to start the day.

As I ate the bread I studied my surroundings. The cell was sufficient for two prisoners, being four metres long by three metres wide and three metres high, with a concave ceiling reminiscent of being inside a railway goods wagon. The peeling paint on the walls was coloured magnolia topped with a dirty white ceiling. There was a battered table and two tubular chairs, a sink and a lavatory. The cell was unbelievably filthy and a health hazard.

Things improved on Monday when Mark was dragged out, kicking and screaming to be dumped into another cell at the far end of the wing. The Shodan screw was responsible for the move. He entered the cell to tell me he was putting an English-speaking inmate with me. He also escorted me across the wing for a shower. This was a treat because inmates were allowed only two showers per week there. He locked me in the shower room and told me to bang on the door when I was ready to come out.

When he took me back to the cell there was a nervous looking man sitting at the table with a holdall and several plastic bags around his feet overflowing with his personal belongings. The Shodan screw introduced me to my new cellmate; an educated lunatic, Doctor Jean Beclet, a hospital consultant no less, who had sliced his wife to death with a butcher's knife as she was serving customers in her chemist shop. He told me his story as we shoved our horsemeat around our plates. I could not eat my food, because it was so awful, not because of his chilling account of attacking his wife. The food was nauseating, so I went hungry again whilst listening to how Doctor Jean walked into his wife's shop and hacked into her with his meat cleaver.

Thankfully, the doctor shared a tin of tuna he fished out of a plastic bag. He had tins and packets of food stashed in plastic bags brought with him from his previous prison. He knew how awful the food in the Douai dungeon was because he was held there three years ago after killing his wife. His nervousness was the result of the bullying and beatings he received from other prisoners who treated him as a nonce. Apparently frog villains do not like their womenfolk getting the chop. He was relieved because I had not beaten him and stolen his food the moment the screw closed the door. Such is life for a frog lady-killer.

I did not spend much time with the doctor because on the following Wednesday, I was trussed in leg-irons and manacles and taken to Douai Court for an extradition hearing. The prison van arrived at the court and, as the general public milled around in the square, I was dragged from the van and escorted across the square in full view of everyone. I was shuffling like a Guantanamo Bay prisoner in leg-irons and jingling chains. The shock was visible on many faces, so I shrugged at the onlookers and gave them my puzzled expression. I was truly puzzled, because why they were treating me like this? I had not committed a crime in France and I was merely being held for extradition to Spain. This would not be the last time I was in chains in France. They put me in leg-irons again when I was taken to Fresnes prison the following week. I had heard about French politicians complaining about the treatment of prisoners at Guantanamo Bay by the Americans. What can I say?

When I shuffled into the courtroom Monsieur Vinsonneau, President de la Chambre de l'Instruction ordered the guard to remove the shackles. The members of the bench seemed uncomfortable when I was taken out to have the leg-irons and manacles taken off. On my return everyone seemed relaxed and treated me to their benign smiles. The President spoke rapidly in French as the interpreter, Madame Vanbecelaere, translated the news that I was to be sent to Spain to serve a further one year, nine months and eight days of a three years and four months sentence. The time spent in French custody would be deducted from the time to serve. That proved to be a lie. The time spent in French custody was not deducted from my sentence. The time spent with the French was not recognised by the Spanish.

When the President finished his spiel the interpreter asked me if I had anything to say. I responded by raising my wrists to reveal the red welts caused by the irons. The awkward silence was broken by a loud harrumph from the President and the guards immediately took me out of the room to again clap me in irons and dragged me to the van. Outside the courtroom people looked at me in astonishment as I was shuffled across the square and shoved into the van. Off we went with all the unnecessary blue lights and sirens and squeal of tyres.

A pleasant surprise awaited me at the prison. Shodan had arranged for me to be moved to a fellow Englishman's cell, but first I had to go through the shakedown procedure of the Douai Dungeon. The irons were removed along with all my clothes. I was told to bend over to enable a most unpleasant screw to inspect my rectum and genitals. This pervert had put me in irons for the journey to court and had never left my side all morning. Here he was now looking up my hole and inspecting my dick and bollocks. Shodan appeared in the doorway and growled something in French. The pervert hurriedly squeezed past him and disappeared along the dim corridor.

"Get dressed!" he snapped, obviously angry about the situation.

"He's gone to play with himself," I said, swiftly pulling my pants up.

"I didn't hear you say that,' he said menacingly. "C'mon, move yourself, you are changing cells," he added, in a more cheerful note.

A colleague joined Shodan and the three of us marched along poorly lit corridors through many iron gates and climbed an iron stairway to the top floor of the wing. Shodan turned his key in a cell door and pulled it open to reveal a filthy cell with a tall man sweeping the grimy floor. The tall man looked past me and growled at Shodan.

"This cell is a fuckin' disgrace," glancing at me but speaking to Shodan, he added, "why the fuck did you put me in here?"

I was so delighted at seeing an Englishman, I simply held out my hand in greeting.

"Nice to meet you pal, I'll help you clean the place up."

He stood gawping at me as his surprised expression changed to joy.

"Are you English?' he asked, his handsome face breaking into a great warm smile. "Fuckin' great! At last, a fuckin' Englishman," he said, grasping my outstretched hand.

"Chris," I said.

"Ian," he replied, as we vigorously shook hands.

"C'mon you two," said Shodan. "You can help him with his things from his cell."

We went down a flight of stairs to my cell and gathered my kit and bedding. I bade the doctor goodbye and clambered back up the stairs to my new filthy cell. I quickly made my bed as my new cellmate, Ian, surprised me by asking if I wanted a brew and was preparing coffee cups. He had a hexamine burner[30] on the floor with a pan of water on the boil in just a couple of minutes. I relaxed on my bed with the best cup of coffee I have ever tasted. We chatted into the night and

---

[30] hexamine burner - a military style camping stove

explained to each other our predicaments. Ian was doing a short sentence for smuggling cigarettes - his first offence. He also told me he was an ex-paratrooper, having served in 1 Parachute Regiment. He stood six feet four inches tall, well built and handsome, an impressive woman trap. During the next six days he cooked many meals and brewed much coffee on his trusty hexamine burner. He was very kind and we shared much of his stash of tinned food. I imagined his family sent in the food. He brought a ray of sunshine to my life during our short stay together. I will never forget Ian the Para - respect mate wherever you are.

Tuesday 16th January was freezing cold as the leg-irons were clamped onto my ankles and the manacles locked my wrists together. I was being taken to Fresnes prison near Paris. I was shoved into the prison van and locked into the rear compartment alone. The escort screws sat up front smoking stinking frog ciggies so it was thick with cigarette smoke and uncomfortably humid with the vehicle's heating system full on. After an hour or so in the van we arrived at a large modern structure, which was obviously a prison. Large steel gates opened and we drove into a secure parking area where I sat locked in the van until the screws were ready to escort me inside.

I was taken into a reception area and the shackles removed. The shouting did not stop until I was put in a holding cell. I was in Bapaume about ten miles south of Arras in what looked like France's newest prison. My cell was clean and bright with new furniture and a television mounted on the long dressing table. I relaxed on the bed and switched on the television. I heard the bolt sliding back on the door and a screw entered with a tray of food. There was a glass of water with salad and hot French-fries which I found pleasantly edible; the first reasonable scran the French had given me in thirteen days. It was to be the only edible meal I had in all the time I spent with the frogs.

As soon as I finished the meal I was taken from the cell to be manacled to a large black man who fortunately spoke my tongue. We were shackled together and shoved onto a large omnibus with ten other prisoners for the ride to Fresnes. The guards were quite friendly with the French prisoners, but to my travelling companion and me they were sullen if not hostile at times.

My travelling companion told me his name. Richard Yaw Serkyre, a resident of Cape Verde, the lovely islands six hundred kilometres west of Senegal in the Atlantic Ocean. He was a well-built man with Raven black skin that was flawless and clean-shaven. His big dark eyes seemed to shimmer with nervousness but held no malice, just like a seal pup's eyes. He had suffered much racial abuse from his captors and it showed. We sat chained together for the hair-raising drive to Fresnes prison south of Paris.

The bus was fitted with sirens and blue lights blazing away for most of the journey because the prison officer driver thought he was in practice for the Le Mans omnibus Grand Prix. He drove like a lunatic and endangered many lives as we sped to Paris. Even in the busy traffic of Paris he bullied and barged across traffic lanes and tailgated and frightened many car drivers. I noticed he did not intimidate truckers. The sign of a typical road bully, a typical prison officer using his blue serge, blue lights and sirens as his armoury. During the three or four hours it took to reach Fresnes the driver showed his poverty of intellect by driving and frightened many other road users. I felt lucky to get there all in one piece.

On arrival at Fresnes we were noisily debussed in the reception area, to be browbeaten through the welcoming process by screaming prison officers who were probably still seething about failing their selection courses for the armed forces and police. My travelling companion suffered much verbal abuse and was roughed up slightly by the blustering screw unlocking our shackles. As he savagely yanked our wrists forward for unlocking, he drove his knee into Richard's bollocks then stepped back sharply as though he was the one being attacked. A nearby screw quickly stepped behind Richard and applied a chokehold, which took him to the verge of consciousness as his colleague removed the leg-irons and manacles. I had to squat next to Richard to be released from the shackles as he lay on the floor.

The moment I was released from the chains I was grabbed and frog-marched into an adjacent corridor and ordered to strip naked. Two shaven-headed louts in blue serge screamed at me as I undressed, but the provocation did not faze me. I knew they were itching for an excuse to give me a beating so I did not respond to their abuse and as I do not understand French it did not affect me anyway. My clothes and holdall were removed and I was put into a nearby holding cell. I was looking for somewhere to sit when the door flew open as a screw threw in my bag and clothes and I was reunited with my belongings.

"Allez! Allez!" he screamed,

I quickly dressed as the lunatic screw shouted his head off. I was taken out and along the corridor. I could see Richard, apparently none the worse for the rough treatment. He was holding his bag and his shirt was hanging out of his pants when he heard my approach behind him. Turning to face me, his face broke into a great smile, showing his brilliant white teeth.

"I was worried I wouldn't see you again."

"Nah mate, you can't get rid of me so easily," I said, grinning at him.

Our smiles vanished as the screaming screws beckoned us to the Formica-topped counter, to throw bedding at us for which we had to sign. We were then hurried out of the store with our arms full of bedding, washing kit and holdall to enter a great wide corridor. This corridor was as wide as a road, with a floor made of polished wooden planking. We were instructed to walk along the corridor in single file with our shoulders touching the wall. When we inadvertently stepped away from the wall we were screamed at. Only screws were allowed to walk in the centre of the corridor.

Fresnes prison was very big. It had one thousand two hundred cells for men, a smaller section for women, and a hospital. It also held the reputation of being the harshest prison in France. I can vouch for that. The famous SOE[31] agent, Odette Sansom had her toenails ripped out in Fresnes by the Gestapo. There are many ghosts of people killed in there and they can be heard in the night moaning. Fresnes was a hundred years old and was built in what became known as the telegraph-pole design, whereby wings extended from a central corridor, which bisected these wings at right angles. I was struggling

---

[31] SOE – Special Operations Executive

along this infamous corridor with my kit and a frightened black man, on my way to one of the many cells in this nightmarish hellhole.

We arrived at our designated wing and were handed over to the wing screws. Gates opened noisily as metal clashed with metal and we were shouted through and bullied into a holding cell before being allocated a cell for the night. After a few minutes I was taken out of the cell and marched in front of the chief screw on the wing. This man was tall, athletic and black. I was made to stand to attention in front of him as he questioned me. On his desk was a document appertaining to me with the dreaded PELIGROSO stamped in red at the top of the page. I guessed I was in for a hard time. He spoke to me in English.

"How long were you in the army?" he asked.

"Twelve years," I replied.

"Rank?"

"Staff-sergeant."

"Okay, do you need anything?"

For a moment I thought I was dreaming.

"A pen and writing pad so I can write to my folks, and something decent to eat," I answered, wondering if I had stepped over the mark.

"I'll bring something to your cell later," he said, beckoning my escort to take me away.

I was taken back to collect my kit as Richard was being hassled to his interview with the chief screw.

"Ask for food," I said as we passed each other.

His face remained blank with fear as the escorting screw screamed at him along the corridor. I was taken to the far end of the wing and shoved into a dark cell cramped with steel bunks from floor to ceiling, three on each side of the cell. I quickly arranged my bedding on one of the bottom bunks and relieved myself into the stinking latrine in the corner. I had just climbed onto my bunk when the door opened noisily and a man was bundled into the cell with bedding and the door closed quickly behind him. The man was a young bloke, nervous and bedraggled, looking at me in the dim light. He started to talk in a low voice but I was not able to understand him.

"Speak English mate, je ne parle pas bien Francais," I said.

"Ah, okay. I speak a little English," he said, less nervous now that we had broken the ice.

Just then the door opened again. Richard was violently pushed into the cell, dropping his bedding as he entered and tripping over it to collide with the other bloke.

"Welcome to the presidential suite Richard," I said, laughing in an effort to lighten things up. "Come on in and make your bed before room service brings our supper."

Richard gathered up his bedding and threw it onto the bunk opposite mine and quickly made his bed. The other bloke made his bed in the bunk above mine, talking all the time in French.

"What's he muttering about?" I asked Richard.

"Something about it being worse here than in Colombia," he replied.

The stranger in the cell was called Gilbert and had been transferred from Colombia to France near the end of his seven-year sentence. He told us that prison life in France was much worse than the primitive prisons of South America. I believed him. The door opened to reveal the chief screw standing there with a writing pad and pen for me. I quickly got off my bunk and took them from him and thanked him. He told me that food was coming shortly and to keep my head down for four days because then I would be extradited to Spain.

"Good luck, Staff. I hope never to see you again," were his final words to me.

That remark was indicative that the best part of his life would be spent in that terrible place and he had no wish ever to see me in there again. I hoped and prayed I never laid eyes on him no matter where the fucking hell he was. It also dawned on me that he could have once been in the British Army because he called me Staff. Shortly after the chief screw departed the feeding trolley arrived with a meat stew and apples for pudding. The stew was atrocious and the apples were bruised and barely edible. Fortunately I had some bread to dip into the stew and Richard produced a packet of digestive biscuits that we shared. We were chatting about our adventures in the dimly lit cell when the light went out. We said our good nights and turned in. I tried to sleep but too many thoughts were queuing in my mind. Also the small cell was so full of iron bars and metal beds it was like being in a steel jungle. Claustrophobia came with the territory, as did the screams in the night, but Fresnes prison wins hands down for harrowing screams in the night and the sense of seclusion and hostility.

In the dark early hours of the morning, the cell door opened and we were dragged from our beds by lunatic screws, shouting, "Allez! Allez!" I was allowed back into the cell to get dressed and grab my bedding and washing kit. Richard and Gilbert had slept with their clothes on so when I came back out of the cell they had disappeared. I was escorted to the other end of the wing and subjected to a strip search and passed through a metal detector frame. There was more "Allez! Allez!" from my escorts as I dressed and put on my shoes. I was then taken up the metal stairways to the upper level where I was shouldered and cuffed into the cell by my escorts, who slammed shut the door with a loud clang of metal and stomped off chuckling to each other.

It was not quite dawn, but in the poor light I could see I was alone in this cold and dirty cell. The cell window was held open with a piece of string, so I quickly untied it and closed the dirty window. I could see this cell had not been used for a long time. It was cold and damp with litter strewn around the floor. The lavatory was irredeemably stained and caked with filth. I found a small dustpan and brush, so I swept the floor and threw the litter out of the window to be carried away on the biting wind.

Shortly after dawn I heard noises outside my cell. It was breakfast. My cell door opened and the screw stepped aside to allow a prisoner to hand me bread and water from a trolley. The bread was fresh and the water lukewarm, so I sat on my bed to enjoy another French breakfast. I spent the rest of the morning cleaning the cell because I knew I had another three days and nights in this hellhole, so I cleaned it as best I could. The midday meal arrived on the trolley and I was given meat and vegetables and a battered apple. I could not tell what the meat was, whether it was formally a creature with two legs or four we will never know. I only hope I never need to eat any such thing again. Writing to my wife and family and making notes for my journal took up my time in that cell. I was locked in solitary confinement twenty-four hours a day for the remainder of my time in France. No exercise, no recreation, no showers or bath and, apart from the prisoner with the food trolley, I saw no one.

I recently read a report by the IOP[32], which concluded that conditions in French prisons are close to those of the Middle Ages. I am not about to argue with them.

My first night alone in Fresnes was unforgettable. The noise from the lower levels was constant until about ten o'clock and then it became quiet. It was then I could hear faint scratching that could have been rats, mice or large cockroaches. The place seemed to creak and moan with the wind, so there was never stillness in the cell. Shouting screws disturbed the peace until about midnight then the place settled to a sinister susurration like the muffled whispers of ghosts in the rafters. Sleep was elusive that first night in the top level of the wing. Each time I drifted into sleep I was awakened by a piercing scream from a disturbed inmate somewhere below me. Somewhere across the wing from me a demented prisoner battered his cell door with a heavy object, probably a chair. I began to wonder if sleep would ever come to me in that cell. I pulled up the blankets to my face and watched my breath on the moonlight shining in through the cell window. My thoughts brought Susan to me and I was stricken with sadness as her predicament became all too clear. The anvil in my chest became heavier and bigger with every scenario I imagined. Tears of frustration scalded my cheeks and I prayed for God to look over her for me and keep her safe. The sensations of hopelessness, guilt, failure and loss combined to tear my mind to shreds with the stress of it all. After several hours of punishing thoughts I fell into a deep sleep.

The arrival of bread and water awoke me to a new day in hell. Time stood still in this pit and the only distraction from dreary isolation was the delivery of very bad food by the duty screw and the prisoner with the trolley. Fortunately I had my martial arts mentality

---

[32] IOP - International Observatory of Prisons

to defeat the onset of mental distress, so I focused on breathing exercises, meditation and military physical jerks. This period of solitary confinement initiated the adoption of a Bushido mindset once more in my life. During previous incarcerations, in order to survive, I had become ruthless with fellow prisoners who wanted to hurt me, rob or kill me. Now I needed to mentally prepare myself to respond with ferocious violence to anyone who confronted me. To achieve this mindset I needed self-discipline and blind courage in order to perform pitiless acts of violence on villains who confronted me, who were armed with stabbing implements and were never alone. In the netherworld of prison, alertness and effective retaliation techniques were essential to my survival. I knew I had trodden this path before.

At last the empty days and nights of isolation passed and I was taken from my cell to be processed out of Fresnes prison. I had become oblivious to the screaming screws as they cajoled me along the sacred corridor with my shoulder to the wall. I arrived at the bedding store to find Richard wild-eyed with fear as his escorts were abusing him.

"Hey, Richard!" I shouted, "Raise your head and give them that big smile of yours."

Dropping his bedding, he gawped at me incredulously.

"Go on!" I said. "Grin at the cunts… we're out of here!" I threw my bedding on top of Richard's, looked at the screw and asked, "What now, you frog cunt?"

At the end of the counter I could see my holdall with papers and my passport as another screw beckoned me to him.

"Come here, you English cunt," he said, "you're lucky your escorts are here waiting for you, something nasty could happen."

These words surprised me because they were said in a Yorkshire accent.

"Yes, something very nasty could happen," I said, looking him in the eye with my nerveless gaze. He was experienced enough to realise I would maim him before I succumbed to the flailing truncheons of his colleagues. He shifted uncomfortably, shrugged, harrumphed and pushed a paper in front of me.

"Sign here," he said authoritatively, "this is for your passport and baggage."

I signed the paper, which could have been my execution order for all I knew because it was in French, then flipped open the passport to check it was mine. I quickly opened my bag to check my kit as the chorus of, "Allez! Allez!" became more urgent.

"The only good thing to come out of Yorkshire is the road to Lancashire," I said, looking at the Yorkshire frog.

I was hassled through the door before he could reply. Four big men in civilian clothes surrounded me and manacled me with chromium-plated handcuffs. Just then, Richard was bundled out of the bedding store to join me. They shackled us together and took us outside to a police van and locked us in. We huddled, freezing in the van for ten minutes until our escorts had figured out the paperwork, then they joined us for the hair-raising journey to Orly Airport with blue lights flashing and sirens wailing.

On arrival at Orly Airport we were joined by two uniformed soldiers who trained their sub-machine guns on us for the dramatic walk through the airport concourse in full view of tourists and travellers. Several tourists took photos, thinking I was a dangerous terrorist or maybe an infamous serial killer. A wide-eyed child clung to his mother's skirt as she gave me a furious look, as though I was to blame for alarming her sissy kid. People made way for us, quickly sidestepping to avoid being shot by the mean looking soldiers, both of whom wore meaningful facial expressions - great theatre. I had seen soldiers like this before; all sharp creases, Brasso and boot polish. They would shit bricks if they were sent to Iraq or Afghanistan where they might have to rough it. They loved this though, real action-man stuff in front of the pretty girls who work in the airport and something to brag about later in the pub.

We were taken to the custodial suite where the Spanish escorts awaited us. After half an hour of paper sorting everything was in order to take us to the aircraft. We gathered outside the custodial suite as the soldiers took post at the rear and front of the procession, with their weapons at the ready in case we were ambushed on the way to the plane. The man in charge of the Spanish contingent suddenly stopped the procession and ordered the chromium-plated shackles to be removed from our wrists. Great consternation ensued for a few minutes as the French argued against such life-threatening folly. The Spaniard produced two looped lengths of nylon cord and slipped them over our wrists then ordered the frogs to remove their hardware. He indicated the nearby metal-detector frame, through which we were about to pass, then smirked and nodded sagely at the frogs. He then turned to the soldiers and dismissed them irritably. The frogs retreated en-masse. Such arseholes.

I have a problem with *Matthew 5:44 'but I say unto you, love your enemies'* when dealing with Frenchmen in uniforms.

Back To Spain

The Spanish escorts were three men dressed in civilian clothes and were having a nice day out. They positioned themselves so as not to draw attention to us then quickly took us through the security set-up and up the stairs into the rear section of the plane. We were the first passengers on the aircraft and we occupied the rear seats. I had seat 25-F next to the window. Richard sat across the aisle from me surrounded by the escorts. I sat alone. Our wrist restraints were removed before the rest of the passengers boarded and the snooty stewardess treated us to newspapers.

The aircraft took off for Madrid and everyone settled down for a pleasant journey. The escorts bought themselves booze and food while I ate the tastiest Mars bar and Coca-Cola I had ever had in my life, momentarily taking my mind off approaching Spain and its shitty prisons.

On arrival at Madrid, we were held in the custodial area until two national policemen arrived to take us to downtown Madrid where we were held in a police station for an hour for processing into the Spanish system. After mug shots and fingerprinting we were put into a cell to await our escorts. Two teenage policemen locked us in the rear seats of their patrol car and we sped away with blue lights flashing and siren wailing. They had a great time showing off, weaving in and out of traffic at high speed. I am sure they drove around in circles just for the fun of it. After twenty minutes or so of sliding around in the rear seat we pulled into the Plaza de Castilla beneath the Juzgado de Instruccion No 19, which I think is better known as the Audiencia Nacional. Richard and I were taken from the car and immediately searched by Guardia Civil officers who were openly hostile to Richard. We were shouted at and separated by the bullying officers, Richard in one cell and me next door in another.

On entering the cell I immediately stood in the centre of it because fresh shit was spread all over the walls. I had problems breathing because I was gagging on the stink. Shit was daubed everywhere so I had to stand to avoid the stinking damp stuff. There was a lavatory in the corner that had also been splattered and the brick bench seating was smeared all over. I was marooned in a sea of shit.

I battered the iron door until it swung open to reveal a tousle haired guard with a red angry face. He blusteringly refused to move me from this virulent health hazard and if I disturbed his sleep again he would chain me to a radiator. I pleaded with him to put me with Richard but the racist bastard vehemently spat at my feet at the sound of his name and slammed the door. After finally leaving that polluted cell I was infected with a stomach bug that laid me low over the next two weeks.

At 3:00 am in the morning I was taken from there by two armed guards upstairs to an office, which served as a late night court room. A female judge and prosecutor awaited me. The judge ordered the removal of my shackles to enable me to sign various pages of documents. After rapid discussions between the two women, the judge handed me a pen and indicated I should sign at the bottom of each page. When I asked what was I signing, a smartly dressed man lounging in a nearby chair told me I was to complete the sentence I was given five years previously. He spoke very good English and informed me that should I refuse to sign the papers I would serve the whole sentence and not be considered for early release with Libertad Condicional. Whoever that man was I owe him a drink because I was eventually released one year early on Libertad Condicional. However, I had a court appearance without a lawyer and an interpreter, which I believe to be illegal. Richard was escorted in as I was going out and he objected to the proceedings because he did not have a lawyer and interpreter. It did not do him any good, but merely caused a delay and a lot of shouting. He came to prison with me.

When the guards took me back downstairs they put me in a different cell and gave me a sealed packet of sandwiches that were three weeks past their sell-by date. This cell had beds in it with mattresses and blankets strewn about. I sat on one of the filthy mattresses to investigate the sandwiches in the dim light. I put them in the rubbish bin and fell asleep.

At dawn I was awakened by noisy guards and given lukewarm coffee in a plastic cup and more out of date sarnies. Richard sat opposite me looking like shit. He had not slept because he was worried about his wife and kids not knowing his whereabouts. I assured him he would be able to call his family from whichever prison we were going to.

"Each wing in Spanish prisons has telephones, so don't show these pricks your distress, they love it. Schadenfreude[33] is the high point in any screw's day, so fuck 'em, don't show it."

We were chained together at 8:00 am and shoved into a police van for the journey to Soto del Real prison in Madrid, which did not take long thanks to blue lights and sirens. Gates opened and closed behind us until we reached the ingreso enclosure. We were hurried from the van into a waiting group of screws who first took our bags then put us in a holding cell with sliding electric doors. The cell was already full of men sitting on the fixed seating that was securely bolted to the floor and walls. Names were called and the door slid open to allow egress for the individual called. My name was called and the door opened for me. I did not know it then but that was the last I would see of Richard.

Further down the corridor was a counter upon which my bag was sitting. Two screws stationed behind the counter beckoned me as one of them called my name. My face was checked against my passport and then my bag was ransacked. My toothpaste, shaving foam and deodorant spray were binned in a plastic refuse bag which was overflowing with other men's shaving and washing kit and items of personal kit not allowed on the premises. I was handed the towel from my bag and taken into an adjacent shower room told to undress and take a shower. The screw watched me shower then told me to bend over so he could look up my hole. He then told me to pull back my foreskin so he could check my dick. Tiny packets of heroin were often hidden underneath foreskins so that fact justified the dick inspection. However, I did not like men up close looking at my dick and gawping up my arse in the war against drugs. This man probably used drugs anyway. He needed to in order to do this fucking job. I

---

[33] schadenfreude – pleasure derived from someone's misfortune

quickly dressed and exited the shower room, grabbed my bag and was sent further down the corridor to another counter.

"Kreestoffer!" shouted the little old screw behind the counter. It was Don Raul, a cruel little shit I knew from when I was locked up in the Carabanchel. Two female screws accompanied him and this gave him the opportunity to puff his chest out and brag about being a screw in the infamous Carabanchel. Suitably impressed the ugly bitches gave me extra soap and toilet paper as Don Raul rabbited away about the good old days when Fanny was a girl's name and he used to strut the wings like Franco with his thumbs in his belt. This horrible little bastard was treating me like a long lost friend, shaking my hand and slapping my back. He was blowing and spluffing like The Great Panjandrum[34] itself, as though he was saying at last we have a real fucking prisoner!

I was relieved when the jefe del servicio shouted for me to join him at the far end of the corridor to be escorted to the upper level and locked up. I picked up my bag and bedding that the ugly sisters had just issued and off I went to be bullied up the stairs and locked in a cell. I was put in cell number 3 on the mid-level of ingreso, where I would remain for the next fifty hours in lockdown.

The cell was clean and of modern design with a fitted shower and stainless steel lavatory - better than I expected. I made the bed and emptied my bag to fold my kit. I shaved and showered and washed my underwear. I felt good but not for long. It was then that I felt the first twinges of gastroenteritis in my guts. Diarrhoea would soon sap my energy. My meals were passed through a hatch in the cell door and though I asked to see a doctor to treat my gastroenteritis each feeding time I saw no one.

After fifty hours in cell numero 3 I was taken to modulo 4 where I was put in a cold, dirty cell with a German called Ernst. He was in a bad way having just suffered a stroke. The poor man was in constant pain and was paralysed down his right side. He was to be extradited

---

[34] The Great Panjandrum - a massive, rocket-propelled, explosive-laden cart designed by the British military during World War II

to Germany where he would pay a fine and be instantly released and returned to his home and business in Tenerife.

That first night in wing 4 was unforgettable. Ernst lay weeping with pain and cold. His right arm was blue with the cold, so I got out of bed to massage his arm and shut him up. It took ages to get some warmth into his arm. I tucked him in, trapping his useless arm with the bedclothes after first wrapping it in a woolly pullover to keep it warm. I was quickly asleep but I had terrible nightmares about the Carabanchel and woke often to hear Ernst weeping. With painful bouts of diarrhoea and nursing poor old Ernst, I was completely knackered, especially with Ernst's snoring when he was not weeping. Thankfully Ernst was extradited to Germany on Friday 26th January 2007 and I had the cell to myself, but not for long.

That night Danny Anderson arrived high as a kite. I lay on my bunk and suddenly the door started to slide open. Getting off my bunk I could hear footsteps approaching along the wing. The duty screw shoved in a skinny black man with a strange hair-do, like he was just starting to grow dreadlocks. He could not stop talking and moving. He was so hyperactive I knew he was high. The door slid closed and we heard the footsteps fade away. Danny immediately dropped his trousers and started shoving his hand far up his arse.

"Oh man, dis is fuckin' killin' me," he said, pulling a face with the effort of burrowing up his colon to retrieve his stash of cocaine. "You might have to help me mate. Dis stuff 'as gone right up my 'ole, it might kill me!"

"You're gonna die pal," I said mockingly as his face distorted with pain.

"Ah, gotcha!" he cried as he pulled out a length of shitty ribbon.

He placed his hands on his hips and bent backwards like he had lumbago and needed a good stretch. Dangling between his legs was the ribbon that disappeared up his arse. Clasping the ribbon between finger and thumb, he gingerly tugged it bit by bit until a shitty white sock dropped out to fall into his trousers crumpled around his ankles. He picked up the sock and hid it in the mop bucket while trying to pull up his trousers at the same time.

"Sorry about the stink mate," he said, chuckling.

"No problem pal, I'm quite used to it," I replied, opening the window as I spoke.

"I'll sort you a line o' Charlie in a minute," he said, washing his hands in the sink. "My name's Danny, what's yours?" he asked.

"Chris," I replied, as he emptied the contents of the shitty sock onto his mattress. "I don't want a line either, I don't touch that shit. Besides, any time now we'll be having an analitico and they'll find shit in your blood."

"Analitico?" he asked, puzzled.

"Yeah, that is the word they use for a blood test in all spick prisons, which tells me you haven't been locked up before."

"Das right bro', dis is my first bird, but not fer long, I'm outta here like lightnin' man."

Danny had wiped dry the edge of the stainless-steel sink and was busy cutting himself a line of cocaine on it.

"Sure you don' want one o' dese?" he asked, looking over his shoulder at me then blocking his left nostril to snuffle part of the thick line of cocaine.

"Fuck off with your shit and don't offer me again," I said.

Suddenly standing upright he shook his head violently, coughed, and then bending over the sink he charged his left nostril along the edge of the sink to snuffle the remaining cocaine. Standing bolt upright, he shook his head again and then sat at the bottom of my bed coughing his head off and gasping for breath.

"Is that good Charlie you've got there mate, or has it been trod on with Vim scouring powder? You're in a right fucking mess." I said, as a trickle of blood ran from his nose.

"Yeah man, it's fuckin' great stuff, but I've had a lorrof it an' I've gorra lot more to get rid of... 'specially dis 'ere.' He said, showing me six small plastic tubes about the size of lady's lipsticks. "Where can I put dese?" he asked.

"Straight back up your hole," I answered, "you can't leave them here in the cell because if we have a shakedown tomorrow, we'll both get fucking hammered, so shove 'em back up your arse when you've made your bed."

"Aw, fuckin' 'ell man, I wanna sell dis shit tomorra. Can't I leave irrin my bag?"

"You've never been in prison before, so you don't know a fucking soul in here and you think you can go on the wing tomorrow and start flogging Charlie just like that? You'll be down the block[35] before lunchtime and I'll have a new cellmate." I said angrily, looking into his crazy brown eyes.

"Well worrama gonna do wid it? My arse is too fuckin' sore to shove it back up."

"Okay, hide it in your bag and bring it down in the morning, I'll point you in the right direction, and remember, never let a spick know anything or you'll be down the block in no time."

During the few days I was there I made a few friends. One of them was Ronaldo, 'Ronnie', a dead spit of Christopher Walken and a high placed Mafioso. He had a couple of pet screws that brought in for him and he knew all of the serious players on the wing. Another new friend was Zehedin Hamid, an Iranian who was the honcho amongst the many Arabs in there; an educated man, quietly spoken, tall and handsome with a dangerous glint in his dark eyes. Apart from Ernst, the sick kraut, these two men were the only men I spoke to on that wing and with the addition of Danny that is how it remained until the day I left.

Danny was so high he had a problem finding sleep and I had to tell him to shut up umpteen times in the night. Motor mouth fell asleep just after 3:00 am and then his nose started a low droning sound that eventually grew to a lion's roar. I had to push him onto his side to shut him up. My new cellmate was in for a rude awakening should this have happened again. A good sleep is essential to staying alert during daylight hours. Being alert is the foundation stone of survival in the netherworld of prison.

At 7:00 am the duty screw came around for recuento, the first headcount of the day. In that prison they were sticklers for having you out of bed for recuento and Danny seemed not to understand the

---

[35] block - solitary

demented screw that was screaming through the Judas hole and banging the door.

"Get out of the fucking bed before he has the door opened and takes you down the block," I shouted, as Danny screamed obscenities at the screw.

Deliberately, in slow motion, Danny climbed down from the bunk and snarled angrily at the screaming screw. In that moment I knew Danny would have a hard time in there. His counterblast showed his naivety and served only to have him singled out for harsh treatment. His colour irritated the screws anyway, so his impetuosity fed the screw's tantrum. I could see the hatred in the eyes of that mad prison officer as he violently slammed shut the Judas hole.

"Fuckin' spick wanker!" shouted Danny as he shuffled to the lavatory to urinate and fart noisily. "Who da fuck do 'e fink 'e is? D'noisy bastard. I'll knock 'is fuckin' block off."

"He's wondering who the fuck you think you are," I said sharply. "The cunt will be back mob-handed to rip this place apart and you've got fucking Charlie in your bag."

"Nah, 'e won't be back... will 'e?" said Danny, the whites of his eyes showing the bright red lines of the cocaine addict. "I'd better 'ave a line now 'fore dey comes."

Danny went through the rigmarole of snorting a thick line of cocaine on the edge of the sink as I waited to wash and shave. He then pulled on a pair of jeans over the combination long johns he was wearing as pyjamas.

"It's fuckin' cold in 'ere," he moaned, struggling with an extra woollen pullover. "Fuck dat shavin' lark as well, my skin is too fuckin' tender," he said, caressing his jawbone.

I shaved and dressed and made ready for going down for breakfast as Danny lay on his bunk gobbing off about spick screws, the few he had experienced had been very unpleasant. He had seen nothing yet.

The cell door opened electronically and we exited quickly to join the throng of prisoners heading for breakfast. The flight of stairs leading down to the sala[36] was a dangerous bottleneck where many

---

[36] sala - recreation room

stabbings happened because it was one of the places the screws do not monitor. However, there was normally a screw stationed at the top of the stairs and one or two at the bottom, never on the landings in between, because the crush of prisoners was too great and they have not the guts to expose themselves to that kind of danger.

Breakfast was bread and jam with coffee dished out from the food-servers counter situated to the left of the entrance to the comedor[37], which was another bottleneck but manned by prison officers who controlled the queue. There were three lines of fixed tables with four chairs to a table - each table a satellite of the occupants' country. Ronnie, who told everyone he was English, occupied the English table. Also on the table was Hamed the Iranian who joined Ronnie weeks before, simply because serious criminals have an uncanny knack of seeking each other out. A strange gravitational pull often shapes the destiny of criminals. Now I was on the table and Danny was about to join us. Ronnie's wide smile quickly changed to a frown as he recognised the bloodshot roadmap on the whites of Danny's eyes. I quickly introduced Danny as a black Englishman with roots to Jamaica. Motor mouth Danny sat down with his jaw flapping wildly, trying to impress us with his petty crime history. Annoyingly he blurted out that he had cocaine for sale and even more of it secreted away in his suitcase, which was held in ingreso.

Breakfast over, we moved to our table in the sala and Ronnie asked if we all wanted coffee. He beckoned me to join him as he left the table to walk over to the economato[38].

"He's a fuckin' liability Chris," he said, through the side of his mouth.

"I know. He's high as a kite and oblivious to what's going on around him. If a spick finds out he's got charlie[39] he'll lose it and get some extra years."

"Yeah, I know," growled Ronnie, "that's why I'm gonna take it off him now an' make some dough out of it."

---

[37] comedor - dining hall
[38] economato - prison shop
[39] charlie - cocaine

Ronnie bought coffee and Kit Kat chocolate biscuits and we headed back to the table. The sala was noisy and full of smoke. Each table was occupied by groups of shifty bastards from everywhere. Hostile eyes averted as I clocked them, envious of our fresh coffee, unable to hide their inextinguishable desire for other people's belongings. If any of these vulpine gits nosed out Danny's cocaine he would not be around for lunch.

"When we get back to the table, you take the shit off him and ask how much he wants. I'm goin' to see a man about a dog," said Ronnie, nodding at someone in the yard who nodded back. "We need to be quick because if that fuckin' idiot has told someone in ingreso about the shit, we'll lose it today," he snarled.

Arriving at the table Ronnie put down his coffee and turned away to walk out to the yard where a large Arab awaited him, after first winking at Hamed.

"Right then Danny, here's a coffee and a Kit Kat," I said as Hamed left the table. "Where's the shit?" I asked, as he tore the foil off his biscuit.

"In da bag under da table. Why?" he asked, giving me a sideways glance.

"How many blokes did you tell about it in ingreso?"

"None mate, I tol' nofukka!" he lied.

"How much do you want for the shit in the bag?" I asked.

"I wanna grand mate. It's worth ten times dat in da street."

"Okay, I'll see what I can do, so grab your bag and put what's left of your biscuit in it and put the shit in this glove," I said, tossing Ronnie's woollen glove on the table. "Do it openly, don't try to do it secretly and don't wait to see who's looking. Do it now."

Our bags were stacked under the table, four of them. Danny pulled his bag out from underneath mine and dropped it on the table in full view of anyone who was interested.

"Don't look around," I said, "just put the biscuit in and…"

Before I could finish he picked up the glove and put it in the bag, he shoved the capsules of cocaine into the fingers of the glove then placed it on the table with other items from his bag, burying the glove as he made a big deal about looking for something in the bag.

I grabbed the glove and folded it with the empty glove. My instincts told me to move now, so I slowly moved away from the table.

"Don't leave our bags unattended. Stay right there," I said.

Danny put his things back in the bag as I made my way to the yard where Ronnie was strolling with the big Arab. The cold wind brought tears to my eyes as I approached Ronnie.

"You'll need these," I said, passing him his gloves, "And that'll cost you a grand mate," I chuckled, made a joke about being out in the cold and then made my way back to the sala.

On opening the door to enter the sala I was hit by the smoke, warmth and silence as everyone stood looking at Danny on the receiving end of a shakedown. The jefe del servicio stood to the side as six cacheros, special search-trained prison officers, were rummaging our four bags and holding down a bare-arsed Danny who was trying vainly to get up off the dirty floor. I turned about and returned to the yard to tell Ronnie about the shakedown. There was no sign of the gloves or the big Arab as I approached Ronnie.

"We better go back in," he said, as though nothing was wrong, "those thieving bastards on the next table will nick our gear."

We arrived back inside to see Danny being frog-marched out and Hamed putting his things back in his bag.

"What happened?" asked Ronnie, as Hamed shoved his bag under the table then started putting Danny's things back in the bag.

"Something about a knife," he said, with a half-smile, "they found nothing," he added.

"So where's he going?"

"Down the block, he bit one of the screws," said Hamed.

"Did he draw blood?"

"No, but he did bite hard."

"Good, he'll be back tomorrow," said Ronnie, as we repacked our bags.

Throwing the bags back under the table, we went for more coffee, leaving Hamed sitting at our table.

"Where's the shit?" I asked.

"On another wing," he whispered, "he'll have 'is money next week... if 'e lives that fuckin' long."

"Why do you say that?" I asked.

"Because 'e's a nigger wid a fuckin' big mout' an' fuck all brains," said Ronnie, looking and sounding like Christopher Walken.

The day passed without further incident and that night I slept like a log alone in the cell.

The following day was a marvellous day because I was allowed to call Susan, my lovely wife, on the wing telephone. Danny returned, but he did not matter, I was walking on air with Susan's words repeating over and over in my mind. Words of love and support and an assurance that all was well at her end, 'just remember how you survived previous prisons and walk tall,' words that fired up my bushido[40] mentality and resolve to leave here unscathed mentally and physically; words that inspired me to get back to fighting fitness and make my body hard again, words that reduced the rock in my chest to a speck of dust. My woman was a diamond. That night I slept a deep dreamless sleep undisturbed by Danny's droning voice, which I left in the distance as I passed into slumber.

The morning started early with press-ups, leg raises, sit-ups and crunches. My abdominal exercise routine would quickly grow to over one thousand repetitions each day along with neck, shoulders and arms routine, which eventually brought my weight down to fourteen stone. Over the next few days I spent my time jogging and marching around the yard to exercise my lungs and clear the shite I had been breathing since my capture. The gastroenteritis seemed to retreat rapidly as my exercises increased and I became fitter. Besides, sitting in the sala was an enormous health hazard with its thick mixture of smoke, communicable diseases like TB, the shuffling zombies with HIV, and fuck knows what else.

On 29th January 2007, I was removed from my cell and taken to ingreso for transfer to Valdemoro prison, also in Madrid, from where I would be taken to Daroca prison in the Aragon region in the north of Spain. As I was being processed out Danny was frog-marched

---

[40] bushido - ethical code of the Samurai

passed me and thrown into a nearby cell. A screw came out of the baggage room with a suitcase that he showed to Danny to verify it was his. He then opened it and produced a spinal support belt in which were hidden twenty capsules of cocaine. Tough shit Danny, your big mouth is your own worst enemy and you have been grassed.

I was put in a Guardia Civil bus with nine other prisoners and taken across town to Valdemoro prison where we were electronically searched and herded into a holding cell. After sitting in the holding cell for an hour with the stink of unwashed gypsies and billowing cigarette smoke, I was taken along the dark corridors of Spain's top security prison and put in a freshly painted cell. The stink of paint was strong, but the cell was warm and had been swept clean. However, the mattress was badly stained so I covered it with a blanket first and then a sheet.

In the evening I was taken from the cell to be fed. A scruffy screw escorted me down several flights of dimly lit stairs to where a trolley was stationed to feed the men on that wing. I was handed a bandeja with stew, bread, a boiled egg and a couple of slices of spam on it. Pudding was a brown speckled banana. I was taken back to my cell by the silent scruff and locked in. After eating what I could I lay in the silence of the cell and remembered the last time I was in that prison. It was in 1998 and I was there with the infamous Mr Kenneth Noye[41] who was actually a gentleman, rather than the total shit the popular press made him out to be. He was kind and generous and pleasant company. He was also fit and hard. I mentioned him in previous journals so I need not say more. The thick silence and sense of remoteness in that claustrophobic cell could possibly distress a first-timer but I had been there before so I slept like a log.

In the early hours I awoke and started my exercise routine after first performing my ablutions. Every morning that I spent in Spanish prisons I washed and shaved if the facilities were in the cell, a quirk of self-discipline. Because this cell denied my visual appetite, I focused my mind on happier times. I was kneeling in the mokuso posture of

---

[41] Mr Kenneth Noye – criminal mastermind and millionaire as described in the book *Kenny Noye: Public Enemy No 1*

meditation when the cell door was pulled open by the duty screw. He beckoned me to follow him and walked away leaving the cell door wide open, indicating I was not coming back, so I grabbed my shaving kit and towel and followed him downstairs.

I was put into a large holding cell with several surly prisoners and fed coffee and plain biscuits. Two prison officers entered and started handing out slips of paper. One of them called my name and beckoned me to him. I went over to him to receive my slip which had my name written in pencil and Daroca stamped in red on it. 'Daroca,' he said scornfully and strolled away with a sardonic sneer on his face. I sat in the holding cell for a few minutes then someone down the corridor and around a corner who I could not see called my name. The big iron door slid open electronically and slid shut again as I passed through it. Turning the corner I was met by a group of screws and Guardia Civil officers manning a metal detector frame and a counter from which I was handed my sports-bag and a plastic bag containing a bottle of water and two bread rolls. I was then hustled into a covered yard where a prison bus belched its diesel fumes in the cold dawn air.

A Guardia Civil officer called me forward to place my bag in the luggage compartment then ordered me onto the bus to be put in a metal compartment with another prisoner. The compartment was too small for two normal sized men. My travelling companion weighed about seventeen stone and so did I, as I had not yet trimmed down, so we were very uncomfortable for the next four hours squashed together in a claustrophobic vault. The bread and water had to nestle on our knees because the floor was running with piss. There was a toilet on board but the Spanish prisoners had urinated on the floor rather than summon the guard to open the metal vault for them to go for a piss. The act of pissing on the floor would prove to be regrettable on this journey.

My travelling companion was a Bolivian, a typical cocaine mule from an obscure village in the arsehole of nowhere. He could neither read nor write and he was lost in the sea of iron bars, blustering prison officers and cadging, intimidating gypsies, so no wonder he looked at me somewhat askance when we first met. I was his first ever Englishman. I admit my Spanish was not good but once we had broken the ice we chatted for much of the journey; but first we had problems with the cruel Guardia Civil officers who thought it was funny to cook the inside of the bus with the hot-air vents on full blast.

I knew I was in for an uncomfortable ride because as we left the ingreso compound the driver irksomely jabbed the brakes several times just to shake us up. The protests from the prisoners were met with derisive cruel jibes and laughter from the guards. The driver hurled the bus around corners and bends until we reached a major road. He then put the heating on full blast. It did not take long before we started to sweat and the protests became louder and more distressing. I stood and undressed down to my vest, folding my clothes and balancing them with my food on my knees as Juan, the Bolivian followed suit. We sat there sweating together, listening to the screaming prisoners being laughed at by the cool screws sitting up front. It was an unforgettable experience for everyone because being winter, everyone had wrapped up against the cold.

I could hear people starting to vomit and Juan came out in sympathy with them by chundering into his food bag violently and copiously. The stink of vomit and piss in the heated atmosphere made everyone bilious. I felt quite unwell and the stab of urgency prompted me to bang fuck out of the door before I shit all over the Bolivian. The bolt shot back electronically and I stumbled out into the aisle after first putting my clothes and food on the seat. The guards were shouting at me to close the door so they could shoot the bolt back to keep the Bolivian locked in. I then went to the front of the bus where a lavatory sat in full view of the guards. The shitter was a plank with a hole in it on which one had to sit. The plank was filthy and caked with shit. I was in so much pain I ignored the onlooking perverts and cocked my arse over the hole and let fly without touching the plank. The relief was euphoric and amazingly there was a toilet roll sitting there on the side.

Feeling much better, I ignored the faces of the perverts and made my way back to the metal cage. The door flew open and out came Juan, vomiting violently into his plastic bag. I needed to get back into the cage before Juan could get by me to go to the shitter, so I had to push him in the opposite direction to which he wanted to go because there just was no room to pass each other in the aisle of this grim, inhuman, Spanish contraption. Not surprisingly, his simple mind did not contemplate the workings of the bus and why he needed to first let me in the cage before he could exit to go to the toilet. He panicked. His eyes widened with the terror of claustrophobia and the urge to shit, his bulk filled the aisle so I immediately retreated, unwittingly breaking transport regulations by having two prisoners in the aisle at the same time. The shitter was only about three metres down the aisle, so I quickly took about four steps backwards and waltzed around him in the toilet cubicle. The guards were screaming hysterically as I went back to the cage and pulled the door closed behind me, then the bolt shot home. I made myself comfortable in Juan's part of the seat, but when he returned, he insisted I sit in my own seat. With some difficulty we changed places then settled down for the rest of the journey. We took turns about to dress because the guards had tired of their fun with the heating system and the inhuman cage on wheels was becoming cold, as were its occupants. At last, after four hours of transit cruelty the bus ground to a halt in the ingreso compound at Daroca prison - Satan's arena.

Welcome To Daroca

I was the only prisoner to be taken from the bus, so the ingreso screws concentrated all their energy on me. They stood in silence as the Guardia Civil officer opened the baggage compartment. I yanked my bag from under the pile that partially hid it as the cold rain of Aragon soaked my fleece jacket.

The Guardia Civil officer hurried me across the concrete yard to the iron-barred gate, which was held open for us to escape the rain. I was taken into a dingy little room where a female prison officer spoke to me in English while two burly screws looked on. The woman processed me in. She took my photo and fingerprints and completed various forms. She was courteous, pleasant and smiled a lot which softened the blow of what was to come. When she finished she nodded at the two screws who took me along a corridor and into a holding cell where I was ordered to strip naked. I removed my fleece and dropped it on the wooden bench next to my bag. One of the screws immediately grabbed it and threw it across the cell into the corner. Then he grabbed my bag and upended it so the contents spilled out onto the floor. He then stamped on my toothpaste spurting it across the ceramic tiled floor. Normally I would hold my temper with screws but the sneer of hatred from the screw holding my bag stabbed my aggression as I inadvertently adopted a fighting stance. His colleague, who was holding my documents, immediately grasped his elbow and pointed to the red ink that spelt peligroso. He reacted instantly and the sneer changed to fear as his bravado melted in his yellow guts. He dashed out to bring reinforcements leaving his colleague alone in the cell with me, so I immediately sat on the bench and continued to undress as though nothing had happened. The screw seemed unperturbed as he spoke to me in English.

"Which martial art do you do?"

"Ju-jitsu and karate, but I like to practise aikido when I get the opportunity," I said, as I removed my shirt.

I looked at him askance as I was about to undo my shoelace. He seemed relaxed.

"Are you Cinturon Negro, a Black Belt?" he asked.

"Why do you ask?" I said, leaving my shoelace intact whilst leaning my elbow on my thigh as I studied his young face.

"I practise Shotokan, so I am interested in people that do martial arts," he said with a half smile on his face, "especially foreigners like you. You are the first Englishman I have met and it is bizarre that you are a martial artist."

"I find that hard to believe," I said questioningly, "you speak English too well not to have been to England."

"My father is Californian and insisted I speak English from the moment I could talk," he said, sitting down on the end of the bench, smiling at the thought of his father. "I have English language television stations at home and English is what we use in the house."

"So your mother is Spanish?" I asked.

"No, she's Mexican, but I was born here in Spain."

Just then four screws piled into the cell with truncheons at the ready. On seeing the two of us chatting amiably on the bench their steam evaporated instantly. I stood to continue undressing and started to pull my shirt off as the argument began between the screws. One of them approached as I was removing my vest and thrust his unshaven face into mine and muttered something rapidly that I could not quite understand, but I knew it was a threat. As I returned his gaze he realised he had made no impression whatsoever and he was playing with fire. As with all bullies a whiff of danger causes the amazing metamorphosis from blustering brave heart to gutful of hot piss in moments. His step backwards was too quick to go unnoticed and caused his colleagues to advance cautiously with truncheons raised. Amex, the English-speaking screw, saved my bacon by stepping between me and the other screws.

"Please sit down and remove your shoes and socks, do not show resistance and do not look at them."

I responded immediately and quickly sat down to undo my laces, knowing in my heart that should any of them touch me four windpipes would be torn out in as many seconds. Bushido is the code of the warrior and from that moment until the day I left there it would fill my heart or I will die there.

The four irate prison officers backed off as the voice of the jefe del servicio softly spoke.

"Que pasa?"

He had silently entered the cell with a female guard who, upon seeing me undressing, excused herself and stepped out. I heard her footsteps retreating along the corridor in the awkward silence.

Amex took my shirt and balled it up to check there was nothing hidden in it. He then took my training shoe and bent it double to check there was no blade in the sole then put it on the bench. Holding out his hand for the other shoe he spoke calmly to his boss as though nothing was going down. The jefe jerked his head beckoning the four screws to leave the cell as he looked into my neutral eyes. All four trooped out giving me scornful looks. As Amex and his boss discussed my situation two screws entered to escort me to the wing, but I had not yet been searched, so they waited until I was completely naked, checked my arse then told me to dress.

I nicknamed Amex for obvious reasons and I was glad he was there to prevent what could have been a life-changing event for me. Between January and September of that year (2007) Amex and I remained friendly. He was the only non-racist prison officer in Satan's arena, the dilapidated, shabby shithole called Daroca. Amex issued me with bedding and ablutions kit and I was escorted to wing 2, the lenient supposedly civilised wing with the least sociopaths, rapists, nonces, AIDS victims and gypsies. Christ knows what the other wings were like if this was the best! I picked up my bedding and bag and with difficulty I tried to keep pace with my escorts as they took me along cold, dark corridors, through many iron gates, up two flights of stairs and along the final corridor to my new home, cell number 39. The screw unlocked the cell and ordered me to throw my bedding onto the bed and leave my bag on the floor and get out. The cell was locked and I was taken downstairs to the yard where all eyes were on me as I strolled around to check out the toilets and showers. I joined the queue for coffee at the economato where I was intimidated by a gypsy armed with a stiletto who poked my chest with his grubby finger - the first of many to get a taste of Bushido.

Bushido Again

Daroca Prison, Spain. Tuesday, 30th January 2007, my first day in Satan's arena.

The smackhead[42] threatened me then poked my chest with his grubby finger, gesturing aggressively in front of his gypsy compadres. I feigned a sorrowful facial expression and raised my hands in a submissive posture. His hard black eyes took on an instant glint of triumph, which was what I was waiting for. I then drove my head into the bridge of his nose with the most vicious, pile-driving head butt I have delivered in years. Simultaneously I thrust my right knee into his testicles crushing his plums into his pelvis. His hooked nose disintegrated internally as my impacting forehead imploded his nasal passage, changing the shape of his face forever. My thumbs drove into the softness beneath his ears where the jaw hinge is, as I lifted him bodily off the floor with my fingers clamped around his neck completely strangling any breath he tried to take. His stiletto clattered on the concrete floor and a nearby Arab quickly retrieved it hiding it up his sleeve and strode away unhurriedly.

This is a take-out technique that I have taught many bodyguards and doormen and is quite effective. If the head butt does not cause immediate concussion the burrowing thumbs will. The gypsy's head lolled in my grip as he dreamt about cooking hedgehogs, and the earth-packed floor of his mother's kitchen, as I dragged his limp body into the nearby shower block just a few metres away from the prison shop. I dumped him into an empty shower stall and retreated back through the clouds of steam into the prison yard, where I clocked the security cameras observing various groups of inmates rather than monitoring the economato queue. Fucking hell, that was lucky!

Good Christ! My first day in that Spanish prison and I had problems with the gypsy inmates already. This incident began as I was

---

[42] smackhead - heroin addict

about to order a cup of coffee at the serving hatch of the economato, when the Spanish gypsy jumped the queue and tried to intimidate me with his threat of violence in front of his tribal members who were gathered nearby. The years of experience inside Spanish prisons influenced my decision to batter this arrogant muckworm in front of his low-bred brothers, in order for them to believe I was a raving nutcase, capable of ferocious retaliation should any of them be tempted to stab me in the back, which is their normal method of attack. I was the lone Brit in this evil place, Daroca prison, Satan's arena. Maybe it is the syllables, but even the word sounds ominous and evil. This was a horrible, dangerous place to be and here I was, alone, amongst murderers, rapists, nonces[43] and sociopaths.

I later discovered my gypsy intimidator was doing a seventeen stretch for killing his teenage niece, after first raping her then ripping out her nipples with a pair of pliers. She died a slow agonising death by first suffering multiple stabbings to her genitals before having her throat slit. I was soon to discover many such foul scum-suckers in here, strutting about as though they owned the place. Alone they were conniving cowards but in groups they were deadly low cunning predators always on the prowl. Before they got much older they would learn that the lone Brit was more deadly than they were.

Daroca prison was just a couple of kilometres away from the village of Daroca situated about one hundred kilometres south-west of Zaragoza in the north of Spain. It was an evil, decaying hole full of stress and misery, which has gouged a scar across my memory that will live with me until my dying day, because that was Satan's arena and I was soon to feel his presence. I started scribbling my journal on Tuesday 30th January 2007, another unforgettable milestone in my life. Nevertheless, I would experience many more bad days and nights before I left that dreadful place, especially the night the Prince of Darkness came to visit, but first I needed to find my way around.

I gazed through the bars of my cell window on my first day. I could just see the barren hills through the three coils of razor wire piled on top of each other atop the concrete block wall, which

---

[43] nonces - child molesters/killers

formed the perimeter of the prison. The wall was eight metres high and on my side of the wall was the exercise yard, best known as the pateo in Spanish lingo. The exercise yard was the size of a football pitch and as I looked at it, it was empty because everyone was in lockdown until 5:00 pm.

A bitter wind blew across from the wilderness because that was all that could be seen from here - wilderness. I was in cell number 39 on modulo 2. I noticed the grey sky met the horizon in the centre of the middle coil of razor wire. I discovered that if I stood on my plastic chair I could gaze through the uppermost part of the iron bars and get an unmarred view of the bleak horizon. I quickly realised the effort was not worth it. It was miserable on the outside as well as the inside of that place, in the arsehole of nowhere.

My cell was cold and damp with one small central heating radiator housed under the ancient sink. There was a concrete lavatory pan, scarred and rotten with many years of use and abuse. A single iron-barred window let in poor light from the grey wintry skies of Aragon. In the poor light I could see the cell had not seen a paintbrush for many years and crispy green bits lay in the corners like old cornflakes. My heart sank even further with the realisation that this pit was my abode. I was to discover that all of the cells on this wing were much the same, so there was no point in trying to change cells. With my chin in my hands and my elbows on the windowsill I gazed out across the yard.

At the eastern end of the pateo[44] I could see the screws' office and next to it the iron-barred gate entrance. The gate swung open as the inhabitants of Pandemonium entered the pateo for their two hours of daily exercise. These prisoners were segregated from the normal prison population because they were a danger unto themselves and to others. Also, some of them were perpetrators of heinous crimes against children and other prisoners would kill them given the chance. Nonetheless they still formed into groups of threes and fours to march around the pateo. I noticed that they were mostly Spanish gypsies. There were fifteen gypsies and just three payos[45]. They all had

---

[44] pateo – exercise yard
[45] payos – non-gypsies

lank, jet-black hair and a darker shade of skin than the normal Spaniard. These inmates were housed on our wing, but locked away in an annex in solitary confinement for twenty-two hours a day. The place we foreigners called Pandemonium was the lair for the scum of Spain. They were herded in and locked down at 4:50 pm. Then we would be removed from our cells and herded into the exercise yard to freeze our arses off until 8:00 pm when we came back inside for feeding.

I could come in out of the cold if I wished. I could use the sala, the recreation room where the television was blaring away at full volume on the cartoon channel, which seemingly was the favourite of all Spanish gangsters. The noise was unbearable with clattering dominoes and shouting gypsies, reminiscent of but noisier than the monkey house at the zoo. Then there was the smoke; a mix of rolling baccy, cigarettes, cigars and spliffs mingling with the stink of unwashed bodies. The room was germ-laden with colds and influenza, tuberculosis, and Christ knows what else. There were umpteen cases of full-blown AIDS and I did not like the idea of brushing up against any of the shuffling zombies in the sala, so I stayed outside in the crisp, cold air of Aragon.

As I wrote the beginnings of my journal I lifted my head to gaze through the window and pondered my words, when one of the Pandemonium nonces clocked me in my cell window. Shouting up at me to attract my attention he yelled.

"Amigo, cigaro por favour!"

As he said this he made like puffing a cigarette with two fingers to his mouth, beckoning with his other hand to throw him a cigarette. He had a face like a plaice, flat and pallid with bulging eyes, reminiscent of a sunburned Clement Freud. I wondered how many children he had interfered with as I shouted and gave him the finger.

"Fuck off!"

Do not be shocked dear reader because in justifying my profanity I need to explain how these people treated me with their innate racism and hatred of all payos. Believe me, the only time they feigned friendship was when they were trying to cadge something from me like ciggies, coffee, or anything of value that could be sold to other inmates, normally for heroin. At any other time, if you were not Spanish, in their eyes you were dog shit. Besides, I did not smoke.

He glared up at me from the concrete yard, his bulging eyes filled with hatred. Had I been down in the yard he would have plunged his pinchou[46] into my back without a second thought. These people were whelped without a conscience. I hated them just as they hated me, it was inequitable, but they were a tribe and I was the lone Brit. Since my arrival I had to tolerate much in the way of racism from the lowliest of Spanish prisoners and funcionarios[47]. On my first day indigenous inmates in the comedor shunned me away from their dining tables. On approaching a dining table the Spanish occupants made it clear that I was not welcome.

"You are a giri[48], so fuck off!" was the collective outcry.

The dining tables were jealously guarded areas of national pride. Each one was a satellite of whichever country the occupants represented. There was no surrogate England in that pit and I was the only Brit, so I needed to find an ally before my scran went cold. I could see there was a Russian table and there was no mistaking the Arab tables, so I opted for a seat with the Arabs because I used to have many Moroccan friends - better the devil you know. Eleven Moroccans occupied the nearest table to the food-serving counter, so room for one more. I placed my bandeja on the table and said, 'Salaam malikum'. A chorus of, 'Malikum salaam,' greeted me in return. At last I had found a place to sit with the Arabs and, when they discovered I was a Brit, they welcomed me with a barrage of questions. On learning that I used to skipper yachts and RIBs working out of Nador and other North African locations, I became an instant hero. In the meantime I tried to eat the swill on my bandeja, but it was only fit for a pig not for an Englishman - a broad hint of future weight loss.

The man sitting next to me was a middle-aged Moroccan by the name of Abdelmalik who spoke a little English and very good German. We became instant friends. He was leaving the next day on

---

[46] pinchou - spike, chiv, shank, stabbing implements
[47] funcionarios – employees, staff
[48] giri - foreigner

a permiso[49], a six-day leave of absence from the prison granted to men of good behaviour who were nearing the end of their sentence. He asked if he could join me in my cell, because if the screws put a gypsy in his cell while he was on permiso there would be none of his belongings left on his return. I agreed knowing the screws were likely to put a gypsy in with me because very few men had the luxury of a single cell. I would be better off with the likes of Abdelmalik than sharing my cell with an unknown scumbag who would likely rob me or infect me with a horrible contagious disease like tuberculosis or even worse.

We finished our meal and went to the screws' office to ask for Abdelmalik to be transferred to my cell. Don Angel was the duty screw. He was a short, chubby, pasty-faced shit of a creature wearing a blue-serge uniform with gravy stains down the front of his light blue shirt. Don Angel sat slouching in his chair with his feet up on the office table and was thoughtfully chewing on his pencil, when Abdelmalik asked politely if he could join me in my cell today before he went on permiso. The response was memorable. The officer's feet slid off the table and surprisingly, quick as a flash, forced Abelmalik to step backwards out of the office with the point of his pencil a fraction of an inch away from his eye. I stepped backwards to give Abdelmalik room to retreat as Don Angel gave him the rough edge of his tongue. The translated vitriol sounded rather like this.

"Fuerra… Get out, you filthy African bastard… and what do you want, you English cunt?"

I expected racist abuse because that was the norm in Spanish prisons. I knew that because I had been inside enough of them to become an expert. Racism arose all the time for lone foreigners in Spanish prisons. My experiences were noted in previous journals written whilst in custody in the Carabanchel, the infamous hellhole in Madrid; Soto del Real and Valdemoro prisons, also in Madrid; Alhurin de la Torre prison in Malaga; La Moraleja in Palencia; and now this evil pisshole, Daroca. Oh yes, experts had racially abused me.

---

[49] permiso leave of absence

So if you are relaxing on the beach do not be upset by my anti-Spanish sentiment. Just stay away from drug deals or you will find yourself experiencing abuse just like I did. Abuse is not only the domain of the Spanish - other EU members are equally as nasty. Prison officers are much the same no matter where they are. I was in the Douai dungeon, a primitive hovel in France, where the screws acted like screaming lunatics who thought they were in the Foreign Legion, with shaven heads and stiff military bearing. They were much the same in Fresnes prison near Paris - martinets, screaming and bullying and seeking an excuse to clout you with a truncheon or give you a good kicking. But I have said enough about them.

I was about to help Abdelmalik move into my cell after that abusive incident with the xenophobic Spanish prison officer. Don Angel who allowed Abdelmalik to move into my cell after the latter had apologised for disturbing the officer's daydreams. My new Moroccan friend followed me upstairs to flit from his cell to mine. He piled his kit into the two empty lockers, made his bed and immediately fell asleep. It was siesta time in Daroca but I was not about to sleep. I needed to focus on my attitude and mentally brace myself for the inherent danger that existed all around me. National shibboleths, to do with race rivalry and hatred, were alive and thriving in this place. Even the screws displayed their loathing of foreigners and dislike for their own indigenous population of gypsies.

Bushido was the focus of my meditation - unbridled violence and fearless retaliation was uppermost in my mind. Awareness and the ability to break bones were the keys to my survival in Satan's arena.

Maricon Africano

Early the next morning, 31st January 2007.

Abdelmalik would soon leave to start his permiso, six days with his family in Girona. I looked forward to spending six days alone in my cell so I could practise my martial arts exercises, breathing exercises, meditate and pray in silence.

The day started with recuento, the first head count of the day. This is the best part of the day for screws because they shout and scream and bang iron doors to get people out of bed. Also, if they are really lucky, this is when they find the dead bodies of suicides. At 7:45 am we were unlocked and had to vacate our cells to go down for breakfast. I shot the bolt on the cell door and went down with Abdelmalik for breakfast. We had coffee and bread and cold cuts of spam. The Moslems were served slices of cheese, but Abdelmalik took the spam for me because he was going home and only wanted coffee. I was the only prisoner on the table eating spam. I was the only infidel. The man sitting next to me elbowed me rudely.

"He is English," he said, pointing to a man walking by with coffee and bread. "Hey, English!" he shouted. The man turned, scowling at the Moroccan.

"English!" he shouted again, pointing at me.

The man stopped, looked at me.

"You English?" he asked.

I nodded because my mouth was full of bread and spam.

"I'll see you after breakfast," he shouted, grinning broadly.

I was somewhat perplexed because I was told I was the only Brit in this prison. A screw appeared next to our table and beckoned Abdelmalik to follow him out of the comedor and escort him to ingreso to process him out.

"Do not let anyone in our cell while I am away," he said, "everybody here is robber. Be careful," then he was gone.

The coffee was white and sweet and I was actually enjoying it when I heard a South African accented voice behind me.

"So you're a Brit then?" more of a statement than a question.

Turning my head I looked up into the face of a broad-shouldered, shaven-headed man who was grinning broadly and holding out his hand.

"Yeah man, I'm a Brit all right, but you ain't, you're South African," I said, grasping his hand and shaking it.

"That's right pal, but these people here think I am a Brit 'cos I got a Brit passport and an address in London."

"I'm just glad to hear English lingo,' I said, shoving up to make room for him on my table.

Instead of sitting down, he walked away from me shaking his head negatively. He came around the table to face me.

"I wouldn't sit on that table with those cunts for anything, so I'll see you in the pateo mate," he said, as he turned to walk away again, then stopped and called back as an afterthought. "The name's Greg, by the way," then he disappeared through the iron gates and along the corridor leading to the pateo.

I finished my breakfast and packed the extra bread and spam in my sports bag. I noticed several bags on a ledge near my table, so I placed mine amongst them. One of the Arabs was eyeing me so I asked him if it was safe to leave my bag there. He told me that it would likely be rummaged for cigarettes by the gypsies, but not while Arabs were nearby it. My bag held washing kit and a towel and my writing pad with a few envelopes, so I decided to leave it with the Arabs for a while so I could check out the facilities.

I walked through the big iron gates of the comedor and turned right to go down the corridor leading to the pateo. At the end of this corridor was the entrance to the screws' office, an iron-gated entrance to the toilet block, a telephone booth and the iron-gated entrance to the yard. There was always a huddle of noisy prisoners at the end of this corridor and much larking about. As I approached the entrance to the yard this group of prisoners fell silent. I could hear the man talking into the telephone and the screws talking in their office as the others eyed me up. At a glance I gathered they were all gypsies. In that moment I resolved to inflict as much physical injury as my years of martial arts training could bestow on them if they should attack me. Their dark eyes were full of malice as they sneered and snarled, but frontal attacks require guts, and besides, the screws were only a few feet away. I need not have braced myself, but I knew I could never relax in Satan's arena.

The bitter cold winds of Aragon whipped around the pateo chilling the few inmates that were jogging around wrapped in scarves and ski jackets. I walked against the flow so I could see the faces of the joggers. As they passed they nodded, waved or winked an acknowledgement - they were the Russians. I heard an approach from behind so I sidestepped and turned quickly to find Greg, the South African, hurrying to reach me, his breath showing white in the cold air.

"Where's yer bag, mate?" he said, all concerned.

In that moment I knew he was an iron[50] and like all irons he would be a pain in someone's arse, but not mine, I am a family man.

"It's on the ledge next to my table in the comedor. Why?" I replied.

"C'mon, let's get it and put it with mine in the sala where it will be safe. You ought to know better than leave it unattended in a place like this!" he chided, unable to hide his kinship with Larry Grayson.

Many will remember Larry Grayson, the Brummy[51] queer, who was partly responsible for altering the meaning of the English word gay in his camp television show. I met many queers during the years I spent in Spanish prisons, even blatant transvestites dressed in skirts and blouses, but none that could communicate in a meaningful way because of language barriers. Maybe that is why I tolerated them. Greg was one who conveyed every nuance in his effeminate nature and would prove to be beyond endurance before I got much older. The tough-guy exterior with shaven head and broad shoulders, clad in a black reefer jacket with the collar pulled up, and his threadbare jeans and Doc Marten boots, could not disguise the homosexuality of his facial expressions. I needed to nip this in the bud to prevent further taking of liberties. Looking him straight in the eyes, I spoke in a serious tone.

---

[50] iron – homosexual, Cockney rhyming slang, iron hoof rhymes with poof
[51] Brummy - a native or resident of Birmingham, England

"Don't ever talk to me like you're my mother… you fucking ain't!" His hand flew to his mouth as his eyes widened in surprise and embarrassment.

"Oh, my! I'm so sorry. I didn't mean anything by it; I'm just trying to be helpful," he said, standing there with one hand to his mouth and the other on his hip.

"C'mon, let's walk, people are looking at us," I said.

"So what," he pouted, "everyone here knows I am gay, so you need not bother yourself with that," he said, striding out to keep up with me as I walked away from him to do a lap of the yard.

"You're not anti gay, are you?" he asked as he drew level with me.

"No, not yet," I answered, "I believe in live and let live, but I don't like missionaries."

"What do you mean by missionaries?" he asked, smiling, but with tears in his eyes created by the bitter winds of Aragon.

"Blokes with an axe to grind," I replied, "blokes who try to convert others to their shitty ways, be it religion, politics or deviant sexual practices. People who recruit children to perform criminal activities and procure kids for paedophiles, blokes who seduce vulnerable teenagers who need fatherly advice rather than the caress of an older male predator, probably a corned beef inspector just like you."

I braced in readiness to punch his lights out should he take umbrage at my speech.

"So, you are anti gay!" he blurted, his round face showing a hurt expression.

"No, I'm anti missionary gay, anti predator, anti seducers of kids. I really do not care who you squirt your AIDS into, just so long as it's one of your own."

"I haven't got AIDS!" he bleated, with a fresh hurt expression on his face.

"Only you believe that," I growled. "Anyone with a pennyworth of sense wouldn't believe a bloke who takes it up the arse.

Just then we were walking past the screws' office and a screw beckoned me into the office. Greg came with me but the screw waved him away. Disgruntled and perplexed he walked away with his hands thrust deep into his pockets, unable to hide the dejected expression on his face, with his head down looking at his feet. I would see much of this posture over the next eight months. The screws' office was polluted with cigarette smoke and body odour so I stood in the doorway rather than enter their obnoxious nest. Inside were four prison officers looking intently at me with hostile dark eyes.

"Ustedes maricon?" asked the fat thug in blue serge.

Fucking hell! He is asking if I am a queer.

"No!" I said emphatically.

My Spanish has never been good, but I did understand quite a bit so I was able to tell them that I am a family man and no way do I bite the pillow. The fat thug was badly scarred around the face and his name was Don Lorenzo. He hated queers, gypsies and Arab Moslems and I would come to know him well. I was studying the concave dents in his forehead where his skull had been pounded with a chair leg, when he asked me if I was a Christian.

"Si," I replied.

The four screws then stood up and approached me to within inches of my face. Don Lorenzo then asked why I was associating with a queer who had recently changed from Christianity to Islam, in order to be accepted by the Arabs because he was shagging a sand boy from Algiers. I would normally have ignored any advice offered by spick screws, but Greg had really shit his nest with these blokes. They were loyal to the Roman Catholic Church and to reject Christ in their prison was a tad more serious than sacrilegious. The enormity of his folly was incomprehensible, especially as it was about the access to an Arab's hairy arse! The screws and prisoners alike referred to him as El maricon Ingles (the English queer). This dented my national pride, so each time someone said this I corrected them with El maricon Africaan.

The screws dismissed me from their office, each of us much the wiser about each other. So I headed for the comedor and my bag. My bag was undisturbed so I settled down to write notes in my journal and letters to my family. It was not long before Greg reappeared. Striding across the fixed bench seat to sit opposite me.

"What happened?" he enquired.

I put down my pen and studied the round face and brown eyes, looking for the something that made him different from normal men. I could see guile in one eye and naivety in the other. Over the next few months my conclusion would be proved correct - that this was one bucket of shit bloke with serious baggage.

"The screws do not like you, do they?" I said seriously. "You took the unprecedented step of changing your religion to become Moslem within the Christian surroundings of a Spanish prison. You must be fucking mad!" I said angrily.

"Why should you take sides against me?" he bleated, his semi pout seemingly permanent as though he wanted to kiss something all the time. "I love my boyfriend and we are to marry just as soon as we can," he retorted defiantly.

"Where is he?" I asked, trying to keep a straight face as I closed my journal.

"He's on modulo 4. He was here with me, we shared a cell, but we had a tiff so we were separated. But he's coming back to me soon and we'll be together again."

"Where did you meet him?" I asked.

"Here, he was put in my cell last year and we fell in love that very first night."

"What happened?"

I could not believe my ears as this strange person who I had only just met started to candidly disclose intimate sickening details about how the South African connected to the North African on their first night together in a shitty prison cell. He got as far as telling me how their foreplay started with the sucking of each other's cocks. I had to close this conversation as he started sighing and making dramatic pledges of true love for his hairy-arsed Arab boyfriend. I could only take so much of this shit.

"See you later," I said, stuffing my journal into my bag and putting it on the ledge, "I'm going for a run around the yard."

I left him sitting there open-jawed. It was cold in the yard so I jogged to keep warm. I did not break into a sweat but I needed a shower anyway so I jogged until midday then collected my bag from the comedor and entered the shower block.

The shower block entrance was in the yard a few metres away from the economato serving hatch, and housed a line of wash hand basins with stainless steel mirrors for shaving in the ablutions room before entering the shower block proper. There were thirty shower cubicles lining the walls with wooden benches in the centre, where blokes undressed and stored their clothes in their bags. White tiles covered the walls and the floor was terrazzo finished and quite slippery. Clouds of steam, so thick that you could barely see across the room, greeted you as you entered. The noise of shouting men and splashing water made normal conversation impossible. One had to shout at one's companion to be heard, as younger prisoners larked about noisily flicking towels around each other's arses in fun.

I found a vacant cubicle and undressed, hiding my gold Omega Sea Master wristwatch in my bag, wrapped in the clean underwear I would use after showering. I bought this watch in Malaysia in 1965 and it is very dear to me. I did not take my eyes off that bag until the watch was back on my wrist. I knew it was waterproof but the old strap needed renewing so I kept it dry at all times.

As I soaped myself I noticed that the Arabs wore their underpants when they showered and some of them covered the entrance to their cubicles with large plastic refuse bags to hide their modesty. When they stepped out of the shower, they wrapped themselves in towels to ensure no one clocked their arses, especially infidels like me, as they fumbled to take off their wet underpants.

Worlds apart the Russians boldly strode about with half erections, showing off their muscular physiques and dangling bits proudly. Curiously they were all big men and about the same age. I would later discover they were ex-Spetznaz[52] and quite ruthless. Each of them was in there for robbery with violence and murder and they were all serving long sentences. Incidentally they hated prison officers, gypsies, Arabs, and Spaniards in that order and, as time passed, I would witness many broken faces at the hands of these Russians. Strangely, they were friendly and kind to me, the lone Brit.

---

[52] Spetznaz - Special Forces

Knowing that the shower block was the most dangerous place in the prison, I showered, dried, dressed and got out of there sharpish. I had gypsy enemies and the shower block was not controlled or monitored by the prison staff. This was the place where scores were settled and unwary men were ambushed, stabbed, raped and robbed by the ever-present predator, the Spanish gypsy.

Exiting the shower block I headed for the comedor to continue writing - but when I arrived the duty screw told me it was closed because the kitchen personnel were getting things ready for feeding time and I must go into the sala where the feeding queue was forming.

I went back into the yard to enter the sala and join the queue, but the smoke and noise was too much for me. So I waited outside in the yard and watched the pushing and shoving of Arabs and gypsies at the front of the queue. Then as the gate opened it allowed the contents of the sala to pour into the comedor. As the queue dwindled I went inside to get some food.

Because Abdelmalik was away on permiso there was an empty space next to me at the dining table. Two new Arabs had arrived on the wing that morning and one of them sat next to me in Abdelmalik's seat. His companion stood behind me and told me to move from the table so he could sit to eat his food. When I ignored him, he made the memorable mistake of spilling some hot soup down my neck. I stood up as if to move and find another table, then tilted his bandeja of food so that it emptied down his front, whilst simultaneously blinding him with a nukite[53] strike to his eyes, followed quickly by shuto[54] into his Adam's apple, and a power punch to the heart. His pal was fumbling for his dagger when I drove my fist through his collarbone and back-fisted uraken[55] his temple, instantly stunning him. He fell backwards off the bench onto his companion with the dagger in his hand, as the comedor screw responded to the sudden disturbance behind him. All he saw was the lone Brit sitting down to his food and two inert Arabs, one with a dagger in his hand, lying on top of the other. I worried needlessly about the other Arabs

---

[53] nukite - strike
[54] shuto - chop
[55] uraken - back-fist

on the table because to a man they shook their heads negatively when questioned by the screws.

The momentary silence in the comedor changed to uproar as four screws removed the two Arabs, each dragging an ankle. As they went through the iron gates on their way to the searching cell across the corridor, more screws entered to calm down the excited gypsies making all the noise. I looked up from my food to see the men on the Russian table wearing enormous grins and giving me the thumbs-up gesture. Amazingly I was not grassed because the Arabs on my table were the only people to see what really happened. The Arabs on my table were Moroccans. The two new blokes were Algerians from another wing and were known troublemakers. I wondered what would happen next. I had been here only a couple of days and my tally was three down and Christ only knows how many to go. It would not take long before my tally grew.

Wednesday 7th February came and England played a football match against Spain at home and the useless bastards lost one - nil to Spain. Oh, fucking hell! The ignominy of it all when I appeared for breakfast the next day - even the screws took the piss! My spirits were low as I walked along the corridor to the yard after breakfast taking a ribbing from everyone I met.

Suddenly, there appeared a spick gypsy pretending to be a Red Indian, dancing and whooping an American Indian war dance. He started to dance around me with one hand to his mouth, whooping. His other hand was held behind his head, making like a feather. He was possibly five feet tall and skinny - a dead ringer for Mahatma Gandhi without his dhoti and spectacles. His Walkman radio hissed techno shite and squelch into the space between his ears full blast as he entertained his tribesmen. Unwittingly I sidestepped him to enter the yard and as I passed him, he struck me from behind. I least expected this because I was right next to the screws' office, the telephone queue and the entrance to the toilets. This would be the last time my mental state of alertness was found lacking in prison, as a double implant and bridge of teeth were knocked out of my mouth by the knuckleduster on the hand of my attacker. The shock waves cleared quickly from my skull as his second punch came into view. It appeared as though in slow motion and I could not quite block it, though I did take it on my forearm rather than my face. The blood trickled down my throat as I stepped into him grabbing his testicles in my right hand and his throat with my left hand and squeezed with all my might, my momentum taking us through the shithouse door away from the screws' office before they could hear anything. I rushed him across the stinking room to the wash hand basin on the wall to smash his face into the tap, taking out most of his teeth by whizzing his mouth around the chromium-plated tap.

During the few seconds it took to finish at the sink, my left hand had prevented him from screaming and breathing so now he was on the verge of passing out. I twisted his head so he could see my face and my mad grin before consciousness left him. As he passed out I dragged him into trap number one and sat him on the raised toilet step and made sure he was breathing all right. There were four toilet cubicles in there and they were white-tiled with a raised dais with a hole in the centre and a ribbed tile on either side of the hole to aid your aim. The smell was incredibly strong and will remain in my olfactory memory for the rest of my life. I left him sitting peacefully listening to his Walkman hissing into his ringing ears as I prepared myself mentally for a trip down the block. Though his teeth were knocked out he did not have any bleeding exterior wounds. Nor did I. So I quickly rinsed my five-tooth bridge implant and stuffed it in my pocket.

I left the shithouse through the yard exit rather than passing the screws' office. As I passed the exit from the telephone corridor to the yard I saw four large Russians blocking the corridor and shithouse doorway preventing any grassing by the gypsies and two more preventing assistance to the sleeping Gandhi. Nevertheless his demise could be reported at any moment because men where continually entering the shithouse using the yard entrance. Just a few minutes later I thought that moment had come because my name was called over the tannoy system. I was marching around the yard stemming the blood flow in my mouth with my tongue as the loudspeakers first began to crackle and then my name was called. Blood was pouring from a split in my mouth along the line of my lip about an inch long.

Blood also dripped out of the holes in my gum where the implants and bridge used to be, leaving a gap of five teeth, which included one of my front teeth, so hiding my injury from the screws would be difficult. I was terribly dismayed at the loss of my teeth because they had only recently been fitted. Most of my teeth were implants and bridges because, apart from a couple of molars, they were all knocked out by the Spanish secret police when they arrested me, prior to throwing me into the Carabanchel prison just a few years previously - but that story is in the previous journal to this one - and so another fucking cowardly spick had knocked them out again! Thereafter these words became one of my favourite mantras at the end of each day when I prayed and meditated before sleep, 'I will never ever be found off guard again and I will brain any fucking gypsy who enters my space'. I walked across the yard to the window hatch of the screws' office, which opened quickly and the duty screw shouted.

"Asistenta social!"

Jerking his thumb vaguely over his shoulder, he closed the window quickly to keep out the bitter wind. The asistenta social had a consulting room in the comedor, as did the psicologa. The social worker and the psychologist visited the wing every day except Saturday and Sunday and today these two women would interview me for the first time. Over the ensuing months they would interview me several times, to justify their existence, and I would discover that the social worker knew what she was about but the shrink was about as useful as a chocolate teapot.

I entered the corridor leading to the dining hall and as I passed the gate to the shithouse, I quickly looked in to find Gandhi was no longer there. Guessing correctly that he was in the enfermeria I made my way quickly to the social workers' room where Greg, the poof, was standing outside waiting for me.

"Oh my" he said, hand to mouth in a dramatic camp gesture, "what have you done?"

His other hand going to his hip, just like Larry Grayson's would have done, to create that goofy, ponce posture much practised by queers. Grabbing my bag I ripped off a yard of paper from my bog roll to clean around my mouth before entering the interview room. I took a swig of water from my bottle, swilled it around my mouth and spat the mixture of blood and water behind the radiator where it could not be seen. I then wiped my mouth and attempted to plug my gum with toilet paper.

"That's better," said Greg, girlishly cocking his head to one side. "Marivi, asked me to interpret for her during the interview."

"Who the fuck is Marivi?" I asked.

"The social worker," he replied, nodding his head at the door, indicating she was in there.

"Okay, is there any blood on my face?" I asked.

"No, but why don't you put your teeth back in?" I curled back my top lip to expose the damage in my mouth and he gasped. "You'll need stitches in that gash and in your gum."

The interview room door opened as a black man came out. Looking at me, he grinned broadly.

"How you doin' man? I'll catch you later for a chat," he said, and then he strode away towards the yard as we went in for the interview.

The social worker was not particularly attractive though she was a Madonna look-alike. She was sitting behind a large desk so I could not see all of her, but her serious face put me on my guard. I need not have worried because she only had good news for me. I understood much of what she said but Greg translated anyway and became quite excited when she told me I was being classified as a third-grade prisoner. This meant I would be considered for parole at the two-thirds stage of my sentence providing I behaved myself and took part in educational and employment pastimes. She asked if I would like to enrol for the Spanish language course - I would begin to attend lessons the following week. I enrolled there and then. Curiously, so did Greg. I then volunteered for work, which she said was necessary in order to qualify for parole. My parole (Libertad Condicional) would be served in my own country and, if I should return to Spain during the period of parole, I would be thrown in prison until the end of sentence. In other words, at the two-thirds point of my sentence I would be returned to the UK and expelled from Spain in October 2008. Yippee!

Interview over I sat at my table pondering the great news I had just received. Greg stayed with the social worker because he had issues regarding his Algerian boyfriend. He was pleading for his return to our wing. Regardless of what anybody told him, I knew the Arab faggot would never be allowed to share a cell with Greg again and that had he not changed his religion to Islam and had the boyfriend been a Spaniard they might well have been allowed to live together in their little iron and concrete love nest. Joining me at my table, rubbing his podgy hands gleefully, Greg blurted excitedly.

"Marivi is recommending my boyfriend, Lhaktar, can return from modulo 4 and live with me in my cell. She's speaking with the sub-director of the prison later today. Oh boy! I am so happy, I must write a note to him now. Give me your writing pad and a pen," he demanded, rudely snapping his fingers, "I'll write it now. C'mon, gizzit!"

Quick as a striking cobra I slapped his snapping fingers away from my face.

"Fuck off away from me you ignorant African cunt!"

His jaw fell open with surprise as it dawned on me that this bloke was used to treating people like shit and making demands without the good manners of saying please and thank you.

"You obviously don't like gays!" he blurted. "I've done you no harm. I've just helped you with Marivi."

"Queers don't bother me," I snapped, "but snapping fingers in my face is something I won't tolerate from anyone. I thanked you for helping with Marivi and if you think I owe you for that, then you can fuck off anyway, and that's nothing to do with you being queer, it is because you are an ill-mannered oaf."

He left the table with a haughty pout but by the time he reached the corridor his hands were deep in his pockets and his head was down and his chin on his chest. A tall thin man sneered at him as they passed each other at the gate. This man then strolled over to me.

"Hello, my name is Willem," he said smiling, "I am from Amsterdam and I just heard about you," holding out his hand for a handshake he added, "you are a big star here. You got rid of Jesus the junkie and everyone is grateful."

"Chris," I said, shaking his hand but not standing. "Who is Jesus the junkie?"

"The gypsy shit you put in hospital this morning," he said, sitting across the table from me to look into my face.

He had a comical face with a big letterbox mouth and a haircut that made him look like the cartoon character Roadrunner. His command of the spoken English word was equal to that of many people I had met from Amsterdam and superior to many people I had met from Runcorn so I knew we would be friends.

"How come he's in hospital?" I asked, wondering about repercussions.

"When you left him in the toilet, one of the Russian guys went in with Jose Louis to check him out, but when they lifted him, he threw up into the face of Ming, the Rusky," Willem started to chuckle. "Ming was drenched in vomit and went ballistic. Jose Louis was kicked out of the way while Ming tore Jesus apart. He did a wrecking job on his head and the earphones of his Walkman are now part of his facial tissue because Ming punched them through his fuckin' eardrums. He's in a right mess."

"Who is Jose Louis?" I asked, slightly relieved that it was not my handiwork that put the gypsy in the enfermeria.

"He's the old guy who cracks the gypsy whip around here," said Willem, more seriously. "He's the jefe, the chief, the king of the gypsies. He's supposed to be the wealthiest gypsy in all of Spain," said Willem, sitting with his chin in his hands, elbows on table, gazing into my eyes. "He will want to talk to you soon so be prepared for a surprise because he's smart and well mannered, most unlike the rest of his fuckin' tribe."

"So, what happened next?"

"The screws knew something was going down in the shithouse and caught Ming before he could get out into the pateo. He's down the block now licking his wounds because he wouldn't go quietly so they piled in on him," said Willem, getting to his feet. "I need a coffee; do you want one?" he asked.

"Yes please, I'll have an Americano and a chocolate biscuit if you don't mind, I'll get them next time."

I was feeling peckish and not too bothered about the soggy gash in my mouth as I ran my tongue along the wound.

"Right, I'll get you a Kit Kat," he said, walking away then stopping to say, "Listen Chris, I don't like to come between Englishmen, but that maricon is a piece of shit and he is hated here. He is a most horrible fuckin' creature, so be careful my friend."

"No sweat Willem. He's not English and I already don't like him mate."

Willem's face lit up as he said, "You can tell me about that when I come back with the coffee," and he scurried away to the economato.

I was writing notes in my journal when Willem returned with coffee and biscuits.

"I guessed you would like sugar if you like chocolate biscuits," he said, placing a plastic cup of Americano in front of me. "So where is that cunt from if he's not a Brit?" Willem enquired, his large mouth forming a grin showing his teeth were the same colour as Roadrunner's beak. At least he has teeth I thought as I ran my tongue over my sore gum.

"He's from South Africa," I said smiling, "so he might have clog blood rather than English blood in his veins," I said, laughing at the hurt expression on Willem's face.

"No mate, he doesn't have a drop of Dutch blood in him, no fuckin' way mate!"

National pride is very strong, even in shitty Spanish prisons, but the clogs are famously liberal to homosexuality so I wondered what Greg had done to upset Willem.

"What has he done to you then Willem?" I asked, tentatively biting at my biscuit and swigging my coffee to soften it.

"He owes me twenty-four euros and simply refuses to pay me back," he snarled, the hurt and hatred showing in his blue eyes. "He needed to make some calls urgently and he pleaded with me to help him, so I lent him two twelve euro phone cards. He swapped the phone cards for cartons of ciggies for his fuckin' faggot, who traded them for smack and now he just stays out of my way. He's ponced off everybody in here so you will be his next target."

"Maybe he has money coming in from relatives," I said, remembering that Greg was smoking a Marlboro ciggie, the most expensive available in the prison.

"No, he works in the lavadero[56] and gets about three hundred euros a month, so he has plenty dinero, that's why I lent him the phone cards, he earns plenty."

"Then why doesn't he pay you back?"

"Because he's a poof and has no values or pride. Fuckin' hell, you should see the fuckin' Arab boyfriend. He's thin as a whip and looks like he's got AIDS. He probably has got AIDS. I like to think he has," sneered Willem. "He's over on modulo 4 flogging his arse to all the fuckin' perv's and this daft cunt sends him ciggies and love letters every fuckin' day," he said, chuckling into his coffee.

"How does he write love letters to a fucking Arab?" I asked. "Does he speak English or Spanish?"

"No, he gets Mad Micky, the Moroccan boss of the lavadero to write them for him. That's how we know about the letters. Mad Micky tells all the Arabs what he's written and they all laugh their fuckin' heads off," said Willem, giggling. "He thinks he's a clever cunt changing to Islam, but they all fuckin' hate him more than they hate the fuckin' nonces, and there's some horrible fuckin' nonces in here."

That last remark pissed me off.

"Tell me this is not the nonces' wing," I snapped angrily.

"Not really, they're all over the fuckin' prison, but there's at least twenty on this wing."

"You need to point them out to me Willem, I can't have them near me mate."

"They're all spicks, mainly gypsies, so you won't be socialising with them anyway,' he said, twisting on the bench to look behind him. "See that fella over there in the corner with the tattoos?" he whispered.

I looked across the dining hall to see a skinny bloke reading a magazine with his head in his hands and the magazine open between his elbows on the table. His oily black hair fell about his shoulders

---

[56] lavadero - laundry

and partially hid his tattooed hands and arms. Just then he sat upright and flicked his hair back and ran his fingers through it revealing a tattoo across his forehead. The tattoo was a strand of barbed wire, the mark of the lifer, the symbol of no parole, the self-inflicted sign of the madman who must die in prison.

"He's a real evil cunt," said Willem, hunching over into a conspiratorial pose to talk out of the side of his wide mouth. "He's done a few kids in, but nobody knows for sure how many. People in here exaggerate all the time so I can't say what he's really done. But I do know he will never be allowed out of prison." Jerking his thumb over his shoulder, he whispered, "See the white-haired cunt with the specs sitting along from him? He killed his missus and cut her up into pieces," turning his head furtively to steal a glance Willem added, "they couldn't find all of her and he said he had burned her bit by bit, but they reckon he had eaten her. Fuckin' hell Chris we have some primitive bastards in here, don't we."

"Why are you here Willem?" I asked, half smiling.

Willem sat bolt upright, "I'm no fuckin' nonce!" he snapped indignantly.

"You wouldn't be sitting there if I thought you were," I replied, chuckling at him as he relaxed his offended expression.

"I was caught down in Algeciras with a parcel of hashish in the trunk of the car. Three fuckin' years they gave me and I didn't know it was there."

"Didn't know what was there?" I asked, waiting for the ludicrous tale to unfold and insult my intelligence.

Willem told me a story of innocence that I did not bother writing in my journal and would not allow him to finish because it was bullshit.

That night I lay awake as Abdelmalik snored softly in the blackness of the cell, not quite a nuisance and not robbing me of the solitude I revelled in, in that evil place. Most people thought of their cell as being the nightmare of prison and I understood their thinking, but I did not share that point of view. My cell was my safe haven, away from the nutters and sociopaths who roamed Satan's arena. The man rubbing shoulders with you in the economato queue had likely battered his mother to death or raped and murdered a child. They were all in there, all around me with their dead eyes, all different in shape and size but the one thing they had in common was the eyes, dead eyes. That was the only way I could describe them. Their eyes seemed to be lifeless and flat, hiding the menace lurking behind them, hiding their hideous crimes and the scenes those eyes had witnessed. During the years spent in Spanish prisons I must have unknowingly rubbed shoulders with many monsters.

These thoughts took me back in time to 1998 and to La Moraleja prison in the Palencia region in the north of Spain, where I was employed as the jefe del polideportivo[57] and the prison martial arts instructor. My dreams took me back through the shrouds of time as the magic carpet of the mind whisks me out and beyond the iron bars of Daroca and sets me down behind the iron bars of La Moraleja.

---

[57] jefe del polideportivo - boss of the gymnasium

La Moraleja

In La Moraleja prison I was the martial arts instructor and the boss of the gymnasium. In that capacity I met every prisoner that entered the gym over an eighteen-month period. During that time I met many monsters. I also met many good men, some of whom became friends and allies - true gladiators in Satan's arena.

One of them, who remains a friend to this day and is now back home in Ohio, USA, was my pal David. He was everything American - big, brash and a great big personality, kind and fun loving. We worked together in the gym and we shared the same cell, until he was released after serving a nine stretch for muling charlie[58] from South America. A mistake he made whilst mourning the death of his father at a truly weak moment in his life. David was over six feet tall and well muscled. His hair was long and brown and he reminded me of Meat Loaf the rock star. His capacity for weightlifting was awesome and his experience as a college wrestler made him quite tasty when it came to aggro. Working in the gym meant we became quite rich in terms of contraband and forbidden items. The reason for this was because the modulos were segregated at all times; so if someone on modulo 2 needed to give something to someone on modulo 3 it would be left with us in the gym and passed to the person it was intended for when modulo 3 next came to workout.

Each of the prison modulos visited the gym twice each week so we were always busy hiding packages and money for various enterprises - a service that had to be paid for. I also operated a booze scam that netted me enormous profit, which I shared with my pet prison officer who smuggled booze into the prison. Don Phillipe, my pet screw, brought in much contraband right up until the day I was released, and then he was grassed by one of his paisanos[59] and sacked from his job, losing his pension. Never trust a spick.

Every day I was approached to pass heroin between modulos but David and I promised never to pass smack through the

---

[58] muling charlie – trafficking cocaine
[59] paisanos - countryman

polideportivo[60]. A promise that was never broken regardless of the never-ending threats from ruthless gangsters, many of whom thought we could be bought or intimidated into handling heroin - subsequent threats invariably ended in much pain and serious injury for the intimidator.

The prison population mainly constituted North Africans and South Americans, but there were a lot of eastern Europeans who placed no value on other peoples' lives whatsoever - a legacy due to the ethnic cleansing and slaughter carried out in modern day Europe. David was the lone Yank and I was one of possibly five Brits. Jean-Louis was the frog who cleaned the swimming pool (appropriate I suppose), and an Ecuadorian by the name of Frank helped keep the place clean. The four of us truly valued our jobs in the polideportivo because we were paid and the gym was the best place to be in the whole prison. Hanging around on the wings was so utterly fucking boring and dangerous. As the boss of the gym I was responsible for the equipment, the cleanliness and keeping order. My principal duty was to teach martial arts to three classes each day and that kept me busy, fighting fit, and ruthlessly violent with many transgressors who thought they could take the piss.

There were many serious faces in La Moraleja who I had to deal with one way or another from October 1998 through to May 2000. But I never once knowingly passed heroin. I suppose there could have been the occasional papelito[61] hidden in the folds of an envelope or in something like a chocolate bar. We refused to handle sealed envelopes and gift-wrapped items that we could not inspect. Everything had to be opened for us to check what we were passing on. Nevertheless lots of blokes tried it on and we consequently found much heroin. The culprits were sent packing and thereafter never given the time of day.

The South Americans were always moving cocaine around the prison and we had our regular movers who always paid the fee; but there were many who thought they could pass charlie without paying postage. Some of them actually believed that threats would be enough

---

[60] polideportivo – gymnasium
[61] papelito - tiny fix wrapped to the size of a piece of confetti

to get their packet through. Back in Colombia they were tough guys with their guns, but here without guns, they bled just like the others that threatened me. Many Colombianos thought they were cute enough to get charlie past us without paying, they could not help it - it was their trait. Just as the spicks could not help grassing, the Colombianos could not help trying to get something for nothing. They thought everyone was like them, thick as pig shit. In all my time dealing with Colombianos I only ever met one educated bloke and he was an ex-government minister that did time with me, so he was not so clever after all. *'Ah, blessed is he who is not caught'* the writing on the wall by an unknown shithouse poet.

Christmas was coming to La Moraleja and I busied myself preparing for it by taking booze orders in advance. One of my regulars came to see me to discuss his Christmas order. Peter du Kuyper, a tall jolly clog, was an influential and wealthy Rotterdam face that loved gin. He always paid me in Spanish currency, rather than the prison Mickey Mouse money[62], so he was of special value to me. Peter was a big time dealer in various grades of hashish and was reputed to keep this prison high with dope. He often gave me a knob of chicha[63]. This day, he gave me his Christmas order and a nice lump of tbezla[64]. David and I would save this for Christmas Eve. I do not smoke cigarettes and nor do I drink alcohol, but at Christmas and New Year I would bend my own rules and share a spliff and some booze with David in our prison cell.

It is not pleasant trying to explain what being locked up at Christmas and New Year is like. I will simply say that there is nothing so sad as that empty feeling in your heart as you imagine your family and friends raising their glasses to absent friends. The pictures in your mind of a groaning table of traditional festive food and silly wines like ginger beer sharing the table with champagne as your loved ones

---

[62] Mickey Mouse money - the prison system produced its own currency known as fiches, little plastic cards of varying denominations
[63] chicha – the high-grade hashish normally reserved for royalty.
[64] tbezla, the very best hashish, sometimes called burbuja in Morocco

salute you and the ladies shed a tear. Oh, fucking hell! I am gutted and I am only writing these notes in my journal!

Peter du Kuyper had more to say than merely to place his order. He was the emissary for a ruthless killer, Alex, a mad Romanian with business interests operating out of Turkey, heroin by the tonne. Speaking softly Peter informed me that Alex had two kilos of pure smack[65] and was diluting it as we speak with a cutting agent. It had to be dished out to his dealers in the various modulos before Christmas. The only way he could move it around would be with the food trolleys running out of the prison cookhouse, or the economato supply trolley that visited each wing to supply the shops.

"Well, let him get on with it then, what the fuck are you telling me for?" I said.

"Because the screws are checking everything in the run up to Christmas and you don't get checked," he said, smirking.

"Two kilos could only have been brought in by a screw," I said vehemently, "so tell him to use the fucking screw to shift it."

"You know better than that," said Peter, feeling uncomfortable now that I was angry.

"He should know better," I snapped. "What the fuck is a wealthy cunt like him fucking around in here with two kilos when he deals in tonnes on the out?" I added, angrily, "He doesn't need to earn in here, he's fucking loaded!"

"He's got it," said Peter, "and it needs to be moved quickly."

Peter's eyes showed momentary fear, indicating the Romanian madman had shanghaied him.

"He's passed it to you when you've been pissed," I sneered, "and now you're fucked aren't you?" I said, unkindly.

"Not exactly," he said, looking at the backs of his hands intently, "but I have got myself involved and you know how fucking mad he is."

"What about your own people? You've got enfermeria staff in your pocket and you must have a bent screw?"

---

[65] smack - heroin

"I'm not as lucky as you with the screws and I've racked my brains with my contacts. I can only shift a bit of it."

"Okay Peter, only because it's you I will try to help," I whispered, "but it is not coming through the poli, and I'll tell you in a day or two if it can be done."

"Fuckin' hell! If it's not coming through here, how can it be done?" he said, sitting bolt upright, unable to hide his relief.

"That is for me to know and no fucker else Peter, and I'm not promising anything, I will sound somebody out and if it's not feasible that's the end of it," I said with finality.

Peter left the gym when the session ended and I discussed the situation with David. We both knew Peter would be seriously injured if not killed for crossing the mad Romanian.

"Why did you hint at a lifeline for him?" asked David.

"Because I might have one," I answered.

"How?" David demanded, obviously thinking I was considering using the polideportivo.

"You know that kraut kid who just joined the combat class, the new bloke from Valdemoro, the blond kid?" I asked, as David studied my face.

"What about him?"

"He was the café fontanero in Valdemoro and he's just got the same job here, he started work last week."

"What the fuck is a café fontanero?" asked David, relaxing slightly.

"He's the bloke who goes around the economatos to service the coffee machines. He'll make a great mule."

"Did he mule in Valdemoro?" asked David, looking much more relaxed now that he could see my plan of action.

"Of course he did, he was bragging to me about it just the other day," I said, "I told him to keep his trap shut and refuse all offers until he knows the score around here."

"I bet someone has leant on him already," said David, wrinkling his brow.

"If they have, he will tell me tomorrow when he comes for training."

"You had better lean on him tomorrow," said David.

"Yeah, we'll discuss this tonight in the cell," I said, as the next modulo entered for training.

That evening after feeding time we were in lockdown in our cell and David was totally relaxed with a luxury spliff of high-grade pollen. Looking at me, he drawled.

"Take a toke on this Chris and stop fuckin' thinkin' man. I can see the steam acomin' outta your fuckin' ears man. Fuck Peter an' fuck mad Alex."

"I don't want Peter to get hurt," I said, reaching across for the offered spliff.

"Don't let it come into the poli' if your kraut plan don't work."

"I wouldn't dream of it," I said, "but I'll speak with our screw tomorrow and get the kraut kid into our wing."

"What da fuck for?"

"Because I've decided he's going to work for me and not the smack dealers," I said, as I studied the spliff emitting its pungent aroma. "What did you give me this for?" I asked David, as I held up the whiffy spliff.

"C'mon man, it's nearly fuckin' Christmas an' it's a beaut' joint. Fuckin' relax!"

"Yeah, fuck it," I said, as I inhaled the hot fumes of the spliff and David's broad grin widened across his big Yank face.

"Yeah man, git that down your fuckin' throat an' fergit that smack shit an' mad Alex."

Taking another pull on the spliff, I held my breath keeping the smoke in my lungs, as my eyes watered and my head spun. The dizziness increased as the goose pimples sprang up along my forearms then quickly dissipated as I went light-headed and relaxed on my bunk.

"Take another toke an' pass it back," growled David, in a mock threat.

I took another deep drag and handed David the spliff.

"Pass me your drink please?" I asked, and David carefully handed me his brim-full plastic tumbler of water, which I gulped, then choked, because it was not the water I thought is was, it was gin.

"Fucking hell!" I spluttered, "I thought that was water!"

David laughed and laughed until tears came to his eyes. My eyes gushed with water as I laughed with him. The spliff and the booze made me feel better but, before I fell asleep, I still felt the emptiness in my heart with Christmas approaching.

The next morning I collared my pet screw Don Phillipe and organised the movement of the kraut kid who was not due for training until the afternoon. We timed his move for later that evening so that I could give him the good news when he arrived for training with my combat class at 5:00 pm.

We all had duties to perform at each gym session. Mine was to ensure that all activities were up and running before I took my own class. David organised the squash courts so people were busy thrashing around in there. My big pal Ali Safave was supervising a basketball game, but would join me shortly for the combat class. Frank the Ecuadorian was refereeing a volleyball game, so the noise of squeaking training shoes could be heard everywhere.

I went upstairs to the first floor where the iron room was, to see groups of men training and coaching each other on the various weightlifting apparatus and to make sure that nobody was fucking around and being a nuisance. Across the room were six men waiting for me to start the combat class. Four of them were sparring while the other two were doing some bag work. They knew my routine so they warmed up a bit whilst waiting for me. I lined them up on the edge of the tatami[66] for my warm up session, which was really a loosening of joints and toning of muscles, especially the neck.

It is my belief that the neck is the most important part of the body to have strong and flexible in the martial arts world of strikes and grappling, especially where judo and ju-jitsu is concerned. The neck is nearly always the cause of defeat in competition fighting, and of serious injury if not death in street fighting. Consequently I would do a lot of neck exercises with my classes and if I saw anyone shirking I targeted them for chokes and strangles sometime during the lesson. This normally drove home the importance of neck exercise. Besides, I

---

[66] tatami - judo mats

would not piss around with half-hearted students because these blokes were prisoners and they did not pay me. Out in the street I had earned my living teaching martial arts to people who would pay me and I would not allow them to swing the lead, so this lot really needed to train hard. I was selective with my students insomuch as I would not teach child molesters, rapists, wife beaters, known bullies, and people with communicable diseases like TB and AIDS, because we sweat a lot and often bleed on each other. The prison authorities would not allow me to teach ETA[67] terrorists.

There were over a thousand men in La Moraleja prison who were housed in the various wings. Each wing visited the gym twice a week, so I was kept very busy dealing with three wings Monday to Friday and two wings on Saturday morning. This meant I took seventeen sessions per week and each session lasted approximately two hours. So I did about thirty hours of intense martial arts training each week, with non-paying men of dubious character and invariably part of the lunatic fringe. I frequently wondered which side of the lunatic fringe I was on because there was never a dull moment. I was always chucking someone out for going over the top, and the number of times I had to stop throttling battles does not bear thinking about. I lost count long ago of the number of times I was attacked and threatened - it went with the territory.

The 5:00 pm class on that day was the usual mixture of international hard men. There was Willy the new kraut kid, Rolf a big hairy clog, Lorenzo a lean muscled Mexican with a terrific droopy moustache, Sergie and Vlad two primitive Russians, and Ronk the blackest bloke in all of Africa. Ronk was darker than black and his abdominals were ripped lean and looked like knotted steel wire rope. He was an athletic, skilful warrior who was fearless and as hard as

---

[67] ETA - pronounced etta, is a leftist group that conducts terrorist attacks to win independence for a Basque state in northern Spain and south-western France. ETA stands for Euskadi ta Askatasuna, which means Basque Fatherland and Liberty in the Basque language

ebony. If I were a funeral director I would want my hearse and fleet of limousines to be the same colour as Ronk.

"Okay, does everyone know Willy?" I said, by way of introducing Wilhelm the kraut coffee plumber to the blokes who would cross his pain threshold very soon. Everyone eyed him up then grunted acknowledgement - they would soon get their hands on him.

"Right then, let's get warm," I said, as I started the old military style warm up of jumping feet astride with arms raised sideways to shoulder height, alternating them from side to front. These ancient military exercises are good for coordination routines. They can be varied to become quite tricky for blokes who need to be coordinated physically. If these exercises were good enough for world-class athletes, then I would continue to use them until someone came up with something better. Many people benefit from these old routines and it did not take long to get warm and to see who was not fit.

Willy the kraut was a young man of twenty years and he was well built with plenty of toned muscles cultivated with prison weight lifting, but aerobically he was a wreck. He collapsed forward with hands on knees choking for breath.

"Keep jumping Willy, else fuck off!" I shouted, as I jumped in time with the others. He started jumping again but was very ragged and out of sync with the group. His face was now quite grey and I could see he was not well.

"Walk around the gym Willy and breathe in through your nose and out through your mouth," I said, knowing that if he was a junkie he would puke any moment now.

I watched him walk briskly around the room as we continued jumping. I was pleased he did not puke because smackheads can never be trusted, and I had Willy earmarked for work that required guile, nerve and loyalty, not the low cunning of a heroin junkie. This was why I was moving him onto my wing and into a nearby cell with Schultz, a fellow kraut, who was on the prison maintenance team and who also worked for me.

"Come back Willy," I called, "we're warmed up now and you need to take part and learn this stuff."

Willy rejoined us and emulated the others as they stretched, loosened up and got their breath back.

"Okay, line up for kicks, blocks and punches everyone. Keep in time with me and kiai on every twentieth kick, block or strike."

A kiai is a shout or loud exhalation of breath when a technique is performed, or when a strike, block or kick is delivered. It is a personal thing that needs to be studied and evaluated by the individual whose sport is enhanced by its use. However, I teach it to all my students because it is an aid to training and I feel it helps increase power and focus. Some famous tennis players use the kiai and shot putters, javelin, and discus throwers have always used it. The only time I do not use it is when teaching silent killing techniques, which I hasten to add, I did not teach in prison. The kiai was an integral part of killing preparation for the Samurai warriors of ancient Japan. Before battle they would kneel in the seiza[68] posture to meditate themselves into a state of trance and become focused in the art of kiai to induce an inner dynamism that enabled tremendous bloodlust and fearlessness in the face of their enemies and victims. This aspect of the kiai is difficult for the modern occidental mind to understand let alone accept. For this reason the methods of heightened power and focus are not generally taught by the martial arts masters who are skilled in the arts, simply because of the possible ridicule from lesser mortals who find it impossible to grasp no matter how hard they try. The practice of kicks, blocks and punches are all part of the warm up routine and serve several purposes. First, it instils discipline in movement and form in a natural way because the squad tries to keep in time with each other without the usual screaming and shouting from an instructor. More importantly it enables the instructor to move about to correct students without bringing everything to a halt. The repetitive aspect of using alternate limbs with equal power is an enormous aid to physical coordination required later in training techniques that must be performed left-handed as well as right-handed. Where teaching children is concerned, it has the added bonus

---

[68] seiza posture - kneeling

of being a good bonding method of togetherness and forming the *I belong* feeling that should be cultivated and coached in all sporting activities including those in prison.

The coordinated cry of the kiai always attracted the attention of the screws, so the CCTV camera was always focused on the combat class. The monitors for the camera were in the screws' office, the director's office and the control tower, so we were well observed, and we always gave a good show because we liked to show our discipline and gladiatorial skills.

After ten minutes of kicks, blocks and punching training I took them onto the mat for ukimi[69] practice, which is learning how to fall or land painlessly from various throws. This was most important to learn before allowing students to perform koshiwaza[70] and seoi-nagi[71] for obvious reasons. The techniques I was teaching this class defence against front strangles and knife attacks. My method of teaching was to first demonstrate the technique to the squad, then have each of them strangle me so that they would know what it felt like to receive a vicious retaliation and find themselves on the ground in a very painful nerve crushing lock. I then paired them off so they could practise the technique on each other while I coached those that needed it.

Near the end of the session I formed them up around the edge of the mat in readiness for hard combat training. Sometimes David and Ali Safave joined in this training because it was enjoyable for adrenaline junkies and skilful martial artists. I nominated one man to stand in the centre of the mat. On my order one man would attack the centre man with a kick or punch, so the centre man had to defend himself with a block and throw or put down technique. The attacker was allowed only one strike, and the moment it was dealt with the next man moved in for the kill, and so on, until everyone had attacked the centre man. Then he changed places so everyone had a turn in the middle.

---

[69] ukimi - break-falls
[70] koshiwaza - hip and loin throws
[71] seoi-nagi - shoulder throws

This hard combat training was fast and furious and required strong control because tempers would flare when a hard punch got past a weak block, and hard men like Ronk and the Russians would lose their cool and want to kill each other. Moreover most of them were tried and tested killers from lands where life has no value, so I needed to be right there in the action to prevent flare-ups. However, it was a most exhilarating method of training and a valuable aid in testing the instructor's teaching skills and quickly exposed airy-fairy techniques.

Normally everyone was worn out at the end of the frenetic combat training but they needed to cool down mentally rather than physically, so we knelt in the seiza posture to practise zazen and mokuso[72] in order to clear the mind and calm right down. At the end of the training session the squad stood to perform a deep bow of respect for the martial arts, and because I demand it as an act of discipline and respect for dojo etiquette.

There were some very hard men in my many combat classes; professional assassins, eastern European gangsters, Sicilian Mafioso, dogs of war[73], ex-legionnaires, ex-paratroopers, ex-boxers, and true hard men. If they would not bow at the end of a session they were told to fuck off.

The session ended and as everyone headed for the showers, I called out to Willy the kraut to inform him of his move to my wing.

"Did Don Phillipe tell you about moving to my modulo?"

"When?" he asked, looking puzzled.

"Now, tonight, you're in with us tonight," I told him, slapping his bulging biceps.

"Nien! He said nothing to me," he replied, beads of sweat dripping off the end of his nose to further drench his already wet T-shirt.

"I fixed it so you come in with us tonight, you'll be sharing a cell with Schultz. Happy?" I asked, knowing full well he would be delighted.

"Oh mensch! Wunderbar, ein froelich Wienachten fur mich. Danke, danke! How you do such thing fur mich?"

---

[72] zazen and mokuso - breathing and meditation
[73] dogs of war - mercenaries

"Calm down Willy," I said as he gave me a manly hug because he was so happy. "You work for me now mate, know what I mean?"

"Ja, ja, kien problem," he chuckled, "I know what you mean," he said, grinning all over his young hard face.

Ali Safave joined us to help me stack the judo mats and do the recuento[74] of the weight lifting apparatus.

"Off you go Willy. Come to my cell later when you've settled in. We have things to discuss," I said.

His smile disappeared when he looked into the fearsome eyes of my great friend Ali Safave.

"I'll go and turn off the califaccion[75] Ali, you go tell the screw we've finished," I said, as we finished recuento.

"Okay my brother, all is accounted for," he growled, and then disappeared down the stairs to tell Don Phillipe to start locking up.

Ali was my special friend from Iran. His stamping ground was all over Asia Minor and he spoke all the various tongues that covered his territory. He was also fluent in English, German and Spanish and his interpreter skills were in great demand in this Tower of Babel. He was fighting fit and an expert martial artist in the Hapkido style of fighting. He was also my Uki, the man with whom I demonstrated throws and techniques when teaching students. This was an honoured position in the dojo normally held by 1st kyu, brown belt holders who were ready for promotion to the coveted Black Belt. He watched my back most of the time, especially when modulos 1, 2, 3 and 4 were in the gym because these modulos housed many sociopaths and raving nutters, mainly Arabs and African Blacks. Ali was of immense value to me in this dark place.

"The German boy needs to be watched carefully," said Ali ominously. "There are men here from Valdemoro who know him and will use him."

"That is why I had Don Phillipe put him in with Schultz, so we can control him."

"He needs to be more frightened of you than them, so I will lean on him first," growled Ali, who always growled or whispered.

---

[74] recuento - stock-take, counting
[75] califaccion - central heating

"I will be talking to him later about a job," I said.

"When?"

"After dinner when we go upstairs, I'll speak to him before lockdown. Actually you can do me a favour and get him sat with the frog at feeding time. Willy can sit right behind me just where I want him."

Jean-Louis, the frog sat alone at the table behind ours in the dining hall. Judging by the expression on Ali's face I knew there would be no problems getting Willy to sit behind me.

"When we get back, I will take him to the little library in the pateo and speak with him," growled Ali.

I felt the slightest twinge of guilt and sorrow for young Willy because being leant on by Ali Safave will likely be something he will remember for the rest of his life. During his working life Ali had had to extract payment from heroin dealers by fair means or foul. I feel the word fair is obsolete with Ali because heroin dealers would not understand the meaning of the word. He is a master at creating pain in the human nervous system and leaving little evidence of his deeds. He told me later that during the interview with Willy he simultaneously crushed Willy's gonads and the zygomatic nerve in his face, causing the most amazing paralysing pain, to underline the penalty for disloyalty to the group of men he had now joined.

"No hard feelings Willy," I said to him after feeding time, "Ali is a big cuddly bear when you get to know him."

Willy's big blue eyes were still watering as he wondered whether or not he had jumped out of the frying pan into the fire.

"Always remember," I said, smiling, "Ali is your secret panzer if anyone threatens you, and now you are in our gang, nobody will threaten you."

After first discussing and then executing the plan to move mad Alex's heroin successfully, Willy led a productive and profitable life in La Moraleja prison until the end of his sentence in the millennium year. I cannot discuss the plan we used with Willy because it is still in operation with our successors, but it is not rocket science is it.

My thoughts now bring me back to the reality of today, as I awake in my cold cell in Daroca.

Sons Of Belial

Tuesday 27th February 2007 and it was my sister's birthday. She was in my thoughts as I gazed across the yard in Daroca prison. I knew my wife Susan had sent her a birthday card so I guessed she might be thinking about me right now. My wife joined her on the screen of my mind as I remembered the New Year's Eve celebrations with my family just a few weeks before.

The vision disappeared as Greg loomed into view. He had just returned from a six-day permiso in Zaragoza. Now he was seeking me out to piss me off with his tales of adventure in Zaragoza. As he walked across the yard he was looking expectantly for people to welcome him back but everyone hated his fucking guts, so nobody gave a shit. Ah, the joys of being a queer. He clocked me sitting on one of the rustic benches in the far corner of the yard and made a beeline for me, with a face-aching grin that stretched from ear to ear.

"Oh, there you are!" he cried, approaching me with his unmanly gait, somewhat exaggerated after being on the out for six days.

I could not endure much of what he had to say because I had no interest in the goings on in the gay bars and clubs of Zaragoza. To listen to a queer mewling about how he had rejected umpteen proposals from handsome young men because he loved Lhaktar, his Arab bum boy, got on my nerves. Adding insult to injury he bragged about spending a lot of money on booze and food, then asked me to buy him a pack of ciggies.

"Fuck off!" I said, and went for a stroll around the yard.

Later that day I was called to the screws' office to fill in a form because the British Pro-Consul had called to say he was visiting me the next day. Mr Adrian Cox was coming from Barcelona. During a previous telephone call to my wife she told me to expect a visit, and that Cox told her he would bring some British newspapers and possibly some books, so I was looking forward to seeing him.

The next day I prepared for his visit by writing several notes about various issues, so I failed to attend my Spanish lesson. I need not have bothered. He did not come. Why should he? I am only a locked up British taxpayer with a few problems.

While I was kicking my heels around the pateo waiting for Cox six new prisoners arrived on the wing. They had been transferred from modulo 4, the wing that housed the worst inmates. One of them was an Arab, the others Spanish and they looked a right bunch of pirates. I had the ability to recognise troublemakers the moment I saw them and these five gypsies stuck out like racing dogs' bollocks. They were of different heights but their features said they were of the same tribe, as did their dress. Each of them wore trainers and trendy threadbare blue jeans with quilted ski jackets. Around their necks were scarlet silk neckerchiefs, the badge of the gypsy spiv, and they were looking for a victim.

My Anglo-Saxon face attracted the spicks like wasps to jam and they buttonholed me on the far side of the yard near the shower block. Their body language was blatantly roistering as they approached, as though friendly and noisy, but their flashy smiles quickly changed to sneers of disapproval as they surrounded me. I noticed the CCTV cameras were focused on groups of men across the yard, as I was explaining that I did not smoke so I had no cigarettes to give them. Three of these pirates were to my front, but two were behind me out of my peripheral vision as the situation became ugly and a sharpened animal bone appeared in the grubby hand of the muckworm to my left. His shifty eyes darted to his right as though signalling something to his compadres. In that moment I knew I was in grave danger. The other two stole a glance at the screws' office to check who was looking, so I used that moment to slam my right fist into the throat of the bone handler, dropping him instantly as my knuckles found the mark. I felt the hardness of his windpipe and Adam's apple, as my fist crushed them deep into his scrawny neck. My left hand swept around blindly as a uraken and, by pure accident, caught one of the gypsies behind me full on his left temple and down he went - his metal shank tinkled across the concrete out of his limp fingers. In fast flowing movements I continued my circular momentum to whack a haito[76] into the throat of the other man standing behind me. The impetus knocked him

---

[76] haito - inner knife hand strike

clean off his feet into unconsciousness as his head struck the unsympathetic pateo floor. My momentum brought me round to face the other two, who were retreating wildly out of reach dancing the back-step to turn tail and run away.

Not sparing a thought for the inert sons of Belial lying on the cold concrete I immediately started jogging around the yard to create distance between the three crumpled pirates and myself as they kissed the dirty floor of the prison yard. I covered the distance around the yard to the telephone gate before the screws noticed anything had happened and slipped into the busy entrance unnoticed - or so I thought. The Russians had watched me defending myself and had positioned themselves near the screws' office to deter any would-be grasses.

Fuck you Cox! If you had done your job this might never have happened.

Mixed Feelings

On the morning of Friday 2nd March 2007 I received the latest edition of the *POWERBOAT & RIB* magazine, sent by my brother John who lives in Penketh, a little village between Widnes and Warrington, two Lancashire towns that somehow moved into Cheshire about forty years ago. The postal addresses changed but not the Lancashire accents. Anyway, this magazine caused such a ripple of interest from the North Africans that I had to make a list of borrowers!

All yachting and boating magazines were of immense interest to high seas smugglers, but any RIB publications caused crowds to look over the shoulder of the reader. There I was sitting quietly at the dining table reading my magazine, when within five minutes I was surrounded by swarthy rubbernecked Moroccans silently gaping at the glossy pictures of up-to-date craft and engines. Most of the Moroccans were in there because they were caught smuggling hashish, either by sea or overland, but at some point in their operation the hashish had to cross the sea - so now I was encircled by bright-eyed men of the sea who wanted to see the latest tools of the trade. The silence was broken when I turned the page to reveal Suzuki's new outboard motor, the DF300. This new four-stroke engine caused much interest, as did the Zodiac Pro-20 Man RIB. Noisy arguments erupted all around me about distances and tonnage from expert RIB jockeys who were probably caught in a rickety patera[77] and had likely never sailed in a RIB. I believed this because not one of them had mentioned the size of fuel tank needed to haul two tonnes of hashish across the Mediterranean Sea from Morocco to Alicante where they all seemed to be living now.

Abdelmalik was not interested in my magazine or my tales of the sea. He was interested only in overland operations and he wanted me to work with him when I got out of prison. He operated out of Algeciras, moving three hundred kilograms of high-grade hashish by car three times a week to Murcia. From there it would be loaded on a

---

[77] patera - wooden fishing boat

lorry with fresh fruit and flowers destined for Amsterdam. Not a bad little number when you think that he handled approximately fifty tonnes a year.

This prison was no different to the others I had been in regarding employment prospects at the end of a sentence. As well as being the University of Crime, prison has always been the villains' jobcentre and the preparation and planning of the movement of serious quantities of drugs were always plotted in the silence of prison cells.

Prison is most certainly the jobcentre for the likes of me: men who are experienced in the movement of hashish by land and sea, men who are known by the wealthy landowners who control much of the movement of drugs, men with reputations of success on the high seas, men who have never lost a cargo. That is why Moroccans who are constantly searching for men like myself welcome me.

I agreed to work with Abdelmalik just to stop him pestering me and, to sound convincing, I had reorganised and improved his operation. Instead of using an ordinary saloon car three times a week, I suggested a tradesman's van, with ladders on the roof and painter and decorator signwriting, to haul one tonne a week in one journey. I would wear white, paint-splashed overalls and the shit would be under the false floor beneath drums of paint and highly flammable thinners. These would be sealed off from the driver's compartment because of the fumes that were so strong and particularly dangerous for anyone with a cigarette in their mouth. This would also piss off any sniffer dogs used at vehicle control points set up by the chain-smoking Spanish police. The floor would be permanently soaked with thinners and stiff with spilled paint - a virtual firebomb, which was part of the plan should things go tits up. I would fit a remote-controlled initiation set to ignite the inside of the van should that be necessary, which would leave no evidence of arson.

Abdelmalik was thrilled with all this planning, but it mattered not to me because I was playing with these people and their plans. I intended going home to England from there, to live somewhere quiet where I could write about my experiences on the high seas and in the various foreign prisons where I had spent so much time. I had come to terms with my God and my conscience and I would never knowingly wrong my fellow man. I would never again allow my adrenaline addiction to rule my adventurous spirit, and I would never be near hashish ever again - the price was too high, prison was not the place to be. I looked around me and I was sharing space with demons; men who should be put to death for the things they had done unto others.

Just a moment before a man asked to borrow my pen. He could see I was using it but he did not consider that fact, so when I refused, the man sneered at me and called me cabron. I made a dummy lunge at him and he back-pedalled furiously into his compadre, knocking him sideways. They both glared at me as though I was the bull and they were the bullfighters. I sat down confidently, knowing neither had the guts to attack me frontally. The cretin who asked for the pen was in there because he took a monkey wrench to his wife and daughter; his pal crippled his own wife with a claw hammer. There were no tools in there so I was on fairly safe ground with these two, though they were both well built and tough looking. They had greasy black hair and dark oily skin. Their eyes were like a stoat's eyes, dark and cold and always on the lookout for something smaller to kill - typical spick gypsies.

I could hear a prison officer approaching. He was in the corridor leading from his office. I could hear his walkie-talkie radio bleeping loudly like something out of the *Star Wars* movies as he got closer. The screw appeared from around the corner as the two gypsies scurried by him on their way to the pateo. As I sat quietly writing my journal in the comedor the screw slowly patrolled between the tables, checking that prisoners were merely writing or reading in this smoke-free dining hall. The nearby sala was smoke-filled and noisy, so the screws permitted the likes of me, a non-smoker, to sit quietly and write. If anyone was caught smoking the dining hall was immediately emptied and locked until the next feeding time. Spanish prison officers loved to exercise collective punishment because they knew the real culprit would get a hard time from the other inmates. Thankfully nobody was breaking the no-smoking rule that day.

Time soon passed as I wrote and at 7:45 pm the screws called us out into the yard for recuento. Everyone formed up in ranks of five so the screws could count us easily, but they never got it right - they were so utterly fucking thick. We all stood still while the screws marched along the columns of five counting as they went. When they reached the end of the column, they compared numbers and argued for a moment before recounting the parading men. When this recuento was finished there was a rush to form the feeding queue at the gate of the comedor in the sala. When the food was ready to be served the duty screw opened the gate and the flow of men barged forward to the food serving counter.

As I got there a kitchen orderly handed me a bandeja with a bread roll and an orange on it. As I moved along with the line of men other orderlies served me lentils, rice and scrawny chicken legs. This was my evening meal. I walked over to the Arab table to sit next to my cellmate Abdelmalik, greeted him in Arabic and sat down to eat my meal. There was blood in the chicken legs and the lentils were undercooked and inedible, so I made do with the bread and orange. The noise in there was really very bad. It was like feeding time at the zoo. There were thirteen tables with fixed benches to seat twelve men to a table, so there were approximately one hundred and fifty men yelling and screaming at each other to be heard above the din. Talking on our table did not usually begin until most of us had finished eating.

I used the prison issue plastic knife, fork and spoon, but the Arabs generally used their fingers to pick up the food and the bread as a sponge for the gravy. There was always a lot of wasted food simply because it was either cooked so badly or low-quality shite that could not be sold elsewhere. I had never eaten meat or fish of such low quality before in my life since being in Spanish and French prisons. I always ate the fruit though it was normally bruised, overripe and the lowest possible quality. The yoghurts were usually past their sell-by dates but I always eat them because they were sealed and untouched by grubby Spanish fingers. The leftovers were tipped from our trays into a large bin and the trays were stacked on a nearby trolley as we left the dining hall to form a queue to go upstairs prior to being locked in our cells for the night.

I entered my cell with Abdelmalik, but he went out along the corridor socialising before the duty screw came to lock us in. It took about fifteen minutes for the duty screw to reach our cell, so I got ready for bed and selected a book to read. Unlike me, Abdelmalik did not like being locked in the cell. He entered just as the screw was about to slam the heavy iron door and slide the big steel bolt. As the key turned in the lock Abdelmalik stood staring at the door as though he could see right through it at the screw on the other side. He turned to see me placing my pillow at the foot of my bed, so I could read by the poor light that shone from the recessed bulb above the sink.

We normally had a brew at this point so he pulled out from under his bed the hidden pulpo - a length of electric cable with a razor blade spliced into each end of the split cable, which was plugged into the wall socket and the dangerous end dropped into a jug of water to boil it. We usually made tea but we often had coffee saved from breakfast and kept in plastic bottles on the radiator. Also on the radiator were bottles of water that I used for shaving every morning. I emptied the bottles into the mop bucket and sat it on the sink to shave with. There was no hot water in these cells in Daroca and I liked a warm shave.

At last we had a brew and a couple of biscuits bought earlier from the economato and Abdelmalik got into bed to lie awake waiting for the final recuento of the day. At about 9:30 pm we could hear the duty screw approaching as he noisily lifted the steel cover of the Judas hole to see the occupants of the cell. If the inmates did not raise an arm when the metal slide noisily opened he banged fuck out of the door, so it was pointless trying to sleep before recuento. One's ears tended to ring with the crash of sliding metal as the sounds diminished with the distancing of the screw.

I felt that Abdelmalik's years behind the door were now affecting him somewhat and he suffered every time he was in lockdown. He lay in his bed with his head close to the cold cell wall as the sensations of claustrophobia enveloped him. He became increasingly restive as I quietly read my book. Suddenly, he got out of bed to gaze through the window.

"Perhaps that is why I feel sad," he said, pointing at the full moon, its pallid light lost in the yellow sodium lights of the prison yard.

"You have just had a permiso so you can't have much time to do," I said softly, "so relax and think about all the money we will make when we start work. All that fucking porro[78] to take to Murcia."

That did the trick. He flashed me his big smile and jumped back into his bed and was quietly snoring in less than two minutes. I turned out the light and pulled the bedclothes over my head and tried to sleep, but pictures of my precious Susan came flooding into my brain, and so began the terrible sensations of loss as the anvil started to press on my chest. The anvil sensation was the first sign of stress building in my nervous system. If unchecked it would rapidly grow to horrible sensations of burning skin on my back and shoulders with intermittent sensations of icy coldness passing under the hot skin, as the anvil entered my chest and started to crush my heart and the urge to weep burned my eyes.

Over my years of imprisonment I had learned to stem this onset of stress and depression by utilising my martial arts knowledge. I silently got out of bed and put my top blanket on the floor to kneel on it in the seiza posture and immediately started mokuso, the martial arts breathing exercise for calming the nerves. After a few minutes of mokuso I changed my breathing to nogare[79] to boost my will power, composure and mind control. These techniques I learned years ago in Thailand with a Zen master to whom I am eternally grateful. I chased away the lingering stress with Ibuki breathing, a type of breathing used to help recovery after a shock to the system, and then I relaxed in mokuso for a couple of minutes prior to hitting the sack with a clear mind. As I succumbed to slumber I wondered at the psychological aspect of martial arts breathing and emotional control techniques. I slept well that night.

On Monday 5th March 2007 Greg the poof sat opposite me at the dining table at breakfast time. He was such a slippery bastard I could not believe the worried facial expression he wore as he looked furtively about him.

"What's up?" I asked.

---

[78] porro - hashish
[79] nogare - power breathing

He then told me a ridiculous story about swallowing a condom loaded with hashish on the day he returned from permiso a week ago, and that he had not shitted it out yet. He smuggled it in because he had done a deal with one of the Moroccans who had paid upfront prior to his permiso. Now he wanted the shit.

"Who did the deal with you?" I asked, wondering who was being ripped off.

"The Rocky on your table, the one who sits next to you," he said, looking askance at the line of men waiting for coffee at the steaming urn in the comedor.

I could see Abdelmalik in the queue waiting to fill his plastic cup.

"Malik?" I asked, surprised that Abdelmalik could be so stupid as to do a deal with this cretin. "Surely not Malik, he hates your fucking guts," I said.

"No, not him; the other one who speaks a bit of English," he said, looking at Ismail waiting with the others for coffee.

"Ah, Ismail," I said, "I'll talk to him and tell him you're constipated."

"No, don't do that, everyone'll know."

"No they won't. He's a Rocky, not a fucking spick, he won't tell anyone," I said.

"I don't care; I don't want you to say anything."

"So why are you telling me?" I asked angrily.

"I might need protection," he said, "and I want you to watch my back."

"You're a fucking liar and a cheat aren't you," I said, "you spent his fucking money on bum boys didn't you, you slimy bastard?"

The look in his eyes told me everything. I then put queers in with spicks in the mental compartment of backsliders in my mind.

"If you don't find some shit for Ismail, he'll slit your fucking throat and you'll deserve it," I said angrily, "and don't give me that bullshit about constipation. Willem was right about you. You're a fucking parasite. Go ask Willem to watch your back," I said, looking across at Willem.

The food queue started to move so I joined it to get my breakfast. As the men shuffled past the serving hatch they were handed a bread roll with a couple of slices of luncheon meat by a kitchen orderly. That morning it was Acid Fran the half-breed French Moroccan, who was badly scarred with sulphuric acid, handing out the bread and spam. He had a ciggie dangling out of his scarred mouth and grubby fingernails on filthy hands. Normally the kitchen orderlies wore polythene gloves and a white jacket, but Acid Fran was permanently stoned and did not care a fuck about hygiene regulations, nor did the screws. Javier, the man in front of me leaned across the service counter and helped himself to a couple of bread rolls and then peeled off a wad of luncheon meat slices. Acid Fran jokingly threw a bread roll at him for being cheeky. Javier ducked out of the way laughing and made a funny remark as he walked away.

Javier was a tall, slim, handsome Spaniard with a runny nose and a runny dick. He had an unusual dose of pox, which was difficult to cure, and full-blown AIDS. Javier was in prison for shooting dead a man who reported him for purposely infecting his sister and others with his morbific dick. He also infected unwary queers in previous prisons. He shared a cell with a fellow queer who was also infected with AIDS, so maybe they would die in each other's arms. I hope so. The sooner that creature dies the better.

I declined the food held out in the hands of Acid Fran and went to the tap for a drink of water instead. I had started to drink water instead of breakfast coffee because the coffee was made in the prison kitchen and was too milky and sweet and I blamed it for producing phlegm in my lungs and throat. The coffee I bought from the economato was pure ground coffee and I took it without milk and just a little sugar. I sat to drink my water and waited for the screw to open the gate to the yard because I wanted to start my workout.

The weather was getting better and I felt the need to increase my physical fitness. I did my ju-jitsu warm up exercises in my cell every morning and enjoyed that, but now I needed to get more serious and intensified my workouts with the difficult military jerks proven to increase fitness levels of commandos and paratroopers all over the world. There were very few young prisoners on this wing, but two of them had approached me to start a martial arts class in the yard. I told them I would consider doing that, but I felt it was not the right thing to do in that prison at that time. I was uncomfortable and unsettled because of the atmosphere; it was evil and unlike other prisons I had been in.

As I wrote that page of my journal there was a man lurking nearby. He was over six feet tall and heavyset and had a big paunch hanging over his trouser belt. His eyes were set wide apart beneath black bushy eyebrows on a big forehead. Words like Piltdown and primeval sprung to mind. He lurched toward me and asked for a cigarette by intimidating me with his gruff demand.

"Cigaro, hombre!"

His mouth was now a threatening sneer and he had balled his hands into fists. His legs straddled the bench on the other side of the dining table upon which I was writing as his upper body loomed over me aggressively. His flared hairy nostrils were the target for my ballpoint pen, as I held the blunt end in the palm of my hand with the pointed end protruding between my thumb and fingertips ready to drive up his nose. I looked up into the mad eyes ready to ram my pen into that ugly face.

"Fuck off cabron," I said, confidently.

He may not have understood 'fuck off,' but the word cabron told him he was not about to get a ciggie. He appeared puzzled for a moment, possibly wondering why his intimidation act was not working. The facial expression softened as the creature recognised potential danger, then he smiled weakly as he moved his face out of danger. Though he was a big man of possibly forty years, I could see he was retarded and I guessed his mental age was ten or twelve years old. He silently stepped back across the bench and shuffled out of the dining hall into the sala.

A screw strolled by with a sickly grin on his thin face.

"Pederaste[80]" he sneered.

He had been looking at us from the back door of the economato, which was situated in the dining hall and had hoped to see my pen disappear up the creature's nose.

---

[80] pederaste - paedophile

"Cuidado Ingles, aqui esta muchos malas gente - careful English, there are many crazy people here."

His words took me back to La Moraleja prison where Don Roberto, one of the gymnasium prison officers, used the same words but he was referring to prison officers, not prisoners. Again my thoughts took me back in time to La Moraleja prison to scenes that are indelible in my mind.

The Gestapo Twins

I talked to Don Roberto, the duty screw in the polideportivo in La Moraleja prison, and told him about the screams I heard in the night when one of his colleagues, Don Adolfus, attacked a young Colombian in his cell. Don Roberto listened attentively as I spoke, the expression on his face resigned to the cruelty in his place of work, as my tale unfolded.

A moonbeam shone through the chink in the bed sheet we hung on the window to keep out the light and, if I listened carefully, I could hear the ragged rhapsody of snoring prisoners. Then I heard the heavy footsteps pounding up the stairs in the silence of the night. The clump of the striding screw passed my cell as I got out of bed to see who it was. Too late, he had passed by. I heard the clunk and whine of a cell door opening electronically and then a muffled, gruff voice followed by a gut-wrenching scream of incredible volume. A loud crack followed, which we all recognised was a hardwood truncheon clouting a head. There was barely an audible whimper and then a heaving grunt, as the noise of the flailing truncheon crunched into its target. There followed an instant roar of outrage from behind each closed door on the wing. Steel doors were bashed with chairs and brooms to produce a cacophony of sound that could be heard all over the prison. The uniformed sociopath with the truncheon panicked and hurried back along the wing and down the stairs, but he was seen and recognised.

"Adolfus! Adolfus!" went the cry, which was taken up by everyone on the wing.

Louder and louder went the cry that followed the brute out of the wing to wake the whole prison. Half an hour later the rumpus had subsided and everyone waited with bated breath, as a squad of unknown prison officers entered with a gurney to collect the inert young Colombian, who had given a bit of lip to the lunatic screw the day before. There was a cry of pity from his paisanos as the gurney left the wing. We all knew he would never be seen again. We could see through our Judas holes that the young bloody face was lifeless as he passed by. Those pitiless bastards had dumped him on the gurney with his bedding caught in his legs and could not be bothered covering him, nor closing his lifeless eyes. I saw the drying blood around his nostrils and mouth and a monstrous bruise on his forehead as the gurney passed my cell door.

Don Roberto inwardly cringed as my tale of murder unfolded to verify what he already knew, as did every screw in La Moraleja. He knew, as I knew, that every Spanish mouth would be closed forever on the subject of Don Adolfus, the lunatic prison officer, who had already been transferred to another prison and would never again be seen in La Moraleja. There was a noticeable depression throughout the prison for weeks after the young Colombian's demise - even the severity and brashness of the screws seemed to soften, but not for long.

Don Umberto and Don Pepe, better known as the Gestapo twins had arrived on our wing. They were transferred to our wing because of the unrest they had caused on their previous wing. These two brutal racists had spent most of their lives in the Carabanchel, so they were unencumbered with a conscience and took great delight in causing suffering. When they were first seen in the screws' office the news spread through the wing like pox in a brothel. Morale plummeted accordingly, especially as everyone remembered that Adolfus and Umberto were big pals before Adolfus battered the young Colombian. We all guessed correctly that Umberto held a grudge against this wing, but his compadre, Don Pepe was equally fiendish.

Normally the screws observed us from their office, but at feeding time two of them would move amongst us and supervise the feeding, leaving two screws looking at us from the office. At breakfast time the cell doors would open electronically and the inmates would throng the stairs down to the dining hall and sala. The duty screws would position themselves at the food serving counter to oversee portion control and jostling, but one day was different. The Gestapo twins had positioned themselves at the foot of the stairs creating a gap just wide enough for descending inmates to pass between them in single file. In so doing they caused a bottleneck, which inevitably resulted in jostling.

These primitive, uneducated dung heads were typical Spanish prison officers regarding their outlook toward foreign prisoners; cruel, racist, and totally oblivious to our needs. Morale on the wing took a nosedive every time these two thugs were on duty. A telephone for prisoners' use was situated outside the screws' office, which inmates could use at certain times of the day. Calls were supervised and recorded by the duty screw. Nevertheless the telephone was the single most important link between prisoners and their families all around the world. Yet it came to pass that whenever the Gestapo twins were on duty the telephone always developed a fault. Their favourite trick was to put the telephone out of order by flicking a control switch in the office. In all the years I spent in Spanish pissholes the telephones always worked except when these two wankers were on duty. Inmates would be brought to the point of despair needlessly, simply to satisfy the shitty whims of these two anthropoids.

Many Spanish screws were small men, runts of the litter if you like, but the Gestapo twins were about six feet tall, broad, hairy and fat-bellied. Their faces were jaundiced and unhealthy looking, due to the years spent in stuffy, smoke-filled screws' offices of the Carabanchel, Satan's lavatory. They were probably much younger than they looked, but the gravy-stained pale blue shirts they wore, stretched across each of their paunches, enhanced their similarity to two sacks of hot shit dumped at the bottom of the stairs, where they were creating problems. The joking and tomfoolery on the stairs ceased immediately as the bottleneck formed. A bottleneck normally meant a shakedown was happening in the sala, so the moment I saw the cause of the jostling I about-turned to gather my friends, the Mezclado.

Enough has been written about the Mezclado in previous journals, suffice to say that Ali Safave, Vito, Abdullah Habbibulla and I were very fortunate to stay together after the upheaval of leaving the Carabanchel. Of course, David the big Yank was now part of our little team, but because La Moraleja had hardly any gypsy inmates we were redundant as a fighting force.

Knowing how unpredictable these two screws were, we formed up at the back of the now silent queue on the stairs. The bloated faces of Pepe and Umberto, in their threatening stance, glared menacingly at the single file of men stepping between them. We slowly moved down the stairs and, as we rounded the final corner, we came into view. Their eyes met with ours simultaneously and their aggressive demeanour changed as our five pairs of hard eyes delivered a message of certain death should things go wrong. We were literally the end of the line, if you know what I mean. Pepe instinctively produced his truncheon but Umberto involuntarily stepped aside as we approached. His vision was that of five large, dangerous men, three of whom had killed professionally over many years and had fearsome reputations formed in the Carabanchel, Umberto and Pepe's old stamping ground. Any fool could see that these men meant business and to make a wrong move now, without firearms, would be foolhardy indeed. Umberto wilted so all eyes glared at Pepe and that was the moment his guts liquefied. I was the last man down behind my four friends, so I observed the traverse of heads from Umberto to Pepe as he crumpled. Pepe's eyes widened momentarily and his truncheon descended to his side as Ali and Vito drew close. Ali's presence was awesome, his Persian ancestry revealed in his warrior's face above a massive powerful neck and shoulders. One look into those dark inscrutable eyes was enough to put your brain into fast forward mode and exit stage left before the curtains came down. Half of Vito's bulk appeared to Ali's right, as though he was about to overtake him on the stairs. I imagined the bright eyes of that Mafioso hit man glittering like diamonds into the face of the hapless screw, sending the hot news of his imminent death directly into his entrails. David had also moved to his right so there was an echelon of three big, talented and dangerous men bearing down on the wilting bully boys. Abdullah Habbibulla moved to his left to gaze into Umberto's grey face with his mujahideen warlord's eyes - those eyes that had witnessed the taking of many lives, especially the Russians who dared to trespass on his dasht[81]. If you could not read the message in Abdullah's eyes you must surely be blind or dead, either way you soon would be if you could not disappear. I hissed loudly as I observed two female and three male screws mesmerised by the sudden malevolent appearance

---

[81] dasht - uncultivated wilderness of Afghanistan

of the notorious Mezclado, a sight they would never forget. We swept passed the deflated screws into the sala to head for the coffee urn. Then an ear-rattling "Yehaa!" from David's big, wonderful American mouth shattered the heavy atmosphere and everything was back to normal. The Gestapo twins had disappeared upstairs to check for stragglers, but we knew there were none.

Later that day in the gymnasium, Don Phillipe my pet screw, told me that Umberto had asked about having me transferred to another prison. The response to his request was his removal from our wing to the prison kitchens.

Reality Martial Arts

I had powerful friends who had a vested interest in my future, but enough has been written about them in previous journals, suffice to say that corruption in the corridors of power in Madrid was far reaching.

My position in La Moraleja as the jefe del polideportivo (boss of the gymnasium), and martial arts instructor was rock solid and would remain so until my Libertad. That position had afforded me many privileges, but teaching martial arts was the real privilege in La Moraleja. The schedule of classes was hectic to say the least and my personal fitness regime was gruelling. The reason for the hectic schedule was because I had to teach a combat class to every wing on each of their visits. My personal fitness routine was so important because I needed to be on a constant state of alert. That prison was full of men of dubious character. Some of them were quite mad and unpredictable. A lot of them were just plain violent with nothing better to do than to take a pop at the martial arts instructor simply to enhance their reputation and standing on their wing.

Whether the martial arts were used for sport or self-protection it always demanded courage and endurance in order to progress and be any good at it. If you attempted to learn martial arts in a prison environment you needed to be aware of the sudden appearance of violent men, who wanted only to achieve notoriety by beating the crap out of you, or by taking the piss to provide entertainment for their cronies. If you practised martial arts in prison you would soon need to discover your killer instinct or you would not survive.

As a teacher of martial arts I was a purveyor of violence. I taught self-protection and that meant teaching some sort of retaliation regardless of style. In prison my teaching methods differed from the way I taught in normal life. Any iffy techniques or fancy and unnecessary posturing would soon be trashed in the harsh reality of prison. Sudden and devastating violence was what prison was all about, so my teaching had to reflect that fact.

The teaching included defence against weapons and multiple attackers, especially from behind. Techniques and drills had to be taught and practised robustly and often. In prison there was nowhere to run and there was usually no time for threat assessment - shit happened fast. If a Spanish gypsy bragged to his tribe about how he could flatten you, you could bet it would not be long before he had a go at you, even if only to save face, which was normally the only reason he had. There were no pre-conflict factors to consider because there would be no dialogue or warning. You would be attacked from behind when you least expected it.

It was essential to be alert and aware of situations and places where violence could take place out of sight of security cameras and prison officers. The obvious ambush sites became second nature to a switched-on chap and a high state of alert was necessary in the showers, toilets, stairwells, dark corners (there were plenty) and areas where Spanish gypsies congregated. If you put yourself amongst them you were a mug and deserved what you got. When the chips were down in prison you had no time to consider how much force you needed to use because it was usually a kill or be killed situation and you hoped to get out of it alive. To consider the wellbeing of your attacker was just so much bollocks, if not suicidal. If you defeated your attacker it was essential to get away from the scene quickly and hopefully escape unscathed and undetected by a Spaniard because he would certainly grass you.

So there were many things to consider when I structured my combat classes and I placed the ability to block a strike high on my priority list of training techniques. Apart from blocking there would not normally be time to think about techniques, so I trained my combat class to use techniques following a block and retaliation came naturally from the block. For instance a John Wayne (roundhouse) punch was blocked using both forearms, the right arm then smashed into the attacker with a fist or chop (shuto) into his carotid artery. From that point there were many follow up techniques to demolish him should you wish to show off. Looking at newsreel coverage of football hooligans or street riots you would see that every punch thrown was a roundhouse punch to the head. One would think then that a high percentage of martial arts training should be aimed at dealing with that kind of attack. Not a bad idea, but your students would soon get fed up and look for another sensei[82].

There were no other martial arts teachers in La Moraleja so I kept my combat class busy with defence against knife attacks, truncheons, bottles, broom handles and chairs. I taught defence against all kinds of attack and the aim was to defeat the attacker and leave him in a bleeding heap on the floor. If the attacker used a knife, chiv, shank, or spike he should be left with broken fingers. If he used a shitstick it should be left embedded in the buttock or at right angles into the pectoral muscle so as not to pierce the ribs. The lowlifes that used these tactics were usually in prison for killing other people and should have been put down at birth. They were not worth doing extra time for, so it was best not to kill the scumbags.

A lot of combat training dealt with grabs because a determined stabber (knife attacker) would grab you with his free hand to control the distance between you, and could repeatedly plunge the weapon into you without overstretching and possibly missing. Most attackers were right handed and did not use their left hand because of the lack of coordination and punching power with that hand, so they naturally grabbed with it to control distance. Consequently I taught defence and attack against grabs and strangles. I ensured my combat class got plenty of practice against the roundhouse punch because that was the prevalent opening attack in that prison. In other prisons where the main population was Spanish, the prevalent attacks were from the rear. However, should a roundhouse punch connect you would go down and lose your shit as the kicks came in. My favourite targets were eyes, neck, solar plexus and testicles. Opportunistic targets like arms, elbows, fingers, wrists and collarbone should be broken or dislocated as violently and quickly as possible. This may seem drastic and a tad over the top, but this was Satan's arena and there were no rules.

That thought brought me out of my reminiscence of La Moraleja and back to the reality of Daroca prison where I was writing my journal and where attacks from the rear were prevalent.

---

[82] sensei - Japanese term for teacher, adopted into English mostly for martial arts

The Prince Of Darkness

As I wrote at the dining table in the comedor an unshaven, unclean man was loitering nearby. I glanced over my shoulder to see him approaching crab-like to look down at me. I put down my pen and twisted on my seat to look up into his dirty face. He rubbed his stubbly lantern jaw thoughtfully before gruffly demanding cigarettes.

He was not a big man but he was stocky and muscular. His eyes were grey and dead looking as though the lights were on but nobody was home, if you get my drift? The combined ugliness of his dead eyes, lantern jaw, bulbous nose, wide forehead and vile smell repulsed me instantly and I knew a miasmal creep had invaded my space. I made a dummy lunge at him from my sitting position and, as he back-danced away from me I stepped away from my bench to adopt a fighting stance in readiness to kick him all over the fucking dining hall. No way was I going to punch this creature and risk breaking my skin on his, my boots would do the necessary. Costas, a Portuguese heroin dealer sitting nearby, called a warning to me that Lantern Jaw had AIDS and TB so be careful. I was being careful. My instincts told me to beware when I got my first whiff of the creepy bastard. Muttering and cursing madly, Lantern Jaw shuffled away into the sala to try his luck there amongst his ilk. I later discovered that Lantern Jaw was a child pederast, a sodomite of little children, the most outrageous, diabolic strain of nonce on the planet. I could not believe I was sharing space with so many loathsome creatures that should have been executed long ago.

I had to control my emotions whilst in Satan's arena, especially as I stuck out like a bulldog's bollocks with my Anglo-Saxon features and attitude. I had no friends there and certainly no one to watch my back, so I relied on my pernicious reputation and bushido mindset to keep safe. If I ever succumbed to the likes of Lantern Jaw then other weirdoes and gypsies alike would have targeted me for the rest of my stay - that would have been life changing. I felt somewhat dirty and mentally contaminated by the incident with Lantern Jaw, so I stowed my writing kit and headed for the shower block. I had to cleanse myself immediately.

The shower block was at the far end of the yard just beyond the economato and was opened each day at noon. The duty screw opened the shower but never entered. There were thirty shower stalls for one hundred and fifty men on that wing and it was the most dangerous part of the prison because it went unsupervised by screws or CCTV cameras. Wet, naked men are vulnerable to a stabbing in the steam-laden atmosphere, the favourite ambush site of the Spanish gypsies and psychopaths in Satan's arena.

Paradoxically it was also good for a laugh because the Moslems do not like to be seen naked and it is an insult to show them your arse. They showered in their underpants and shielded their modesty behind black plastic dustbin liners draped across the opening of the shower stalls, to prevent the ever-present perverts getting a glimpse of their nudity. Over the years I received many complaints and sometimes threats because of my flagrant nudity, but I admit to being an infidel and proud of it, so fuck off!

It was on that day that Greg the poof had the temerity to complain about nudity because he was an Islamic convert from Christianity and he and his fellow Moslems do not like to see gonads and arseholes in the showers. I explained to him that I was insulting Moslems long before he became one and, seeing as how he was a practising queer, he was a liar and hypocrite because he loved arseholes, especially male arseholes.

"I hide my arse from you, but not because you are a fucking Moslem," I said. "You shower twice a day, and that tells me all I need to know about you."

The smirk on his silly face told me I had hit the right nerve.

"Oh, and what's that?" he asked petulantly.

"You are a fucking pervert and can't help yourself from ogling hairy arseholes. That is why you spend so much time in the fucking shower," I retorted angrily.

I remembered him ogling Sam the giant Ghanaian, whose cock dangled down to his knees. Realising that I could read him like a book he walked away head down with hands deep in his pockets.

Funnily enough, it was in the shower where I first met Black Sam. It was a bitterly cold day and the water in the shower block was cold, but nobody knew that until the miserable screw opened the big steel door and everyone rushed in. Because there were only thirty shower cubicles and one hundred and fifty men on the wing, there was a mad rush to get undressed and into a cubicle before they were all occupied. I undressed quickly and was the first to get wet, so I was the first to discover there was no hot water. I wet my hair and put on a spurt of shampoo and lathered vigorously as other blokes jumped about with one outstretched hand feeling the cold water and cursing loudly. I gritted my teeth and stepped under the cold deluge, which took my breath away with the shock of it. I rinsed myself off and stepped out, completely invigorated but freezing my nuts off. By this time, everyone was pissed off and getting dressed again without getting wet and leaving the shower block disgruntled and grumbling about the mad Englishman.

"Anglo-Saxon mate," I said to the coal-black Ghanaian waiting for the water to come hot, shivering like a leaf in the wind, his big black dick dangling half way down his thighs. "Get in here and shrink your dick," I joked.

Surprisingly, he understood me and burst out laughing.

"Fuck dat!" he said laughing and started to dress. "See ya later man," he said, as he walked out. "Sam's the name," and there he was gone.

I enjoyed Sam's friendship. He was a no nonsense hard case and hated the Spanish. He suffered three years of racial abuse for possessing a few ounces of hashish. Apart from the few months he spent in prison in Tenerife, he spent his three years in this pisshole and hated every minute at the hands of uniformed racists.

I was sitting at my table in the late afternoon writing letters when Greg the poof sidled onto the bench opposite me. He was carrying a pair of jeans that he placed on the table.

"I'm altering these for one of my friends," he said. I ignored him. "Writing again?" he asked girlishly. I did not respond. "Oh dear! What have I done now to get the silent treatment?" he asked, in his ridiculous camp voice.

"Have you got needle and thread for those jeans?" I asked without looking up.

"Of course!" he replied sharply.

"Give it to me so I can stitch your fucking yap up," I growled.

"Oh we are chivalrous today," he bleated, as he arranged the trousers on his lap. "Two packs of smokes I got for doing this," he said, with a needle in his mouth.

I put down my pen and started to read the letter I was about to seal and send to my mother.

"Fancy you reading and me sewing. Does it remind you of anything?" There were a few seconds of silence as I thought about his words. "It does me. It reminds me of couples," he then said in a soft voice.

My right hand grabbed his windpipe and I yanked him across the table as his eyes rolled in their sockets. My left forearm quickly replaced my right hand across his throat to form a hadake jime[83] from which there was no escape as I choked him to the verge of unconsciousness.

"Any talk or suggestions like that again and you'll be chatting up Larry Grayson, you fucking maricon."[84] I released him slowly, allowing the blood to flow again through his carotid arteries and the air to reach his lungs. "Sit still for a moment, you'll be all right," I said, my anger receding rapidly. "Take deep breaths through your nose and relax," I said, as I sat him back on the bench to recover.

After a minute of wheezing and coughing he whispered.

"You could have killed me," he gulped a few more deep breaths and said, "you did that so quickly and easily, you must have killed people before?"

"I've never killed anyone," I replied brusquely, "but you may well be the first, so shut up and relax."

"You're the one that needs to relax," he said. "I don't fancy you, you're not my type. I was having a joke with you."

"There won't be any more fucking jokes then will there," I said, my temper cooling now that I had made my point.

---

[83] hadake jime - strangle hold
[84] maricon – Spanish word for homosexual, faggot

"For a split second, when I felt your hand on my neck, I thought you was going to kiss me," he joked, "but it was the kiss of death wasn't it?"

"It will be if there's a next time," I said grimly.

"Don't worry, there will never be a next time," he said, the joke now dead. "Are you reading or writing?" he said, gathering the jeans to him.

"A bit of both," I said, "why?"

"Oh nothing, if you're reading, I might talk, if you're writing I'll remain quiet."

"Writing," I said, with finality as he busied himself with needle and thread.

The sun shone through the glass roof of the dining hall making the place bright, as sparrows flitted about the empty tables searching for crumbs. Only four men sat quietly writing or reading, as Greg repaired the jeans and I wrote my letters.

The din from the sala seemed to diminish as my thoughts turned to my wife Susan, her lovely face filled my mind and my thoughts were of yearning and absence and sadness. Mood swings were a fact of life in prison. Oppression always kept you on the edge no matter how long or short your sentence was, especially when held in pits like that one. Happiness was a personal affection crushed beneath the weight of self-reproach and bitter regret. Apprehension was a sensation that rarely left me, and the absence of liberty was a constant irritant that would stay with me until the day I walked into freedom. I fervently hoped the black bile of melancholy would leave me soon, as my mind remembered the words of W.B. Yeats:

Others because you did not keep
That deep-sworn vow have been friends of mine;
Yet always when I look death in the face,
When I clamber to the heights of sleep,
Or when I grow excited with wine,
Suddenly I meet your face.

Susan is my Angel of Light or maybe I should say a goddess in my melancholy state of mind. I reflect on past joyous times and imagine what my homecoming would be like. I remember a previous reunion when I found her face amongst the throngs at Malaga railway station. The apprehension, then the pang of recognition flooding my heart and soul as my eyes feasted on her searching face. Maybe that was why Yeats came to mind. I think he was downhearted when he penned that poem, just as I felt then as I entered my cell after the evening feeding time.

I plugged in my battered reading lamp and selected a book while Abdelmalik socialised with his countrymen out in the corridor before lockdown. I prepared a brew and waited for the duty screw to lock up before I produced the forbidden pulpo to boil the water. As soon as the screw locked us in, we had a brew of tea and settled down for the night. I read my book as Abdelmalik wrote letters. Just before midnight Abdelmalik stowed his writing kit and got into bed. I put away my book and pulled out the plug of my reading lamp and quickly got back into bed because it was bitterly cold outside and not much warmer inside.

I could see condensation on the glass, fogging my view of the stars through the bars of the cell window. The pale glow of the sodium security lights shone through the droplets on the cracked glass creating a ghostly shimmer. My heightened sense of imagination played havoc with my mind's eye as I peered through the sparkling glass to see two shimmering points of light that slowly changed colour to that of red glowing coals. Pinpointed in the centre of each red glow was a glittering diamond, which formed the eyes of Satan. He was there hovering over the prison sinister and threatening. His murky features taking shape and form with the movement of cloud and the upward glow of prison lights. El Diablo was there spreading his evil shadow over Daroca. His fangs moved as though he gnashed his teeth and every sinew of his monstrous form dripped with evil. I realised this was his new home now that Carabanchel was devoid of humans. I was frozen with fear as I felt his force searching my soul.

"My God and His son Jesus Christ are in here, so get ye behind me Satan!"

The prayers spilled out of me as the fear intensified, and terror gnawed into my heart as the evil loomed over Daroca. My heart was racing as the monster's face descended towards me. My chest felt crushed and my stomach started to liquefy as the brilliant white light hit my face.

"You are dreaming my friend."

It was Abdelmalik shining my reading lamp into my face to waken me from my nightmare. I was drenched with sweat.

"I will make tea," said my cellmate softly, his voice somehow reassuring after the humming drone of Satan's growl, "and I will play some music, it is only just after midnight," he added cheerfully.

The clever music of Dire Straits filled the cell as we enjoyed a sweet brew and Mark Knopfler lifted my spirits with his guitar. Deep sleep engulfed me as the music embroidered the beginnings of dreams, dissipating the fading foul stench of Satan who I now knew lived there in Daroca. The visit from the Prince of Darkness haunted me for a long, long time, but then I prayed fervently to eradicate the memory.

My Nightmare

THE NIGHT I KISSED THE DEVIL

The night is coming in fast as the evening light fades to complete darkness with the coming storm. I keep stretching my body to get a look at the last glimmer of daylight and the falling snow through the cell window. I become mesmerised as the snowflakes settle on the coils of the razor wire mounted on the high walls of the prison. The lightning creates strange momentary visions of prisoners that were here before me, and their last messages on the walls that faded long ago. I put down the small journal I've decided to write in order to help my mind and body to survive; the light slips away and it is hard to write anyway. Now I'm left with this horrible ache of what I anticipate will be the beginning of my insanity. My mind screams, why am I HERE?

I am disheartened to see the shadows dance across the bleak countryside through the wire and my spirits fall to a new low. The silence in between the loud snaps of thunder screams into my ears, as I realise it is my screams that compete with the thunder that wins and fades out into the night; screams that no one hears, or if they do they don't care.

"God, you must be pissed with us tonight?" I whisper, as the deafening crack of crashing thunder shakes the window, and again the lightning illuminates the dank cell walls like an evil disco strobe light as the torrential rain washes away the snow.

Even the name of the prison sounds ominous. Daroca. Say it to yourself. Daroca. It's not a nice word is it?

"Daroca!" I scream again and again. I laugh as I realise it goes well with the bleak landscape and the raging storm. Is it thunder or the distant screams from the dark cells housing very dangerous men? Most of the inmates here have committed the most atrocious crimes, and here I am sharing my space with cannibals, child sex killers, murderers, and rapists. Men who should have been put to death for their barbarism are just on the other side of these urine-stained walls. That smell still fills the air with their internal evil. My prison cell is my safe haven, or so I thought.

I climb into what they call a bed, as the night envelopes the prison and the volume of the rumbling thunder increases. Pulling the dirty stained blanket around me to get some warmth and comfort I listen to the sound of the night in this evil place - thinking about my day and the people I now share my space with in this dark corner of the world as I try to slip into the welcome escape of sleep.

A face looms into my thoughts, an eerie calm face with bushy eyebrows over large ice-blue eyes. He stares at me across the dining table in the comedor, his eyes cut right through me as if he is elsewhere, but he just keeps staring. He reminds me of a wild Arctic Husky dog with his salt and pepper hair, ice-blue eyes, intense stare, and the way he eats the meat, tearing into it as if he had not eaten in weeks, and grunting with sounds of great satisfaction that are almost sexual.

I have a strange realisation. I'm breathing the same air of a man who ate his wife – very slowly, a finger, a toe, arm, leg – as she still lived, and then slowly cutting her open to take slices of her liver and kidneys – a cannibal – and here he is within touching distance, chewing on a piece of meat and looking at me! A sub-human that is pure evil! My mind wonders if, like a virus, I too could become this monster by just breathing in close proximity to this cannibal.

Oh wait - he's talking to me now, as he prods his food with his plastic fork.

"This is my wife's arse, sliced thinly and cooked rare," he grunts then pokes another piece. "This piece here is the first slice of her breast. Look how beautiful it is with the nipple in the centre, cooked exquisitely in butter. I would offer you a piece, but she's too precious to share - especially with an Englishman such as you."

My stomach turns over and I swallow my own bile, as the nausea sweeps over me and I stem the urge to puke. Bizarrely, this is the moment I felt great sorrow for a woman I never knew. Even more strange is that he devours everything put in front of him thinking it is his wife he is eating. He would not have been caught but for the police finding her fingernail at the bottom of the freezer. After she finally died he then butchered her into sizeable chunks ready for the frying pan or the oven. I wondered what he did with her bones. Why did I think that? His name is Emilio, the Spanish wife eater.

Sitting at the table in this insane canteen my hunger dissipates as I realise who I share hell with. I am surrounded by evil and wonder if this is some kind of sinister, satanic ambush. To my right is a young man who calls himself Julio. He chopped off his uncle's head with a Samurai sword. He chats amiably to the man next to him who raped and mutilated his thirteen-year-old niece. Thirteen was unlucky for her, and especially considering the length of time it took for her to die, after being raped and her nipples ripped out with a pair of pliers and her genitals torn apart by secateurs.

I could continue describing the creatures around me, but it would become unbearable for me to go on and survive even my own mind. Is this kind of evil catching? Will you doubt my word? There is, however, another I can't leave out of my notes. A necrophiliac who killed his child victims and sexually assaulted their little dead bodies until the stink of decomposition necessitated burial. He calls himself Brujo – the Warlock.

The storm is now a tempest and the thunder is reminiscent of ice cracking across a pond but a million times louder. The lightning is alarming and illuminates my decrepit cell, giving me the forlorn feeling that it's heralding the arrival of something evil and malevolent.

I can hear Herbie the giant cockroach scratching the floor under my bed as he searches for food, and beneath that I hear the susurrations of the sleet and rain as it runs in rivulets down my cell window. Sleep eludes me. My brain is surrounded by thoughts of evil.

The thunder and lightning just gets louder and louder and it seems the lightning strikes are inside my cell, just missing me.

WHACK! Again and again, crashing thunder shakes the window and lightning illuminates the walls, but now brighter, showing photos and a calendar in stark detail. I turn to look at the calendar hanging there. A black cross is drawn on 14th February.

"Oh bloody hell! It's Saint Valentine's Night. My missus will be heartbroken. I didn't send her a Valentine. Oh, Christ almighty!"

The thought occurred to me that I should make one for our wedding anniversary. Feeling guilty and depressed over the Saint Valentine's card I hear the large cockroach noisily crawling around the cell floor looking for food that isn't under my bed. Funny I can still hear him above the thunder. How is that possible? I tried to clean the floor today and it did look better. I tried to clear the stench of shit and urine that is now part of the cement. The cockroach, still looking for food, seems to be unafraid of me as I look down on him.

"Hello Herbie, I must have upset your meals today, sorry. Look at the storm hey – looks like we won't sleep tonight mate."

The muffled sounds of the screams of madmen are barely audible through the thick walls, but they are there - the storm taking its toll on the warped minds of my fellow prisoners.

I feel sleep is finally starting to close around me so, like a baby I curl into my foetal position before taking a last look outside. I can see condensation on the glass fogging my view of the night sky through the bars of the cell window. The pale glow of the sodium security lights shine through the rain onto the cracked glass creating a ghostly shimmer, as I slowly fall into welcome peaceful sleep.

Or so I thought! Damn! My heightened sense of imagination plays havoc with my mind's eye, as again I open my weary, sleepy eyes and peer through the glass. The rainwater distils what seems like two shimmering points of light, which slowly change colour to that of red, glowing, piercing coals. Pinpointed in the centre of each red glow is a glittering diamond, which form the eyes of Satan. He is here, hovering over Daroca prison – sinister, hostile and threatening.

His murky features take shape and form with the movement of the outside cloud and the upward glow of the stark prison light. El

Diablo is here, spreading his evil shadow on the netherworld of the hell called Daroca. A numbing sensation sweeps over me, paralysing me with a feeling of total helplessness as the fetid face looms nearby. His fangs move as though gnashing his teeth and every sinew of his monstrous form drips with evil. I realise he has come for me... ME!

An evil silence descends. I freak out internally and choke on the scream that won't come out. It's as though I am lying face down on a waterbed that has suddenly flipped over suffocating me with its weight. The terrifying emotion of stress and panic creates a feeling of intense heat across my back followed by ice under the hot skin. My arms and legs feel like they are covered with raspberries because of the size of the goose bumps. I am frozen with fear as I feel his force searching my soul.

"My God and His son Jesus Christ are in here, now get ye behind me Satan!" I scream.

The prayers spill out of me, the fear intensifies and the terror gnaws into my heart as the evil looks over me trying to consume me. I cannot move.

"Of all the evil in this place why are you here for me?"

My screams now blend with the thunder – loud, deep, cracking – the beating of my heart grows louder and louder. My heart races as the monster's evil face slowly descends toward mine.

"Why me? Why me?" I cry, as my mind races back in time seeking a reason for this catastrophe.

The kaleidoscope of visions slows to a halt just where Satan wanted it to - now I am on the deck of the yacht *Harlekin* somewhere in the Mediterranean Sea several years ago. Another nightmare on top of the one I am already in. A davit swings out over the stern with a body hanging from it, hands and feet tied to a rusty old anchor. A deckhand lowers it into the sea and completely submerges it for a minute before cranking it back out. He leans over and rips off the gag. The spine-chilling screams coursing out of the doomed man will remain with the crew members forever. A reminder not to be seen talking to a policeman. The screaming man was again slowly lowered into the sea cutting off the screams. Moments later he was raised again to scream for all he was worth, until eventually being released to plummet to the sea bed strapped to the old anchor. I was witness to that man's death, ordered by the boss - a Dutchman who hates police informers, because four of his crewmen received long prison sentences due to the dead man's low cunning and deceit.

It seems now is my turn to pay for my sins and that rusty old anchor is coming my way. My chest feels crushed as if an anvil is in there slowly pressing harder and harder. My insides start to pop, my stomach starts to liquefy as those horrible lips descend to touch mine; and then a hoarse, guttural sound, words and weird noises, a garbled message telling me to be calm.

"That heavy anchor is not for you Christopher, though you do deserve it because you didn't try to stop it. No, I need you just for me. It is many centuries since I had a Christopher just like you; a being who can soothe me and praise me just like you do with the other monsters."

"What other monsters?" I hear myself reply.

"Jesus, Mary, God the Father. He's not your father. He's nobody's father. You have prayed to them all for years and what have you got in return? Nothing! You are here because the Angel Gabriel guided you here."

"Why would he do that?" I asked.

"Because he knows you are mine and he will fight me for you."

The sounds from Satan's lips change to a whining, purring sound, like that of a wild cat-like creature, as he closes his lips on mine and whispers.

"Come, feel me. Join my soul where I can love you like no other, my beloved Christopher. You don't really know the monster in you yet. Kiss me. Kiss me."

I tense with trepidation as his lips cover mine and immediately relax as they mollify me with their softness. I feel a strange, exciting sensation as his tongue seeks mine and the excitement intensifies beyond anything I've ever experienced. His honey-tasting tongue slides further down my throat igniting powerful, erotic sequences of delight, and I feel the electricity in my loins that wants to explode with pleasure. His kiss like no other induces affectionate feelings of Svengali charm and seduction. I am amorously smitten by him and totally bewitched, but something in my mind is warning me to back off. A shock, like a bolt of lightning, brings me to my senses but I fear it is too late as Satan draws me further in and he whispers in my ear.

"You're not strong enough to withstand the storm."

Then I shout back into the Devil's ear.

"I AM THE FUCKING STORM!"

My lips, teeth and tongue melt and flow down my throat, then my nose, eyes and face are drawn into the space between Satan's dribbling lips as the rest of me enters the place of fallen angels. I am on my way to hell. The noise is like nothing I've ever heard before - akin to prehistoric beasts bellowing in savage combat as they tear each other apart, mixed with a clatter of giant cymbals echoing in my molten ears. A vision appears above me with Satan ferociously attacking the Angel Gabriel. A great swirl of fire and smoke engulfs the two combatants and I am alone and moving at great speed.

Thoughts elude me on this journey to hell, as ghostly unrecognisable faces flit through my vision, distorted by the raging turbulence of evil wrath. Suddenly the aroma of sulphur and volcanic ash are in my senses as another world begins to appear, with horizons and oceans and tsunami giant waves crashing over seemingly flaming seas - but no sign of life, just a maelstrom of exploding energy.

Suddenly I find I have the power to think for myself again and realise that Satan is not a being but a parallel universe and I am helpless within it, hurtling around encased in a capsule of invisible energy powered by Satan. I am orbiting his world.

The distorted faces again come flitting through my vision and I sense something familiar about some of them as they are whisked away in the opposite direction to me. One of them has a vague resemblance of my grandmother and similarly others like my uncles and friends who died long ago.

In my terrified mind I reached out to catch one of them, a woman, a beautiful woman, of such beauty I could not believe my eyes. I realised she has passed me several times during this passage around hell. She slipped away giving me a sad smile. I knew I would see her again because she was orbiting in the opposite direction to me. I will be prepared next time.

Myriads of mountains are spewing flaming lava as I pass above them. The air I breathe is getting hotter and the burning feeling of hopelessness and distress grows stronger from gazing at these distorted faces.

The beautiful woman comes near and I manage to catch the invisible bubble in which she travels. I now experience telepathy for the first time as she speaks to me.

"Touch my husband Emilio with your little finger when you see him. I ripped off my little fingernail when he put me in the freezer. He butchered me when I was frozen but I knew they would find the fingernail. He is the cannibal at your dining table."

"Why are you here, circling hell?" I asked.

"We are in purgatory awaiting entrance to paradise."

Suddenly a beautiful sound - a sound like no other - was heard as she was whisked away before I could reply. It was at that moment I heard the sound of a key in a door and the crashing sound of a great bolt opening a metal gate. I could see an enormous sun rising beyond the horizon with a light so bright I thought it would burn out my eyes.

"Recuento, recuento!" Shouts the prison officer as he performs the final head count of the day. He opens all the prison cells one at a time to check the inmates are alive, or dead. His voice and bright light dissipates the evil red eyes of Satan who is gone in a flash. In his accented English, Don Gabriel the duty prison officer speaks to me.

"Good night Christopher, the storm has gone. Sleep well. You are still under my wings Englishman."

He slams the big steel door and noisily crashes the massive bolt home as he goes to chase the demons from the minds of his inmates in the cells on his wing of the prison. I look under my bed to see Herbie the cockroach looking back at me.

"That was the Angel Gabriel, the angel in a prison officer's uniform."

At breakfast I asked the man opposite if he was Emilio?

"Si," he replied, "por que?"

I shook my head and answered, "Nada," as I touched his hand with my little finger. His look was one of terror as his heart stopped and I knew that the Devil had returned for his new recruit – one he did not have to kiss.

That night as I lay in bed I smiled as the screaming began in my neighbour's cell. The Devil had come for Emilio. I looked for Herbie the cockroach and he was nowhere to be seen. It was at that moment I realised I have something the Darkness could not take from me. My soul.

Nutmeg And Arabs

Nutmeg (Greg) was becoming more and more irritating. He was leaving on another permiso the next day - six days on the out. He was going to Zaragoza to stay with his newfound friends - perverts and sickos who could not wait to get their paws on him.
    He joined me at my table as I was writing in the comedor and he made sighing and huffing noises around me as he thought about his six days of freedom. He was quite frustrated because he knew he could not drool about his sink of iniquity in Zaragoza with me. Also, he needed cigarettes and some postage stamps and was waiting for the right moment to sponge them off me, so I kept my head down supposedly writing and pretending to concentrate on my work. He needed the stamps urgently to send letters to weirdoes in Zaragoza arranging meetings over the next six days. He shuffled the letters noisily and I knew he was about to ask me for the stamps. I quickly got up and grabbed my bag of laundry to throw on the pile of bags at the bottom of the stairs just a few metres away, because today was Tuesday 13th March 2007 and it was laundry day for this wing.
    Nutmeg's chin dropped as his hands went to his hips in that ridiculous camp posture which was de rigueur for homosexuals when annoyed. Looking at him, I realised it was so unfair to suggest queers have female traits - they don't, they have queer traits. They do not behave like any women I have known and this popular misconception should be righted as quickly as possible because of its affect on children. This particular queer would never be allowed near any children of mine.
    As I returned to my table the sun suddenly shone through the high glass roof and the voices below echoed above the talking heads.
    "English!" shouted Malik the Moroccan. "Venga! Come here!" he cried as he beckoned me to a table where two young Arabs were sitting with him.
    Ignoring Nutmeg I quickly put away my writings and went across to Malik and his young friends.
    "Que pasa hombre?" I asked, more a greeting than a question.

"You teach us karate today?" asked Malik, the younger Arabs' eyes bright with anticipation.

Taking care not to spill my coffee I straddled the bench.

"No amigo, aqui es mucho pederaste y es no mi gusta," I said, in my shite Spanish, pointing out that there were many nonces on this wing.

"Oh sheet!" he said in his shite English, catching my drift as he realised the paedophile population would take great interest in learning restraining techniques and hold downs.

In the silence of the moment my mind went back to La Moraleja prison where another North African asked me the same question, but this man was an Algerian, not a Moroccan. Not that that made any difference, but the Algerian was a nonce. He was also very big and powerful, a veritable beast of the worst kind. He stood head and shoulders above me and had very big hands, as though he had been shovelling sand all his life. He was an inmate from modulo uno, the worst wing in the prison.

Six prisoners from that wing were members of my combat class. I had taken them on after first checking their form[85]. They were villains all right, but acceptable for training because they were lifers and long-term inmates convicted for various offences, none of them related to offences against women or children. They were hard men doing hard time. The discipline of martial arts training suited these difficult men, uplifting them from their forlorn existence and giving them something to look forward to twice each week. It was men like this with long sentences who begged for instruction regarding the esoteric aspect of the martial arts - the psychological meditating Zen aspect that westerners ridicule because they have not the mental agility to digest it, simple as that.

The Algerian beast standing in front of me pointed his grubby finger in a threat inches away from my nose. Big mistake. Like a striking mongoose I bit into the snake-like finger with the stumps of what remained of my teeth (my teeth were broken by the Spanish secret police during a pistol whipping as described in a previous

---

[85] form - rap sheet

journal). I was trying to bite off the finger at the first joint whilst stabbing his eyes with an open fingered nukite. The fingers of my right hand plunged into the eye sockets of the big skull, as my right knee jerked up into his gonads with a sickening crunch. Releasing my fingers, I stepped back into zenkutsu datchi[86] and drove my bare foot into his testicles. He doubled over holding his testicles with his bitten hand as his other hand massaged his eyes. That was the moment my instep crashed into his throat.

Dealing with the lumbering Algerian nonce took all of four seconds. Luckily the combat class had not yet started so the security camera was still focused on the weight lifters. The combat class quickly scooped up the groaning nonce and carried him down the stairs to the first landing then threw him down the remaining steel steps to the ground floor level where he rolled to a crumpled halt just as the duty screw, Don Phillipe, rounded the corner. Fortunately he only clocked the rolling over bit from the bottom of the stairs. The men in the combat class quickly descended the stairs to help the poor man who had fallen. They fussed around the nonce busying themselves whilst stage-whispering the words 'heroin' and 'junkie' just loud enough for the screw to hear, but not intentionally if you know what I mean?

"Okay you lot, back upstairs," I spoke. "Don Phillipe can take care of this prick."

Phillipe's English was quite good so he gave me that old fashioned look with one eyebrow raised, letting me know he knew what had just happened. Shrugging my shoulders, I turned to run up the stairs.

"C'mon," I called, "we haven't got all day!"

"I need a statement from witnesses!" Don Phillipe shouted.

"I'll do that!" I shouted over my shoulder.

Later that evening seven statements were on the screw's desk stating that the Algerian nonce seemed drunk when he fell down the stairs. A subsequent blood test proved positive with heroin and hashish in his bloodstream. It mattered not what the nonce had to say after the blood test.

---

[86] zenkutsu datchi - forward leaning stance

My thoughts returned to Daroca and I left the young Arabs with the thought that maybe soon I would accommodate them with a few lessons.

The sun was shining brightly but there was still a nip in the air. It was Wednesday 14th March 2007 and Nutmeg was going out on permiso today. We were walking around the yard quite briskly because I needed the exercise.

"Why are we walking so fast?" bleated Nutmeg.

"Because I need to stretch my legs," I said. "I always walk like this."

"I'm going to sit down and have a smoke," he pouted, "I'm nervous."

"Why would you be nervous?" I asked. "You've got one leg out of here already."

"I'm nervous anyway," he said, fumbling for his ciggies.

"Why would you be nervous," I asked again, "you gonna do a runner?"

"No, I'm coming back on Tuesday."

"I know you are, you haven't got the guts to fuck off."

"I can't fuck off 'cos I plan to stay here in Spain with Lhaktar," he said.

"What kind of life will that be? He is a wog Algerian and you are a South African and you are both queer." We stopped to face each other and I looked him in the eye. "You know how racist this fucking lot are. They already hate you for what you are, so how will the locals like it when they discover you changed from Christianity to Moslem," his eyes widened as I added, "because they will find out you know, they always do?"

"The Spanish are a modern thinking society now," he said defensively.

"Oh yeah, take a look around you. They all hate your fucking guts and these are just screws and spick scum. What do you think the people on the out will think, you know, the ones who think their shit don't stink?"

"Well, I can't do a runner, I love my Lhaktar and I must wait for him and prepare a home for him for when he gets his Libertad."

"If they let me out on permiso I would be away like a fucking long dog, I wouldn't give these fuckers another minute of my life."

"If you did that, Interpol would soon pick you up," he said with a sneer.

"No they fucking wouldn't," I growled, "not with a new identity."

Cupping the cigarette lighter in his hands he lit his ciggie and coughed loudly as he tried to speak.

"I'm sitting down," he spluttered.

"Yeah, you do that, catch your breath," I said acidly, envious because he would be on the out any minute.

I walked a few more laps of the yard then they called him over the tannoy. He dashed across the yard to me with his hand held out for a handshake.

"See you next week!" he cried.

I couldn't tell whether the tears in his eyes were caused by the cold Aragon wind or his excitement at being allowed out.

"Yeah mate," I called after him, "keep your cock in your pants, there's a lot of dirty arses out there," I laughed to myself as he looked back over his shoulder at me.

"Oh you!" he cried coquettishly, grinning all over his face and there he was gone.

The big iron gate clanged shut behind him and the escort screw took him away to start six days of freedom. I strolled briskly around the yard alone with my thoughts when Miguel, a young slim Spaniard with pugilistic features caught up with me.

"Your amigo is gone?" he asked.

"Si, el tengo permiso para seis dias," I replied, telling him that Nutmeg had gone for six days.

"Oh bien," he said as he tried to keep up with me. We walked in silence for a few minutes, then he asked, "Yo tengo hashish, you buy some?"

"No, no tengo dinero," I lied, "and I don't smoke, yo no fumar," I said truthfully. He turned sharply to target others with his wares. He knew not to lean on me.

There was hardly any cash on the wing because the economato did not take cash. When a prisoner was processed through ingreso he was issued with a debit card that had a barcode and code number on the reverse. This was swiped through the till in the economato and a receipt given itemising the purchases and stating how much money remained in your peculio[87]. Family and friends could top up the prisoner's account. I was indebted to my family for sending money orders to the Foreign Office in London from where it was sent to the local embassy, which in my case was Barcelona and the consul there sent it to my account in Daroca.

This method effectively prevented open trading with cash and drugs like it used to be just a few years earlier. Nowadays small trading was done with fixes being sold for telephone cards, ciggies and various items available from the economato. Everyone seemed to be stoned and there were enough zombies around there to make a Michael Jackson video, so there was a lot of smack and hash on the wing. I suspected much trading happened at visiting times between families and friends who came on regular visits, probably just to do business with other inmates' families. I had not become part of the system in Daroca and I did not intend to, so anything I have said was an educated guess and, unless I discovered how they operated around there, I would say no more about it.

I continued walking around the yard with my thoughts. I have walked around a few yards in my time and this one was par for the course with goal posts at either end and basketball nets at each side. There were ten park benches fixed into the concrete at intervals around the perimeter and eight large rustic tables with benches fixed under the wing awnings out of direct sunlight or rain. Before sitting on any of these seats I always checked for phlegm gobbed out by peevish gypsies who purposely spat on furniture, walls, water taps and windows, but particularly these outside seats. Maybe their misguided minds thought that their vandalism and gobbing was hurting the system, but they knew only inmates used these things they gobbed on - so I will leave you dear reader to figure that one out.

As I walked around I could hear the security cameras whirring on their mountings scanning the yard. I could see the screws were

---

[87] peculio - account

watching from their office. I followed the gaze of the screws and the bearing of the cameras as they converged on Miguel, the man who had just approached me to sell hash. I was pleased I did not spend more than a minute with him because they were obviously onto him and he would fall into the hands of cacheros at any minute - I found it strange that some dope dealers thought they were fireproof and ignored the obvious. The security cameras followed Miguel for ages. I heard my name called for Spanish lessons and, as I was leaving the wing, I clocked a team of cacheros coming from ingreso. I knew Miguel would not be on the wing when I returned at feeding time. As was normally the case he was grassed by one of his paisanos, a client who owed him money for hashish. The Spanish always did that. They would smoke the shit, run up a bill and then grass the dealer when they knew he had a lot to sell. Typical spicks.

The Arabs traded lots of hashish but I never saw them trading with spicks. They knew what would happen and they did not give credit. Besides, the Moroccans were a vengeful race so there would be a dramatic increase in the death rate, because in their eyes chivatos[88] were lower than a mole's arse.

---

[88] chivato - informer

The School

The escuela[89] was the place where contraband, dope and messages changed hands and the place where I learned Spanish. In my classroom Arabs sold lots of hashish from various modulos, which was then sold on when the lesson was over and we all returned to our various wings.

Screws did not supervise the classrooms; the teacher was in charge. My teacher was from the nearby village and while he was there teaching Spanish the village was bereft of its idiot. He taught us by reading aloud from his book and scribbling nonsense on the board as everyone did deals behind his back. There were no cameras or screws in the escuela, only stupid teachers who could not get a job elsewhere. So trading was rife in there because most of the students were Arabs. Classes ran from Monday to Friday and I never witnessed a shakedown. Nobody had yet been searched on the journey from wing to school, even though the walk-through metal detectors were in each corridor and we walked past them each way every day of school.

A semblance of order was kept in the classrooms because nobody wanted to fuck up the trading, not that that affected the standard of teaching. The young fellow employed as the teacher of my class must have thought he was teaching chimpanzees because most of his class were Arabs who could not read or write anyway, so who cared a fuck around there, seemingly no one? I looked across at my neighbour's textbooks and saw drawings of Iraq and portraits of Osama bin Laden or some other Ayatollah wielding a Kalashnikov rifle or an RPG-7 anti-tank weapon with the stars and stripes ablaze in the background.

I remember the atrocity of 11th September when the Twin Towers came down in New York. I was an inmate at Malaga prison at the time. I witnessed the celebrations as every Arab in that prison danced and cheered in the yard. They screamed and danced like Dervishes in front of the appalled prison officers and other shocked European prisoners. Like me the screws could only look on with hatred in our

---

[89] escuela - school

hearts as these people celebrated the carnage of that unforgettable, unforgivable day.

Anyone who tells me that Christianity and Islam can live in harmony would be told to stop dreaming. I know the Arabs tolerated me because I was a means of transporting their hashish; but in their eyes I was a Christian, therefore an infidel, therefore no better than a dog. The women in their lives were treated no better than their dogs, so where did the infidel rate in their order of things? Dog shit, that is where.

The class ended so everyone dutifully put away pens and papers into their carpetas, blue coloured file folders with elastic corner fasteners to keep them closed with names proudly scrawled in Arabic across the front cover. Mine said simply *69* any way up, who gave a shit. I could pick up any chimpanzee's carpeta and the teacher would never even know. We filed noisily out of the classroom to descend the stairs where the pungent stink of hashish wafted through the primitive lavatory blending well with the smell of real shit. We lined up at the big iron gate where the duty screw called out the various wing numbers in order to count the heads from each wing as they passed by him. I was the only Brit in this prison so I was the odd one out. I was also the odd one out because I refused to mule hashish from the school to the wing. Practically every student was a mule for hashish, that being the sole reason for enrolling for Spanish lessons.

A little Chinese bloke walked alongside me. He was nervous because he was loaded with all kinds of shit for the wing and he knew the cacheros had visited our wing earlier to shakedown Miguel. He knew they could still be there searching inmates, because it was not their practice to go straight for the man they wanted. They did not want the target to think he had been grassed, so they would do a large group of suspects knowing that Miguel was in their net. This small man was the only Chinese in the prison, so he stuck out like a Panda's bollocks as his nerves were getting the better of him. Sweat ran down his face on that chilly morning. As we approached our modulo down the long dim corridor we could see movement beyond the myriad of iron bars that formed the partitions and gates to our destination. Fuck! They were still there! The cachero screws were in a group, smoking and noisily chatting with our regular screws. The Chink looked like a duck heading for Peking, about to start shitting and squawking at any moment. The screws clocked our approach and started to put out their cigarettes in readiness to deal with us. Realising that quick thinking and drastic action had to be taken to save the Chink I called out to him.

"Hey Chino!" I snapped.

He turned to face me, his face looking more and more yellow under the poor lights. His eyes widened as he watched me shove my hand down the back of my pants to my arse. I lunged at him and shoved my fingers down his throat. He gagged and puked all over his shoes just as the screws opened the big iron gate. I shoved him along the corridor away from the screws in the direction of the enfermeria.

"Cabron!" I shouted, as I gave him a hard push toward the gates of the sick bay, "get in the enfermeria rapido, ahora!" I shouted as I pushed my fingers into his mouth again.

His breakfast chundered through his gizzard with a vengeance as he escaped into the enfermeria. You owe me Chino I thought as I entered the gauntlet of cachero screws.

"Ah Kreestoffer," beamed a familiar bearded lantern jaw, "venga amigo!" the noise boomed out of the beard. "It is I, Don Geraldo!" his big paw held out for a handshake.

"Christ! What are you doing here?" I asked incredulously, as I recognised a screw I helped to learn English nearly ten years before in the Carabanchel prison in Madrid.

"I might ask you the same question," he said in good English.

"You learned my lingo then," I said, as his big hand shook mine.

"C'mon, let's get a coffee," he roared.

As the other poor sods were stripped for a body search we walked through the comedor to the rear door of the economato, but it was closed.

"Fuck! Merde!" he cursed, then slammed his size twelve into the iron door.

Mario, the shopkeeper sat in the comedor looking at the mad screw.

"Senor Functionario," he cried, as the boot went in again.

Geraldo the screw spun around to face Mario then pointed silently at the door with his forefinger twirling, indicating to open it. His eyes bore into Mario's wide eyes like lasers trying to cut his brain out. Mario lost his bottle right there and then, as his bottom lip started to tremble in time with his knees. The time was 1:00 pm and the dining hall was bright and airy with sparrows twittering in the eaves, and Mario was shitting bricks.

"Dos cafelitos hombre," snarled the lumbering Geraldo; then looking at me as Mario fumbled with the lock, he said in good English, "now I know where the shit is on this modulo. This Mexican cunt has more than coffee and cakes in there."

"I wouldn't know," I said, "I have fuck all to do with anyone in this pisshole."

"We already know that Kreestoffer, your reputation arrived before you, so you have been well looked at," he said, as he stooped to enter the rear door of the economato.

"Oh well, that's all right then. I can go home now then?" I joked.

"We'll have coffee first," he chortled, calming down now that the steaming coffee machine was gurgling.

He beckoned me into the rear of the economato to sit on cardboard cartons with my back to the wall.

"Help yourself to whatever you like. Cakes, chocolate. He's too busy shitting his pants to care."

"I'll just have the coffee thanks. Americano por favor Mario," I called.

"Dos!" snapped the screw. "Y dos cortado para mi," he added, ordering two black coffees for me, and two half and half with milk for him.

We sat there like a couple of old pals swigging hot coffee and chatting about the Carabanchel. But feeding time was drawing near so he had to go back to his lair with the other cacheros. He nodded at Mario and spoke to me as he left.

"He knows you pay for nothing now, but don't do it when others can see."

This was like having a blank cheque for the economato.

"If you give him a spin everyone'll think I am a chivato," I added cautiously.

"Do not worry, nobody but me suspects him, and I do not care at this time, but if problems arise with heroin on this modulo he will be my target," he said knowingly.

I could not tell Geraldo the screw that I was now an author because nobody in Spain knew about my books, so I had to tell him I was still messing about in boats. I knew he would come to see me when he could, even if it was only to practise his English.

Mario the Mexican was so pleased he did not get a spin he kept sending me Americanos, little plastic cups of coffee just how I like it with sugar but no milk.

The Chinese bloke returned from the enfermeria and offered to buy me coffee and ciggies, anything for saving his yellow skin. He explained that, in all the years he spent in Shanghai's prisons and the time in filthy Spanish prisons, he had never had such a filthy trick played on him like what I did to make him sick, but he was ever so grateful. I explained as best I could that it was an Anglo-Saxon trait to use shitty solutions for shitty problems, because had the chink been caught he would have been in very deep shit indeed. He did not quite get the gist of things because he asked what Michael Jackson had to do with it - hmm, Michael Jackson, Anglo-Saxon? I really did need to improve my communication skills!

The silence of my cell welcomed me as I closed the big iron door to shut out the noisy antics of the unsupervised chimpanzees larking about in the corridor trading drugs and pushing each other around before lockdown. The shrieking and door banging caused an instant headache so I shut it out. The duty screw would be along presently to lock me in, then twenty or so minutes later there would be a recuento, another headcount. I organised the making of a brew and set out a book to read and my pen and paper for writing the day's notes. There was a knock on the door. It was Mickey from across the corridor offering me his radio because he wanted to sleep and did not need it. I knew there was an ulterior motive for his kindness. I gratefully took it from him and quickly found the Classic FM channel and relaxed with Chopin in my cell.

Mickey's real name was Abdelkader and he was a short fat Moroccan who nowadays lives in Holland. He was very kind to me because he required my skills as a skipper. I expected a proposition at any time over the next week because blokes like him did not like wasting time in prison. Time spent in prison must be used to cultivate business contacts with the likes of me - people he could only meet in prison. The chances of meeting a traficante skipper on the out is like finding Lord Lucan down the pub, so he had to make use of his jail time by seeking out men of good skills and reputation.

Mohamed Skandiri, a friend of Mickey's, recognised me when I first came to Daroca and told him about my work. Mo Skandiri hailed from Berkane, a small town situated between Nador and Ouzde, near the Algerian border with Morocco. He recognised me because he was part of the loading gang at Mar Chica from where I used to set sail with the cargo he helped to load. He could not believe his luck. The only Englishman in the prison happened to be a skipper of repute, well known amongst the Barons of Nador. So Mickey would soon pounce. His round face and bald head gave him a pleasant outlook and his rolling gait told me he had spent many years at sea in pateras, little Moroccan fishing boats that can be seen all along the North African coast.

Mickey's facial features and pleasant outlook reminded me of a man I once knew along that coast, who nearly ruined a job because of his pleasant outlook. The job was at Saidia on the North African coast, not far from Oujde, and Mickey's doppelganger was reluctant to disturb a group of campers sleeping on the beach just a few kilometres away from Saidia. The beach at Saidia is beautiful and popular with tourists and locals alike, so it was perhaps not the best place to load a ton of hashish onto a RIB. However, from mid-September through to May the place was deserted. The cargo of hashish arrived early at the western extremity of the beach where it was quite remote and normally isolated. The RIB was late because of engine problems so the job had been postponed for twenty-four hours. There was a new moon and sea conditions were perfect as I hit the beach at 2:00 am. Instead of the usual mayhem of phantom ragheads of the night frantically loading bails of hashish, there was only the sound of the sea rolling onto the beach. In the starlight I could see a haggle of men standing silently around what looked like a tent. One of the ragheads detached himself and tiptoed toward me, as he approached he broke into a run and gasped.

"Problems!"

"Okay, see ya!" I said.

I slammed into reverse because the water at the stern was deep just there, so I had not needed to tilt the engine when I ran aground. I slowly and quietly left the beach, skinning my eyes for patrol boats when, splash! Someone had jumped into the sea and was swimming madly toward me, his robes and turban making it difficult for him to make headway. My first thought was illegal immigrant hitching a lift.

"Francois! Francois!' he called, as he was drowning.

I held out a paddle for him to grab and levered his arm onto the sponson[90], raising his torso from the sea and sending the RIB back onto the beach. He found his feet he scrambled onto dry land.

"Do not go!" he cried, choking on salt water.

"Right!" I shouted. "Hang on to this," I ordered as I handed him the painter to hold the RIB close to the beach, "and don't fucking move!"

I raced up the beach to find my loading gang huddled near a tent from which the sound of loud snoring could be heard.

"Tourists," whispered the Mickey lookalike, "they are sleeping on the hashish."

Nearby stood a beat up VW bus with kraut number plates. As I looked at it I lost my temper.

"Fucking raus! Raus! You fucking arseholes! Get out of there!" I screamed.

The shocked krauts thought they were being robbed as they scrambled out of the tent.

"Get the fucking shit down to the water now!" I roared and headed back to the RIB as the ragheads tore down the tent and started digging the bales of hashish out of the sand.

---

[90] sponson – inflatable tube

The frightened krauts came running down to the water's edge struggling with bales of hashish alongside the Moroccans. They loaded them into the RIB then ran back for more, wearing only their underclothes and frightened out of their wits - two men and two girls running with the Arabs to lift bales of hashish from underneath their fucking groundsheet. All the bales were loaded and the boat roughly trimmed, so I took my two guards-cum-crew and told the frightened krauts to go back to bed with a two hundred and fifty gram bar of Morocco's finest. They thought they had won the lottery and the pot party they would doubtless have would surely never be forgotten.

I bet they got many steins of kraut ale while telling their story when they got home. Of all the miles of remote beaches on the North African coast, they pitched their fucking tent on a million pounds-worth of hashish buried in the sand in the arsehole of nowhere!

Welcome Mike

On the evening of Thursday 15th March 2007 I collared Mo Skandiri in the prison yard and asked if he had told Mickey (Abdelkader) about me working out of Nador. He told me that several Moroccans knew about me, especially as I was the only Brit in there. Also someone from Caba Negro had recognised me.

"Why do you think they welcomed you at their dining table?" he said in fair English. "And Ahmed with the broken mouth? You don't recognise him?" he asked.

"I don't know who you mean," I said, puzzled.

"El sits across from you," mixing Spanish with English. "Ahmed Ghzeli with the broken cara (face), el trabajando con Bougnoch (he worked with Bougnoch) in Alicante with you," he added.

I remembered Bougnoch very well, but not Ahmed Ghzeli. This puzzled me, especially as he sat opposite me on the dining table. As I visualised Ahmed who sat across from me at feeding times, I saw the bashed in lower right part of his jawbone and the missing teeth but it did nothing for me. I visualised the oily brown eyes and the bushy black eyebrows, then it dawned on me.

"Barba! He had a great black beard when I knew him and I called him Barba," I said, looking at Mo Skandiri. "He must have done something bad to shave that fucking great beard off."

I would never have guessed he had a disfigurement under all that facial hair. Then I remembered him. He worked with the unloading team on the rocky shoreline behind the casino just to the east of Benidorm. The landing bay was cut out of the rock face and was just a bit awkward when the sea was choppy. Actually it would shrivel the guts of most skippers because, with two tonnes of happy herb on board and no leeway or room for error on approach, and the main highway just a few hundred metres away, one's sphincter muscle was sorely tested. Barba would leap on board from the rocks and throw out the painter and stern line in a flash. Two men would hold the lines, as six men frantically unloaded the cargo, then loaded the twenty litre containers of fuel that I needed for my return journey to

Morocco, along with a hamper of food and anyone that wanted to come back to Morocco with me.

If there was no fuel at the unloading point I would go out to sea and clean all evidence of cargo, then come in for a recovery at a pre-arranged RV[91]. This would normally be a quiet dock somewhere along the coast, where the RIB was craned out of the water and loaded onto an articulated lorry to be taken to workshops for a complete overhaul and servicing. The RIB was covered with a tarpaulin sheet and I would be whisked away to a nearby hotel for a shower, change of clothes and a decent kip. The kindly Arabs would offer me a young girl or boy and champagne and caviar, because in their eyes I was the mutt's nuts for delivering their precious cargo all in one piece.

"I'm going home to my wife, roast beef and Yorkshire pudding," I would tell them.

Take my new Mercedes, or take my new BMW they would say, keep it until the next voyage they would say. I always went home in style with fresh new clothes and a flash motorcar. I would call Susan to let her know I was safe and that I would be home whenever.

"We'll go out sweetheart," I would say, "don't bother cooking, just put on one of those slinky black numbers and leave your knickers in the drawer."

We would laugh at that but I knew she was laughing with relief, because she knew how dangerous life on the ocean waves could be, especially for the lonely RIB jockey whose voyages were fraught with danger. She knew that a special kind of lunacy was required to do that job. A lunacy that was now no longer with me. I had made my peace with my God and repeated my Act of Contrition in my daily prayers. I knew that God would let me out of this pit soon. I had confidence that God would keep me safe because I had survived the horrors of prison life and the terror and danger the high seas had thrown at me and, because He gave me the serene equanimity to face my nightmares and foes like an Englishman should. I sometimes wondered if God allowed me to survive so that I could write these journals, to deter would-be drug smugglers and weak-willed mariners

---

[91] RV – rendezvous

from putting to sea to haul the happy herb for the drug barons of this world. I knew God was near because this was Satan's arena and He would never be far from him.

"Why did he shave off his beard?" I asked Mo Skandiri.

"You must ask him yourself," he replied, as the tannoy crackled and hissed - the duty screw was fiddling with the prestle switch prior to shouting.

"Recuento! Recuento!"

We all traipsed out to the pateo for the headcount. Standing in one of the ranks of five men I noticed a new face. I could see he was not Spanish. Under the yellow sodium lights he looked like he had a sickly complexion, but so did everyone. His hair was iron grey and trimmed short, giving him what some people call a salt and pepper effect because of the feathered appearance of grey and darker grey. He stood about five feet nine inches tall and looked fit with a weather-beaten face. I knew he was a seaman. He found a place in one of the ranks of five and looked around to see if he knew anyone, as the screws ambled down the ranks counting them. Miraculously the screws got it right first time.

The duty screw shouted, "Vale!" then we all dispersed.

I made my way to the comedor to pick up my pen to finalise then close my journal for the day. Feeding time was drawing near and I would continue in my cell after eating whatever shite they would feed us for the last meal of the day. The duty screw entered the comedor to order us out to join the food queue in the sala. The door from the sala into the comedor was kept locked but you could see the head of the queue through the bars. We had to walk out of the comedor and along the corridor into the yard then into the sala to join the food queue. I did not see the new face until I had eaten and emptied my bandeja into the swill bin. He was standing near the swill bin looking slightly bewildered. He carried a sports bag and wore a short ski jacket, light grey jeans and sports boots. We eyeballed and knew immediately that we were of an ilk.

"Where're you from mate?" I asked, smiling.

A great, relieved smile spread across his face as his hand grabbed mine in a vigorous handshake.

"The States, man, California," he beamed. "You're a Brit, right?" he added.

"Yes mate, I'm Chris," I said.

"I am Mike Sherman, pleased to meetcha."

"Have you got a cell yet?" I asked.

"Yeah man, number thirty eight."

"Oh fucking hell," I said, "you're in with the nonce next door to me."

"What da fuck's a nonce?" he asked, looking alarmed.

I explained that my nextdoor neighbour lived alone because he was a filthy spick giant who picked his nose all the time and often shitted his pants, but he was here because he sexually abused and throttled to death a little girl.

"Oh, you gotta be shittin' me!"

"No, I ain't pal," I said, "you're sleeping with a monster tonight." Pausing for effect I added, "he's a big version of Igor, Frankenstein's helper. Remember, Boris Karloff's mate?"

"Can I get it changed?"

"Too late mate," I said, "we'll all be locked up in a minute, and the Poison Dwarf is the duty screw and he wouldn't change your cell unless he knew someone worse to put you with."

"Why would he do that?"

"Because he's a racist. He's a spick with gypsy blood in his veins. You know, one of those unfortunates, born with the sadism touch, everything he touches turns to rat shit instead of gold."

"You gotta be shittin' me," he said again, as I shook my head negatively.

"Wharram I gonna do?"

"I'll give you the head off my sweeping brush," I said seriously.

"What for?"

"To batter his teeth down his fucking throat! What do you think you would do with it, fucking sweep up?" I said, realising my joke did not make things any easier.

"You gotta be shittin' me," he said, for the third time.

Just then Igor shuffled up to the swill bin to empty his bandeja.

"This is him," I said, nodding my head at the nonce.

"Holy snappin' catfish!" Mike cried, as his jaw dropped open in disbelief. "I can't sleep with that thing in the room! Wharram I gonna do?"

"Relax, I'll find something for him." I said, as I looked around the food counter for Acid Fran the boss of the comedor destinos[92].

"Fran!" I called, as I clocked him talking to the duty screw.

I did a deal with Acid Fran who gave me a very potent sleeping pill. Blokes around there gobbled up pills like kids with Smarties, so I took the wrapper off the pill and held it in the palm of my hand in front of Igor the nonce. He looked at my face then at the pill in my hand. He took the pill from my hand and without even looking at it, popped it into his great mouth and swallowed. I looked into his eyes. They were cold, dead eyes like the eyes of a corpse. Oh how I wanted to blacken them. He about turned and walked away without so much as a kiss my arse or a thank you.

"You owe me a pack of Winston ciggies," I said to Mike Sherman. Then I explained what I had done to ensure a good night's sleep for both of them. I also asked Mike if he needed anything like postage stamps or telephone cards but he did not need anything. The duty screw then herded us upstairs to our cells.

Mike had his kit already stowed in his cell. He had a couple of large holdalls full of books and things he had garnered during the previous two and a half years spent in Font Calent prison on the Costa Brava. I helped him drag his kit across the cell floor, as Igor the nonce shuffled in and blocked the doorway. The big lug let fly with a monstrous fart like a slide trombone and ended with a wet raspberry. In the confined space of the cell the fumes would make a pig puke.

"Open the fucking window, quick!" I cried, as Mike looked unbelievably at the hulking creature blocking his escape from the gas chamber. He quickly yanked open the window and a migrating flock of geese broke formation overhead, as we both barged past Igor into the lesser-contaminated air of the corridor.

"I'll get that brush for you," I said, as we stood in the corridor.

"What for? You gave him a Mickey Finn didn't you?" he asked.

---

[92] destinos - kitchen porters

"Yep, but you'll need something to shove up his fucking arse, especially as how you are in the top bunk."
"Oh, fuckin' hell man, what a night this is gonna be."
The duty screw was nearing our cells with slamming doors loudly heralding his approach.
"Leave the window open Mike, your cellmate is full of gas."
"It's fuckin' freezin' man."
"Yeh, I know mate, see you tomorrow," I said as the Poison Dwarf neared my cell.
"Yeah, good night mate," he said, using the word mate for the first time in his life in the way we Brits use it.
The Poison Dwarf put the wing in lockdown as I busied myself with a brew, set up my writing table and selected a book to read after writing in my journal. I could hear Mike nextdoor pulling stuff about and talking to Igor. I made myself comfortable and started to write. After a while there was silence and then as the night bore on a deeper silence settled on the prison. I continued to write until I began to feel weary.

It was just before midnight when I got into bed with James Clavell's *Whirlwind*, a book I was enjoying because it depicted a strife-torn Iran in 1979 which interested me simply because my good friend Ali Safave was Iranian. I adjusted my reading lamp and took a final look at the stars in the sky then opened the book. In just a few minutes my eyelids started to droop, so I dropped the book onto the empty bunk beneath me and leaned across to turn off the reading lamp.

I do not know why but I had a feeling that the prison sodium lights shed a gloomier light than usual. I looked to the sky to see the stars but there were none to be seen. In the stillness the night moved stealthily around the prison seeming to swamp it with dread. I sensed a tingle of fear down my spine, which grew rapidly with apprehension as I imagined an evil omnipotence surrounding me. My cell changed atmosphere, as though I was in very deep water and I could feel pressure in every pore of my body. I pinched my nose and blew hard to equalise the pressure in my ears but it did not work. As I started to panic the harder I blew. An invisible force tore away my hand from my nose and through my ringing ears I heard the rasping voice of Satan. I could not decipher the words as I furiously rejected the whispering overtures by calling to Jesus. The haunting voice was growing in sound and dominance and seemed to be echoing as though something was getting in the way.

Suddenly there was a great crash and I sat bolt upright in my bed, perspiration dripping off my chin. Crash! Another bang. Thick silence as I held my breath, listening. Crash! It was Mike nextdoor sorting out Igor's snoring and farting problems. There was a long drawn out groan then silence.

"You okay Mike?" I yelled.

"Yeah man, no problem!" he yelled back. Silence again.

I checked my watch. It was 3:00 am. Christ! I've had a three-hour nightmare, I thought, as I climbed down from my bunk to use the toilet. The toilet flushed noisily as I threw a blanket on the floor and knelt in seiza posture to begin breathing exercises and meditation. I was worried about stress affecting my mind and what to do about these Satan hallucinations should they increase. I did not know it then but that visit from the Prince of Darkness was to be his last. It left me with a strange thought that, if the stars were an excuse for a universe, was life a will-o-the-wisp excuse for death. Hmm, strange?

Calmness came over me as the Lord entered my thoughts with the words from a psalm.

> *Hear, O Lord, when I cry with my voice!*
> *Have mercy upon me and answer me.*
> *When You said 'Seek My face' my heart said to You,*
> *'Your face Lord, I will seek.'*

I felt then that I would never again get a visit from imagined djin[93].

---

[93] djin - demons

The Mad Arsonist

St Patrick's Day 2007 and snow was falling in northern Spain. The window in my cell was warped and the icy draught had chilled my face, so I pulled up the bedclothes to cover my head. Moments later the bell rang for recuento, the first headcount of the day and time to check for suicides and murders.

I got out of bed to switch on the light, so the duty screw could see me when he slid open the Judas hole in the big iron door. He had to see my face and see me move, so I always raised my hand when I heard the Judas hole slide open. I could hear the noise of each cell being checked and the shouts of the screw at the prisoners who were still comatose from last night's smack or knockout pills. My door rattled as he noisily moved the metal slide.

"Solo?" he yelled, asking if I was alone.

"Si, mi amigo es permiso!" I yelled back.

"Venga! Okay!" he yelled and continued his headcount.

I stripped off and poured my two bottles of warm water into a plastic bucket to wash and shave. The cruel bastards had turned off the central heating during the night so my shaving water was barely warm - but it was better than the icy water from the tap, which I would use after shaving to rinse my face. I could use the pulpo to heat some water, but I preferred to make a brew with that rather than use it for shaving.

When I finished my ablutions I got dressed in tracksuit bottoms and trainers to start my daily routine of stretching and ju-jitsu warm up exercises. There was not enough room in my cell to jump around so I made do with sit-ups, press-ups, crunches, and umpteen other exercises I could do in this confined space. I checked my watch as the bell rang for unlocking and desayuno[94]. The cells were quickly unlocked and everyone poured on to the corridor to head downstairs for breakfast.

Breakfast on St Patrick's Day was a bread roll and two slices of spam. The spicks loved that shit. The Arabs did not touch it in case

---

[94] desayuno - breakfast

there was pig in it, so they ate the bread roll soaked in olive oil and dunked in coffee. Some of them ate leftover food from the previous day and enjoyed that with their hot coffee. I ate a bread roll with a tiny wrap of margarine and a bit of jam, as the noise reverberated around the dining hall. The sound of feeding Arabs and Spaniards, in this large room with its high ceiling, was deafening. Everyone was shouting to be heard and the noise bounced back from the ceiling to irritate one's ears and fuel the beginnings of a headache. I could have moved into the sala but that room was full of billowing cigarette smoke, hashish and heroin fumes and coughing, sneezing zombies.

I quickly ate my breakfast and strolled out of there, down the corridor and out into the yard. I moved quickly along the corridor because it passed the lavatories and that was the busiest time. There was a queue of Arabs and spicks waiting their turn to shit. They seemed not to notice the incredible stink of fresh shit and lots of it. I quickened my pace to get past the door and, as I did so, I saw a spick gypsy pissing into the only sink, his piss splashing over the taps. Such is life in this appalling pit of Spanish iniquity.

As I entered the yard on that bitter Saturday morning, a blast of cold air hit me hard in the face and I welcomed it by gulping it down deeply and completely exhaling to clear my lungs of the fug of the shithouse corridor. I strode out briskly to loosen up and breathed in the cold fresh air through my nose, as powdery snow swished this way and that in the blustery wind, sometimes causing a vortex, like a miniature whirlwind that can only be seen when it snows.

I used the loneliness of the snowy yard to speak to God. I did not actually talk out loud, though a murmur sometimes escaped my lips, nor did I discuss things - but I did ask for strength and comfort for my loved ones, and to make them aware of their blessings, and to please increase my blessings, and to help me get the fuck out of there. What use was God if I could not talk to Him? There was nobody in there I wanted to talk to, so I talked to Him. He answered me by giving me mental strength and courage to conquer the ever-present evil that lurked in every passage and corner of Satan's arena.

I held my head high as I marched around the pateo, my face exposed to the howling wind and swirling snow. I embraced the elements and strode out manfully, reminding myself of my army years as a professional soldier - proud of my Englishness. *Mad dogs and Englishmen* and all that old bollocks passed proudly through my mind. Never did it matter so much as it did then, as the stoats' eyes of the Spanish nonces, gypsies and zombies peered at me from the fuggy warmth of the sala.

The hard eyes of the prison officers were also focused on the lone Brit marching around their bleak yard. Look at the crazy Englishman, they all thought. That is right, the operative word being crazy because, if you entered his space threateningly, he would likely rip the flesh from your skull.

I started jogging and enjoyed my exercise as my out breath appeared as mist through the snowflakes that swirled around me. I was careful not to break into a drenching sweat because the shower block was not yet open, so I practised stances, kicks, blocks and punches under the awnings where the rustic tables and benches sat empty and forlorn. Only the screws could see me under the awnings because I was out of view of the sala. The screws' office extended further into the yard enabling them to see each corner and doorway. I could see four of them huddled, gazing out of the smoke-filled office, their pallid complexions ghost-like as they discussed their English prisoner alone in the yard. Ignoring them I continued my training and was truly enjoying myself, when the tannoy crackled and announced that the prison cinema would be showing the latest Stallone film *Rocky V* in twenty minutes time. So I left the lonely yard to join the back of the stampede.

The queue snaked from the main gate back along the corridor, where I had to endure the unrelenting stink of the lavatories, until the head of the queue was allowed through the main gate and along the corridor to the cinema, which was possibly sixty metres away. At the entrance to the cinema a team of cacheros manned the walk-through metal detector set up with tables where metal objects like watches and cigarette lighters were to be placed. If it did not bleep as you passed through you collected your bits and entered the cinema. If it bleeped you were stripped and searched by the hated cacheros.

A central aisle divided the cinema. A burly prison officer indicated that I should sit on the right side of the cinema because a different wing would occupy the left half and I must not cross the central aisle. I sat alone on the back row as the remainder of modulo dos (wing No. 2) crowded to the front, jockeying for positions nearest the central aisle.

My mind flashed back to when I was a kid going to the Saturday afternoon flicks in Widnes, my hometown. I used to go with my pals to the Regal cinema, or the Premier cinema, which was directly opposite on the other side of the main road in the busiest part of town. Tom Mix or Roy Rogers would decide which one we went to. *The Three Stooges* was always showing no matter which cinema we attended and the place was bedlam. Just like then as modulo cuatro (wing No. 4) inmates entered the prison cinema.

Though the place was illuminated the screws carried those long heavy torchlights that could be used as clubs, and they used them unsparingly to keep the two groups of inmates apart as they spilled into the aisle to greet each other. Several prisoners tried to reach their friends across the aisle for a hug and handshake as the pushy screws attempted to separate them. Prisoners at the front caused a rumpus as prisoners at the rear exchanged drugs while the screws were diverted to the front. This happened each Saturday so it was well rehearsed.

Everyone settled down as the deafening introduction to *Rocky V* started and the lights went down. The volume was so high the speakers rattled and shook as the decibels loosened my earwax. But it mattered not that the voices were distorted. I could not understand Sly Stallone's Spanish lingo as I have a problem understanding his English! I sat on my own on the back row and enjoyed the performance of an ageing athlete making it back to the top. Great! It should give old has-beens inspiration to get fit again. I loved it. That man Stallone inspired me with his superb fitness and dogged attitude to endurance, a magnificent role model for mature men.

The film ended and I was first in the queue to get out because now was the time for the final exchange of drugs to take place and phoney fond farewells happened in order to distract the torch wielding screws. Stallone must have stirred the blood of the belligerent screws because the torches were being viciously thrust into ribs and kidneys to separate embracing poofs and friends alike. The screws thought they were on fairly safe ground because the metal detectors ruled out the use of metal spikes and knives; but the bone pinchou (shank, chiv, spike) would not be found with a metal detector.

The pinchou was a stabbing weapon fashioned from an animal bone normally found in the prison cookhouse. The sharp end was usually grooved to house rat shit near to the point, or shit from an AIDS victim, which was left inside the wound after a stabbing. The embryo left in the wound would cause major problems to the victim. This was the most favoured weapon of the Spanish gypsy. The pinchou was normally used on fellow prisoners to settle scores, rather than on prison officers because the thick blue serge is hard to penetrate. Also, the most vital commodity, courage, is lacking in the Spanish gypsy psyche, unless the victim is unaware of his attacker when his back is turned.

I could see the tussle in the aisle had escalated to a mini riot, so I sneaked out into the corridor to avoid being called as a witness later. The sounds of battle echoed past me and along the corridor to the open gates of my wing from where a group of screws came rushing toward me to join the melee. From the opposite direction came more screws, hell bent on cracking skulls with their big sticks. The metal detector frame was parked against the wall, so I stood next to it out of harm's way. Looking at the approaching faces converging on me, I could see some of them were scared, but most of them were snarling with rage and adrenaline. Both groups of screws barged into each other at the entrance to the cinema in their attempt to get there first. An older screw shoved me away toward my modulo, so I strolled along the corridor and waited at the gate. He obviously did not want me to witness what was about to happen. Don Eugeniol, a young pasty-faced screw wearing a poncey hairstyle that made him look feminine, minced to the big gate and let me in. I immediately went to my table to write this down in my journal on St Patrick's Day.

The next day was Mothering Sunday and I was allowed to call my mother in Widnes. She was in bed but so glad to hear my voice. I was allowed five minutes to speak with my mother and five minutes to speak with Susan my wife. Ten minutes of ecstasy for me and a good start to the day for them. The duty screw tape-recorded our conversations then ordered me to write down the telephone numbers to attach to the cassettes. In January when I had first arrived, it was necessary to contact my wife and mother and ask them to send copies of their domestic telephone contracts, so I could present them to the chief security officer before I could use the wing telephone. The telephone was then programmed to accept these numbers and allowed exactly five minutes per call then automatically cut me off. The duty screw sat in full view and recorded my calls. Maybe they thought my eighty-six year old mother was a drug dealer, or maybe they had no right to eavesdrop electronically and record a call that I was paying for - take note Strasbourg. Are there copyright rules regarding these tapes? Hmm... anyway bollocks! I was so pleased to have a chat with my wife and my mother.

Mothering Sunday was very cold and nobody was in the yard. The sala was crowded and full of smoke and fumes. The television was on full volume as animated conversations and noisy arguments clashed in a cacophony of disharmony in the competition to be heard. Groups of hard-faced men huddled over the pachis[95] tables noisily slamming dice and arguing, as others played draughts and chess with spectators standing and sitting around offering expert advice. Other men read quietly, while agitated men padded up and down like caged tigers. Some of them wore hissing Walkmans on their heads and nodded to the rhythm, moving their heads from side to side like those little toy dogs seen in the rear windows of motor cars. Fucking hell! It was like a scene from *Star Wars*.

There was a shortage of chairs so nobody wanted to lose theirs by going to the stinking lavatories. I waited for the inevitable hostility as the morning wore on. I was in the comedor where there was no smoke but the stimulating stink of hashish was virtually impossible to avoid anywhere, on any wing, in any prison, in Spain, so I was quite

---

[95] pachis - tables

used to it. I am certain the same smell was in many a royal palace and staterooms, only a fool or a liar would disagree.

Standing near to me was a furtive, shifty-eyed man of about fifty years. His beard was rough and untrimmed and his body odour was reaching my nostrils. He moved his weight from one foot to the other so he was in constant motion like a metronome. He was an arsonist. He torched a finca[96] as the occupants slept; the family perished in the blaze. There seemed to be an innocent evil about him as though he was childish or mentally retarded and possibly did not realise the consequences of his actions. But as he shuffled toward me showing his brown tombstone teeth glistening out of the big hairy hole in his face, I noticed his eyes were without expression and lifeless. Suddenly, his mouth formed a sneer and his eyes transmitted threat and evil.

"Cigaro hombre!" he growled.

"Fuck off!" I said, contemptuously.

"Deme cigaro, ahora!" he demanded, his grubby fingers reaching for me.

I cocked my left leg over the bench so I was straddling it and then slammed my fist into his approaching sternum. He flew backwards to land on his arse between the tables. He sat with his back against a table gasping for breath as he shook his head incredulously. I sat watching him as he slowly recovered and looked at me with a hurt look in his eyes, the evil had momentarily gone. He had difficulty getting to his feet so he pulled himself upright by grabbing first the bench and then the table. Turning unsteadily to face me he revealed the evil that had returned to both his eyes with a wicked glint. I instantly regretted not battering his eyes, because as he transmitted a threat to me I realised he could stab a pinchou into my back in revenge. The duty screw walked into the dining hall so I was unable to correct my mistake.

I believed that when a prisoner attacked my person, I should leave that prisoner in a bleeding heap, crumpled on the ground with painful and lasting injuries, so he would realise the consequences of assaulting the lone Brit. Their terrible pain and the scarred eyebrows

---

[96] finca - farmhouse

should serve as a deterrent against any future act of revenge. I was aware that if the miscreant had had the use of a gun, then my deterrent action would be redundant - but there were no guns in prison, so the reputation of the unbridled, berserk Brit must serve as the deterrent.

The shuffling arsonist made his way to the far end of the dining hall to sit rubbing his chest and glaring at me from the tables furthest away. Other prisoners sat quietly reading, looking over the tops of their books and newspapers at the lone Brit who they all knew to be dangerous and deadly when cornered or threatened.

I picked up my pen to record the happenings of the morning when a rumpus started in the sala. As usual the scuffle began with a dispute over a chair. I could see part of the sala from where I was sitting in the dining hall through the bars of the gate that separated the two rooms. I could see the edge of the table tennis table, which was piled high with holdalls and sports bags. Nobody plays table tennis. A tangle of bodies slammed into it, as the melee resembled a rugby scrum. This was no slugfest, it was more a rough and tumble, that was until a piercing scream rented the foul air of the sala. The bodies quickly disentangled to slink away as the screws entered the sala. One of the younger men in there had been stabbed in the back and was writhing in agony on the filthy floor. His hands were trying to reach the wound but could not quite reach the animal bone protruding between his shoulder blades. The screws ordered two prisoners to support him and move him quickly to the enfermeria, where they could remove the pinchou and deal with the implanted rat shit.

Everyone was quickly herded into the gloomy yard for a recuento and to wait for the inevitable shakedown by the cacheros. We did not wait long out in the cold. A team of cacheros took station in the corridor where the telephone was and we were sent in ten at a time. My turn soon came and I stood in front of a young prison officer who ordered me to empty my pockets. He picked up my wallet and opened it revealing my membership card of Departmento Nacional Buguei Ju-Jitsu with my mugshot and cinturon negro (Black Belt dan grade) thereon.

"Cinturon negro?" he asked incredulously.

"Si," I replied, "no necesito cuchillo, I don't need a knife."

"Venga," he whispered, then handed back my wallet and pointed to the dining hall, indicating I should go back to my writing.

I could not see the cacheros at work from where I was writing but there was plenty of drama emanating from around the corner because the surprise shakedown was turning up street money, hashish and other illegal objets d'art that could not be shoved up arseholes quickly enough.

The cacheros finished at feeding time so I was first in the queue today. I got a pear, bread roll, two fried eggs, and a fish and rice fuck-up from the cookhouse. The shakedown had no effect on the noise. The monkey house still had to be fed and these incidents happened so often it was not worth discussing at the dinner table. Certainly my fellow diners, the Arabs, were too busy scooping the food into their mouths with bread in their fingers rather than using the plastic forks. They would break a piece of bread then shove it with their fingers into the mess on the bandeja, lower their faces to shorten the distance between bandeja and gob then shove it in. Animated chatter ensued and the stabbing was forgotten in the sands of Algeria and Morocco as they talked of family and home.

Feeding time ended and we were herded upstairs to our cells for siesta. I would be in lockdown until 5:00 pm, so I settled down for the afternoon by first preparing a brew. I took the pulpo from its pug. Pulpos are not permitted in prison because they had a tendency to electrocute the unwary and fuse the lights, so a good hiding place was necessary, because if one was found it meant a spell down the block. Any Heath Robinson contraption that used electricity to boil water was treacherous in the hands of the dopey spicks and Arabs, consequently, the lights went out quite often and many fingers were treated for burns.

I relaxed with my brew of tea and my James Clavell book until 05:00 pm when the bell rang to end siesta. I stowed my writing kit in my sports bag with my shower kit (towel, shampoo, fresh skids and socks), then tidied up and listened for the approaching screw crashing open the big steel bolts on the cell doors - a noise I would never forget. Crash bang went my cell door, so I exited, closed the door and silently slid home the big steel bolt, proving that the noise created by the screws was not necessary for the egress of prisoners - it was simply another psychological truncheon to bludgeon the mind.

I arrived at the bottom of the stairs to the cries of 'ultimo, ultimo' as agitated men were trying to find their place in the telephone queue. Ultimo means in this case 'who is the last man in the queue?' The telephone queue was another prime site for scuffles because of queue jumping by gypsies and Arabs who did not understand the concept of queuing, or simply thought they were above waiting in line to use the telephone. So the telephone was a daily bone of contention in Spanish prisons.

I pushed through the gaggle of arguing men to make my way to the comedor to arrange my kit on the dining table. I took out my writing kit and made myself comfortable by putting a blanket on the hard seat and sitting with my right side close to the white tiled wall. I could only be approached from the left-hand side, so any would-be attacker could not surprise me nor stab me in the back - just another precaution in Satan's arena. I continued writing my journal until 7:00 pm when I packed everything away to go for a shower.

An impatient crowd waited for the duty screw to unlock the shower block as the bitter wind blew with a vengeance, chilling all the hard faces gathered around me. The duty screw, a short-arsed nasty piece of work known locally as Senor Costra (Mister Scab), ambled slowly across the yard twirling a bunch of keys around his forefinger. He silently threaded his way through the crowd, holding the keys to his front like a blind man with a white stick expecting men to make way for him, which they did instantly. He deliberated for a moment then slowly inserted the key and turned it, withdrew it and stepped back out of harm's way as the big steel door opened outwards against the flow of pushing prisoners.

I went with the sudden surge and snaked through the two doors leading to the shower stalls. I quickly found a space for my kit and was naked in a moment. Rushing into a vacant shower stall I pushed the button recessed into the white tiled wall to start the water flow, which was cold. I dodged the cold water and waited for the hot water to appear. The hot water soon arrived and I immersed myself, soaping my hair with shampoo. The water suddenly became scalding hot and, as I leapt backwards out of the shower, I collided with the mad arsonist, accidentally knocking the bone pinchou out of his hand. Cursing myself for not being on red alert in the dense steam of the shower block, I squatted and retrieved the weapon before he could reach it. Christ! This is the most dangerous place in the prison and I had my back to that shuffling thug. I could see the needle-sharp point had been smeared with human faeces, probably from an AIDS victim. The boiling water had rapidly filled the shower block with steam and yelps from scalded inmates as they leapt out of the shower stalls. The mad arsonist grabbed my wet hair as I spun around to face him. I effortlessly shook my head free as his big fist sailed by, narrowly missing my nose. I slammed his shitty weapon into his groin, embedding it possibly three inches into his flesh and left it there as he caught me with a hefty punch to my ear. My head rang with the impact of his punch but my open fingered nukite found both his eyes. Standing there solid and stocky he rubbed both fists into his eyes and screamed like a pig. His cries melted into the shouts and screams of remonstrating inmates, complaining about the scalding water. He stood there fully clothed rubbing his eyes, when I punched into his guts just beneath his sternum. He went down instantly without a sound so I pulled him easily across the wet floor to the corner shower stall and shoved him in and pushed the water button to drench him in scalding water. The jarring scream drowned out all other noises, so I quickly pulled him into a sitting position, delivered two very hard punches to each eye, broke his nose with my knee and dislocated each of his thumbs. Turning to exit the shower stall I found three grinning Russians stark naked and dripping water. They reached in to grab the mad arsonist and hoisted him shoulder height and rushed him out to dump him headlong onto the cold concrete of the yard.

By now the hot water had cooled somewhat so I quickly showered and was dressing when the screws entered mob-handed to chase everyone out for a recuento and body search. The mad arsonist was in the enfermeria having his thumbs fixed and the shitty bone removed from his groin. I did not lay eyes on him again but I knew he would remember his attempted ambush on the deadly Brit for a long, long time. Had that scalding water not made me leap backwards into my backstabber these words would not be here. That night I said prayers of thanks, for I am beholden to Him for my survival in that dreadful place called Daroca.

That evening at feeding time I noticed the duty screw, Don Angel, the venomous runt who hated all forms of life within these walls, was looking at me eating. I wondered if the mad arsonist had grassed me from his hospital bed. He needed only to whisper the word Inglese and I would have been nailed. The mad arsonist had no friends. He was hated and not mentioned on my table during feeding time but somehow Don Angel made me feel uneasy. I noticed that some of my Arab friends had observed his interest in our table. Their eyes went from him to me as though they knew something I did not.

After feeding time we were herded upstairs and put in lockdown at 9:00 pm sharp. I did my usual things like make a brew and did some writing while waiting for the final recuento of the day. Recuento happened at 10:00 pm and I lay on my bunk waiting for the duty screw to check me out by peering through the Judas hole in my door. I heard his footsteps approaching and as they became louder I became more nervous. There was silence for a moment, then crash, as he yanked back the metal slide to reveal his glittering eye, unblinking, boring through me like a laser beam. I met his gaze and held it for what seemed like ages, thinking to myself, if you come in here with your big stick I will shove it right up your sick arse!

Several times in the dead of night I heard the approaching footfalls of the duty screw doing his rounds. I held my breath as I first heard the sound of movement on the wing. Then the footfalls would become louder as they neared my cell. Apprehension danced in my mind as paranoia fed the furnace of dread. Fear and dread enveloped my mind. I doubted if I could sleep but, if I did, I would have terrible nightmares. Realising this was a condition of imprisonment I got out of bed in the middle of the night and did some breathing exercises to calm my raging thoughts and prayed for courage. I climbed back into bed and went quickly into a dreamless sleep.

Nuradin bin Sahara

Tuesday morning saw the return of Nutmeg the queer. I was writing my journal in my usual place in the comedor when he arrived exasperated and spluttering about cacheros taking away his new radio and other bits and pieces he tried to bring into the prison.

His facial expression seemed strange, camp but not feminine, scowling but not masculine either. This creature was not a woman locked in a man's body. He was simply a man with damaged genes, just like a cleft palate or blindness at birth. A gene that emerged at puberty that created an unhinging of his sexual development during puberty was what he suffered, which created an impulse to mount a man instead of a woman, to poke into that which God designed as an exit hole for human waste. His facial expression served only to irritate me because he was neither effeminate nor masculine, but somehow unmanned and mentally emasculated.

Before the blubbering alien finished complaining the tannoy crackled and I was called to the screws' office. I quickly scooped everything into my sports bag and made my way there with Nutmeg following on and bickering about cacheros. I turned on him and stopped him dead in his tracks just outside the screws' office.

"You have just been out for six fucking days and you're back here whinging and whining like a fucking Aussie squaddie! Why the fuck did you come back in?"

Without a word he about turned and scurried away, mincing in a gait unlike any man or woman I have ever seen. I reported to the duty screw.

"Analitico!" he shouted.

Another screw with a familiar friendly face emerged from the office.

"I am your escort," he said, grinning.

It was Amex, the screw who helped process me in on the day I arrived.

"Come on, I am to take you for your blood test. How are you doing? I hear many stories about you my friend."

Looking into his young, clean-shaven face I could not help but like him.

"Whatever you've heard must be lies," I said, "I haven't done anything here yet, apart from write letters."

"Oh, I've heard about your letter writing, everyone here knows about that and how you behave when someone disturbs you," he chuckled as he slapped me on the back. "You have injured some very bad men, but you are clever, you do not get caught, but we do know about it you know."

"Yeah, this place is full of grasses, you should rename the place Hotel Chivato. I can't piss without someone telling the screws."

"A lot of people are waiting for the results of this analitico to see if you take drugs Kreestoffer," he said with a wry smile on his face.

"Is anyone betting that I do?" I asked.

"Oh yes, Don Angel is taking bets that you are a junkie."

"What about you?" I asked.

"I don't gamble my friend."

"You do now mate," I said, unable to conceal the glee in my heart. "Put your pay-packet on me. I'm clean. I don't smoke dope, I don't smoke ciggies and I'm never in a place where I get passive smoking, so put your money on a clean result."

"I will do that and tell my friend Ramon as well, he is an enemy of Don Angel."

All of a sudden I felt good about the dreaded analitico, the taking of blood that exposed any secret bad habits to the prison authorities and those facts lived in your documents forever. Amex took me to the front of the queue in the enfermeria and a horse-faced nurse quickly pushed a needle into the crook of my arm and filled six vials with my blood. Five minutes later I was back on the wing.

When I arrived at the screws office with Amex there was some consternation because Abdelmalik had been arrested whilst on permiso and was now languishing in a police cell in Girona. The screws were discussing who should be put in with me because a two-man cell must have two men in it. Amex told me to find a cellmate to move in with me. In the meantime I had to go to my cell and put Abdelmalik's kit into plastic bags and put them in the corridor so orderlies could take his kit to ingreso. Amex and another screw accompanied me and sealed the plastic bags when I had finished.

I moved my bedding from the top to the bottom bunk because whoever came in there could have the top - the bottom bunk was best for me. When I finished Amex took me back down to the pateo and wished me luck finding a cellmate.

"Don't forget to put your bet on," I reminded him as he walked away.

Nutmeg made a beeline for me the moment I stepped into the cold wind on the pateo. I momentarily shivered then strode away clockwise around the yard. He converged on me as I passed the economato queue.

"Get me a coffee!" he said, loudly enough for the men in the queue to hear him.

"Fuck off!" I replied, loudly enough for the whole yard to hear.

Crestfallen he tried to keep up with my pace around the yard.

"Why are you so mean?" he asked sulkily.

"I'm not fucking mean," I replied. "You are an ill-mannered oaf who doesn't say please or thank you, so fuck off!"

"But we are in prison!" he bleated.

"Fuck off!"

He fell back as I quickened my pace around the yard. My thoughts were about choosing a cellmate from this reprehensible bunch of scum suckers. I would have approached Mike Sherman because he was a gentleman of the sea and a good man, but I withdrew him from my thoughts because he was comfortable with Rudi the Cuban who was in there for cocaine trafficking. I also helped Rudi with his English lessons, but he was a lazy sod and would not take much in. Maybe that was because he was stoned all the time. I faced a problem because I did not want a gypsy or a nonce in my cell. Abderrahim sprang to mind as I saw him throwing a basketball up at the net and missing it each time. I watched him alone in the yard following the basketball as it bounced off the backboard. He was a quiet man who did not smoke and he spoke a little English and some German, and he spoke Spanish like a native. He was also one of the diners at my table. The biting wind had numbed my cheeks, so I decided to go indoors to the comedor. As I passed Abderrahim I called out to him.

"Venga amigo, yo abla contigo!"

My spick lingo was quite crap but I still liked to practise it occasionally. The basketball was thrown at the net and missed to bounce and roll forlornly across the blustery yard.

"Que pasa, Kreestoffer?" he smiled, glad that someone had invited him in out of the cold. We sat at our table and I explained the situation regarding Abdelmalik and how I needed a cellmate. He was delighted I had asked him because his Moroccan cellmate was a camel herder and he snored and farted like one.

"Mucho ronca y gas," he said, pulling a face and pinching his nose.

I told Abderrahim to inform the duty screw of his change of cell, so off he went to do just that, but it was very near feeding time so the screws chased him away. He told me as we dined that he would see the duty screw after feeding time and before we got banged up for the afternoon. Unfortunately the screws had other ideas. They moved me out of my cell during lockdown and put me in with Luis Quero, a sordid little Spaniard, a muckworm who dealt heroin to school children in an effort to lure them into a paedophile ring in Madrid. The screws knew he would be very uncomfortable living with me. I guessed this was a set-up for me to beat the crap out of him, so I decided, wisely, not to touch him. My plan was to find another cell as soon as possible, but until then I must share his space. From the moment I set foot in his cell he was terrified. He lay on his bunk with eyes and mouth wide open as I threw my kit through the iron door then made my bed. The grinning screws locked me in and listened at the door before strolling away a few minutes later. I said nothing as I made my bed and stowed my kit. When I had finished putting everything away, I took my James Clavell book and climbed up into my bunk. As I clambered onto my bed he muttered something unintelligible in Spanish. I leant over the edge of my bed to look into his sallow face.

"Callate la boca! Shut your mouth!" I said.

They were the only words I said to that creep because I was not in that cell long enough to say much more. Amex heard about my predicament and had me moved that same day. He was waiting for me in the screws' office when we were unlocked at 5:00 pm. He told me to find someone else quickly so I immediately told my Arab friends to pass the word.

That night would find me in a different cell with two Moroccans as my new cellmates, but before that I continued writing my journal in the comedor whilst I listened to Nutmeg talking about his six days of debauchery in Zaragoza. As I wrote he excitedly spilled his beans and I braced myself mentally as I heard about things I could not comprehend. Like the mating games they play with introductions to each other in faggot discos and bars in Zaragoza. The emasculated facial expressions and cheek kissing and fairy handshakes. Oh, fucking hell! Why am I listening to this namby-pamby shite?

"My doctor friend took me to a brothel and treated me to a beautiful Brazilian boy," he said coyly.

"Oh, so Lhaktar is history then?" I snarled.

"Oh no, we didn't make love," he whispered. "He only sucked my dick and fondled me."

"You didn't make love!" I growled. "Make fucking love! You call sticking your dick up a spick's hairy fucking arse in a faggot brothel making love?"

"Actually, he wanted to enter me but I was true to Lhaktar and stopped myself and settled for the suck, but it was so difficult because the boy was beautiful."

"I don't believe you," I said. "You let a bloke, a complete stranger, suck your dick? I reckon you'd let the village donkey up your fucking arse!"

"You don't understand," he said, dangling his limp wrist.

"I don't want to understand, you horrible cunt! Fuck off away from me, you might have something contagious!" I growled.

It was not often that someone made my flesh creep but I had had enough of Nutmeg, Greg the South African poof. Piqued, he left the table and minced out into the yard as I dismissed him from my mind and thought about the next day, Wednesday 21st March, my mother's eighty-sixth birthday.

I was thinking about my mother when Nuradin bin Sahara came to sit next to me. Nuradin was another Moroccan who shared my table and he had heard about my need for a different cell. I was surprised when he spoke English to me. Not good English but better than most people around here.

"You come my cell my friend? We have clean cell, nice cell, smell very nice with fruit and bread. You like my cell." The hands and mouth were working like a souk carpet seller in Tangier. I could not get a word in edgeways as he babbled on with his sales pitch. "You come live with me, Nuradin bin Sahara and Ahmed, my friend," he said, animatedly.

"Yes," I replied, "I would like..." he talked right across me.

"Ahmed, my friend, he work in lavaderia[97] and he do all our things special with nice smell, not with other man's wash, and you not clean celda[98], we clean room, you relax, do nothing, we do something all time, you read, write, no work, we do everyt'ing mister!"

I could not resist! I had seen so many of these blokes on my travels around the North African coastal towns who treated me like royalty just because I was a skipper. I simply could not refuse him.

"Okay Nuradin, later you can help me to carry my things to your cell, but first I must tell the funcionario about your cell, what number is it?"

"I go now, tell funcionario and then get coffee. You like coffee or tea? I fix now, you relax, coffee or tea?"

His face was a picture of relief and happiness. I wondered why as he scurried away to inform the duty screw of my move. A few minutes later Don Jose Maria, a brutal racist, was standing next to me looking down at my writing.

Looking up into his hard face I asked, "Que pasa, jefe?"

He wanted to know why I had asked to be moved in with Arabs. He was confused because he thought Englishmen were fussy about who they lived with and, in his eyes, Arabs were lower than a mole's arse. This was one of those moments in life when one knew it was prudent not to reveal one's true thoughts. I felt it best not to say how

---

[97] lavaderia - laundry
[98] celda - cell

much lower than a mole's arse most of the Spaniards in there could descend. All of the Arabs were in there for smuggling offences - none of them have committed offences as heinous as the Spaniards. There was not one nonce amongst the Arabs, yet this prison officer would have a problem finding someone who was not a nonce amongst his paisanos.

A few minutes later Nuradin bin Sahara returned with coffee and chocolate biscuits and right behind him was the reason he was so anxious to have me in his cell - eight inmates, transferred from modulo cuatro (wing No: 4), the worst wing in the prison. He knew about their pending arrival and knew one of them would be put in his cell. I could see why he wanted me to share his cell because the eight new boys were straight out of the *O.K. Corral*. The group dispersed as they searched out friends or relatives amongst their tribe. They were also looking for men to share cells with. If they could not find someone willing to share by feeding time, the duty screw would allocate them willy-nilly into cells with empty beds.

Nuradin was delighted and it showed. He was bragging to fellow Arabs about having the English balandrista[99] in his cell. He must have thought there was kudos in securing my residence. I suppose there was if the Arabs thought I was going to sail his hashish across the Med. I drank my coffee, ate some biscuits, scribbled some notes and went to the screws' office with Nuradin to get the register changed to show that I had moved to cell No: 31 - a large cell with three beds and six steel lockers, two for each inmate.

At feeding time the table was unusually noisy with chatter about how Nuradin had managed to get me instead of one of the inmates from modulo cuatro. Animated conversations in Arabic ensued concerning the reputations of some of the new inmates. Apparently, some of them have been on the wing before and because of stabbings and smack dealing they were removed to modulo cuatro to teach them a lesson. was supposed to be hell on earth, especially for payos.

The mood on the wing had changed already and they had only been there for an hour or so. It felt as though something bad was

---

[99] balandrista - yachtsman

about to happen and the apprehension was showing on the face of the young screw in charge of the food serving. There would probably be a turf war regarding the sale of drugs and other scams on the wing, but I felt it would be over quickly. The Russians ruled the roost and they did not take prisoners, if you know what I mean? Pun intended.

Feeding time ended and we were ordered upstairs. Nuradin and Ahmed helped me gather my kit from the cell of the wide-eyed Luis Quero and lug it to cell No: 31 and stowed it neatly in my two new lockers. I folded various items of clothing to stow in my lockers, while Ahmed made my bed and Nuradin prepared a brew and rolled a spliff whilst waiting for the water to boil. The duty screw came along to lock us in and slammed the door and crashed the bolt loudly then turned the key in the lock. I was then given the grand tour of the cell.

There were cardboard cartons of soft drinks, boxes of dates and other fruits, cases of non-alcoholic beer in cans, boxes of cakes and biscuits. There was fresh bread and butter with slices of processed cheese, foil wrapped portions of cheese spread and fresh goat's cheese. Small jars of honey, jam and marmalade sat on a shelf and tea, coffee, sugar and milk were on a metal tray. All of this was hidden behind a clean bed sheet fixed on the wall and draped over everything. A pile of fresh bed linen was folded and piled neatly on one side of the makeshift table and a pile of laundered bath towels and hand towels on the other. These were obviously the fruits of working in the laundry. The cell was spotlessly clean and smelled pleasantly of fabric softener and soap powder. Nuradin proudly showed me a shelf on which to put my washing kit and Ahmed presented me with a beautiful all wool Moroccan blanket, which he dramatically threw across my bed and made it neat and folded in all the edges around my bed. Wonderful!

Ahmed spoke no English but was fluent in Spanish and spoke a little German, so we communicated quite well. He told me he would change my bedding every week and my laundry would be done any time I liked. The towels were for my daily use, so I could shower each day with a fresh bath towel. Nuradin handed me a cup of coffee as Ahmed gave me a plate of vanilla and chocolate cakes with a few biscuits.

I relaxed on my bed feeling like the Aga Khan when they produced the piece de resistance, a television hidden behind a bath towel near the foot of Nuradin's bed. Bloody hell! Much to my delight Ahmed switched it on and the Euro Sports channel appeared on the screen showing a football match. Ahmed demonstrated the other eight channels, so we were spoilt for choice. Suddenly prison life had improved for the lone Brit, as we three new friends toasted each other with cans of non-alcoholic beer.

Ahmed remained my friend until he got his Libertad on Sunday 1st July 2007. He served three years and one day of a three years and one day sentence. Not a single day remission did they give him and he worked all of his prison life and was a model prisoner. Had he been a Spaniard he would have only served two years of that sentence. He despised everything Spanish when I knew him. I wonder if he still does?

I slept soundly that first night with my Arab friends and I was pleasantly surprised to wake up to a cup of sweet coffee in the morning. I was also surprised to find Nuradin had gone to work at 06:00 am and I had not been disturbed by his exit at such an early hour. The duty screw silently opens cell doors to allow working inmates out of their cells without disturbing the rest of the wing each working day.

Nuradin worked in the tallers[100] fabricating electric fluorescent lights. He earned about €300 per month so he could afford his daily consumption of porro[101] and all the extras they had in the cell. Ahmed worked six days a week so I imagined he got the same amount as Nuradin. Because of their 'extras' they were very careful not to allow Spaniards to see the inside of our cell, so that was the only rule in No: 31, no spicks! That suited me anyway, but I could understand why they hated the Spanish, they had been victims of racist abuse from prison officers and Spanish inmates since the day they arrived.

As I sipped my coffee I cast my mind back to the time I shared a cell with two Arabs in the Carabanchel prison in Madrid nearly ten

---

[100] tallers - workshop
[101] porro - spliffs

years earlier. How kind and protective they were with me in that terrible place. The Carabanchel was General Franco's favourite torture chamber. Many lives were lost in that Godless pit. I remembered the band of brothers that I formed. A group of international villains with one thing in common, we were foreigners in a xenophobic Spanish hellhole. We grouped and bonded to protect ourselves from the unwashed rabble of Spain, the uneducated gypsy inmates with monstrous egos. My small platoon of professional killers defeated all attempts to kill or injure us and we became known as the Mezclado the Spanish word for mixture. We were all from different countries: China; Afghanistan, Sicily, Iran, Belgium, and I was the lone Brit. I wondered where they all were now? Good luck and respect wherever you are. Carabanchel was a stain on my life that I cannot remove, as were La Moraleja and Malaga prisons. I feared Daroca would also be in my dreams long after I had left.

Touching the wall next to my bed I felt it was damp and clammy - Satan's sweat, just like the cell walls of the Carabanchel. I sensed the onset of stress, the featherlight ripple of goose pimples across my shoulders heralding its approach, the incomprehensible state of mind, triggered by unguarded thoughts. I quickly sat cross-legged on the bed to start a deep breathing exercise and forcefully visualised myself standing under a waterfall. The water was soft and cool in my imagination as it cascaded onto my head and shoulders. The water had a magic cleansing property, an inherent power to cleanse without detergent, so there were no suds, just cool clear water. In my imagination the water began to seep slowly through my skin to pass through my body and out through the soles of my feet. The flow quickened as the cleansing water sluicing through my being washed the sensation of dread away. A warm sunbeam dried my skin as I heard the tinkling of a bell in the distance.

"Que pasa, Inglese?"

It was Ahmed shaking me awake as the bell rang for unlocking and breakfast. After my cleansing meditation I felt cool and fit as I left Ahmed to clean and lock the cell. I briskly walked downstairs to grab a coffee and get my place in the telephone queue. Today was special, it was my mother's birthday and I was first in the queue. At 09:00 am the computer activated the telephone and I called my mother.

"Happy birthday to you," I sing, as my Mum wondered who could be calling at 08:00 am because we were one hour ahead of UK, "Happy birthday to you..."

"Oh Chris!" she cried into the telephone. "I'm still in bed!" she said happily.

"You stay there Mam," I said, as I looked at the fat screw tape-recording our conversation.

We chatted happily for the allocated five minutes and told each other how we all loved each other dearly in my family and how pleased everyone would be to hear I called to wish her a happy birthday.

"Happy birthday Mam, I love you," I managed to say, and then we were cut off.

The fat screw called me in to sign the recording slip and verify my mother's telephone number on the cassette. I really did not like those earwigging bastards.

Mental Cruelty

A nasty surprise was in store for me on my mother's birthday. I was called to the social worker's office for an administration correction, a euphemism for mental cruelty, a favourite weapon of the civilian staff. I will explain.

One month before on 20th February 2007 the social worker informed me that my release date would be 26th July 2007 and I happily signed the authorisation paper. That was the day I was told about my 3rd Grade classification. That was the day I joyfully wrote and told my wife and mother that I would be home during the last week in July. I should have known better because I had seen this act of mental cruelty performed many times on foreign prisoners. Now it was my turn.

I entered the office to find the psychologist and the social worker flanked by guards. I immediately knew all was not well. I was told to sit as the two screws then positioned themselves on each side of me. In slow enunciated words the psychologist spoke first to inform me that the release date of 26th July had now been changed to 5th September 2007. The social worker then started to speak, but my world had just crashed around my ears as the realisation hit home. Stunned, I simply signed the new paper and left the room showing no signs of distress as I went. I hoped I had ruined their day by not showing any of the emotions that provided them with entertainment.

I blindly made my way to the yard with what felt like an elephant on my back. I was crushed inside and I needed to run around the yard to vent my spleen. I prayed that I would not bump into a Spaniard because for two pence I would tear one limb from limb. Such was the venom in my veins. My hatred boiled over as I realised what they had tried to do. In my mind I was no more than a bit of experience for the naive young Spanish girl who was trying to be a psychologist. Fuck! Fuck! Fuck!

Emotions were amplified in the unnatural surroundings of prison. The need to tell someone was truly pressing on me as tunnel vision came and went every couple of minutes and the blanket of depression wrapped itself around my shoulders. I strode out aggressively and accelerated to a pounding run as my breath puffed out white in the cold Aragon air. My lungs sucked in the crisp air as my arms pumped and my legs pounded and propelled the rage from my mind as I came to terms with the disappointment.

An incident like this might possibly seem small potatoes to people who have never experienced prison. After all, what were a few weeks extra to someone who has been in several prisons? Human beings, like machines, do not function well when taken out of the environs of their design. A man could adapt to his surroundings especially when they were of his own design no matter how harsh they were. However, when the situation was not created by his free will the stresses were somewhat different. Just like a Rolls Royce engine would break when given inferior oil, or not enough coolant, or used for something it is not designed for, a man could be affected by seemingly minor problems when locked in a prison with all the alien aspects of its population invading his space.

The problem expanded as I wrote the letter to my wife informing her of the extended stay. Visions of her opening the mail and reading the sad news crushed my heart as I saw her burst into tears in my mind. Such were the thoughts in the cramped mind of a prisoner. I would not have thought twice about inflicting pain on scumbags in there, but I was a coward when it came to telling my family about my own misfortune. I could not bear to tell my mother, so to lessen the blow I asked Susan to tell her about the postponed release date.

I somehow got through the day and had a hard night trying to sleep as pictures of my loved ones flitted through my mind, as I imagined their emotions on receiving the bad news. Prison was cruel to the innocent families of inmates, just as violent crime was cruel to the families of victims. But where lay the solution? Hmm. Who would throw the first stone?

Shit happens so I climbed out of it as fast as I could. By the next morning it was out of my system and I got my head around the new release date. Only twenty-four weeks to do, easy fucking peasy. But beware! Any problems with screws and they would make me do the whole sentence and that meant my Libertad would not happen until October 2008.

I ate my breakfast as the Arabs chatted quietly around my table. My thoughts returned to the heartache I had caused to my family and the guilt swamped my conscience yet again. But it was forgotten in an instant, as a fox-faced gypsy sneaked up behind Jamal Afkir sitting on the opposite side of the table from me and stabbed him in the back. Jamal was a big man, hard-muscled and athletic. He roared with pain as the faeces smeared bone slammed into his broad back between his shoulder blades and the swarthy muscular gypsy swiftly slunk away to mix with his tribe in the sala.

Jamal was the boss of the destinos[102] that cleaned the wing every day. He was tough but fair with his workforce, which were predominantly Arabs, but no gypsies. Like most men here he hated the Spanish gypsies and refused to employ any of them, simply because his experience of them proved they were worse than useless when it came to cleaning duties.

I leapt from the table and grabbed Jamal's arm and lifted him from the bench with his arm around my neck. Ahmed swiftly grabbed his other arm and we rushed him to the main gate shouting at the screw to open it so we could get to the enfermeria. Orderlies took Jamal from us and took him into the treatment room as the screw ordered us back to the wing. The bone pinchou was still embedded in his back. I did not know how deep it went or what damage it had done.

On returning to the wing I could see immediately a hostile mood divided the Arabs and gypsies. The Arabs were in the comedor and in the yard, while the gypsies were in the sala. No Arabs were in the sala. They were in groups at strategic places on the wing. One group covered the entrance to the lavatories and another stood near the economato. All bases were covered. An ambush awaited any gypsy that needed a piss, a coffee, fresh air or anything that required him to leave the sala. The screws were aware of the situation and reinforcements had arrived from other wings. Amex, my friendly screw had arrived with some of his colleagues from ingreso and he sought me out to chat with me.

---

[102] destinos - orderlies

"This is very bad," he said, as he found me sitting in my usual place in the comedor.

"Yeah, the fucking yellow spick pikey stabbed Jamal in the back," I replied.

"Which one?" he asked, looking at me with no hope of an answer.

"You'll find out soon enough," I said, "the Arabs will produce a body for you shortly after you lot go back to your normal duties."

"Cacheros will tear this modulo apart today, so there will be no weapons here," he said sternly, as though he was warning me personally.

"The Arabs don't need weapons, they'll simply tear him apart."

"We will soon know who stabbed the Arab," said Amex, "someone will talk."

Looking past Amex I could see through the barred gate of the sala and the fox-faced gypsy talking animatedly with senior tribesmen, who were berating him because they could not get coffee or ciggies from the economato. They could not have cared less about the injured man. Their only concern was the lack of coffee. Amex followed my gaze to the foxy face framed with long black curly hair. He could see the grubby fingernails bitten to the quick on the large dirty hands. He knew the dirt floor he normally lived on was a million miles from there. He was happy in prison with regular food and a bed.

"He raped and murdered a child, and I hope it is him that stabbed the Arab," he said, and I could see the hatred in Amex's eyes.

"You'll find out soon enough," I said, a bit more cheerily.

"Recuento!" shouted the agitated screws.

So we all shuffled out into the chilly yard to form ranks of five. I felt an air of trepidation growing as I strolled outside. The atmosphere in the yard was explosive. The gypsies came out last to form up at the rear of the parading inmates, their posturing and bravado an attempt at masking the fear in their guts. Nobody was talking. It was like a silent protest and it showed on the stern faces of the Arabs. Not a word was heard. Apart from the low shuffle of feet and the occasional twitter of a bird all was hushed as the apprehension grew and grew.

In the silence I could hear the sound of approaching men. Boots could be heard pounding along the corridors as extra prison officers converged on our yard. Cacheros burst into the yard brandishing large wooden truncheons. Apprehension swept through the ranks as they took station under the wing awnings to use the rustic tables as places of search. It seemed all the screws in the prison were in our yard and ready for a fight. Their body language expressing their mood, cocky, and aggressively slapping truncheons into their hands as they flashed threatening looks into the parade of prisoners. An air of fee-fi-fo-fum was apparent and fear shone in the eyes of men as the volatile situation grew more and more sinister with each passing second.

Suddenly, the first rank of five gypsies was hustled forward to the rustic tables and quickly stripped and searched. It took only a minute before the next rank was roughly rushed across the yard to be searched. Foxface was in the fourth rank to be searched and as soon as he reached the table he was attacked by a group of screws, overpowered, pounded with truncheons and carried away screaming by four burly screws. All eyes were on Foxface as he was unceremoniously hauled out of the yard with a screw lifting each of his limbs to carry him off. The look of fear on his face and the terrified screams were worth buying a ticket for. The parading prisoners turned as one to see the going of the hated gypsy.

I realised the screws had saved the day by their actions. Foxface had been grassed by one of his own and the unrest between Arab and gypsy had been settled as Foxface was sent to another prison. The search took on an air of half-heartedness as the mood on the pateo changed as screws tried to joke with inmates. The stick of gelignite was now a damp squib.

Amex joined me as I was about to be searched. He nodded at the cachero who waved me through his tables without so much as a patting down.

"C'mon," he said grinning, "I'll get you a coffee. The back door of the economato is open for prison officers."

Satan's Elves

British summertime began one Sunday and the world's clocks put forward an hour so I could look forward to an extra hour of daylight. I marched briskly around the yard and was about to break into a jog when Mike Sherman appeared next to my shoulder.

"Hey man! Where's the fire?" he chuckled, breathing hard as I slowed the pace to accommodate him and enjoy his company.

Mike's life had been a wonderful adventure and he was blessed with the art of storytelling. I would be the first to buy his book if he writes one. Over the coming months we would tell each other stories of our past lives and we both realised how lucky we were to have had so much adventure. Mike's stories of adventure on the high seas thrilled me, which may seem strange seeing as how much of my time had been spent smuggling at sea just like Mike. We talked about hair-raising situations as though they were humdrum events in the average working man's lifetime. Nothing seemed to faze Mike. He calmly told me he had a thirty-year sentence awaiting him in France when he finished in Daroca! Fuck me! I would be out of my mind! Seemingly the frogs had made a hash of their extradition application to have him removed from Spain to France, so there was a chance he would walk out to freedom instead of starting a thirty stretch in France.

Mike's thirty stretch was for a bit of puff. Fancy getting thirty years for hashish? Not even murderers get thirty years. There were blokes in Daroca that should have been executed for what they had done to children, but they would be out on the streets after doing just a few years. Bollocks! I bet the frogs that sentenced him smoked hashish. Ah well, blessed is he who is not caught. But Mike was not caught. He was tried and sentenced in his absence. How shitty was that? Thirty years on the word of grasses trying to save their own arses.

Mike's casual outlook on life was admirable, although I would not have expected much else from a man who spent his life sailing the vast oceans of the world. Mike and I became good friends and we shared many hours of storytelling entertaining each other. Later on we would share the same cell - but first I needed to start a new training routine and it began on Sunday, April Fools' Day.

I was waiting for Lorenzo, a half-breed kraut-spick to return from permiso in Barcelona. He was bringing me a new pair of trainers because my Reeboks were breaking up with all the physical jerks. Old military exercises like jumping with feet astride, and stretching in martial arts stances, and hard running soon took it out of old training shoes, especially when on the feet of a seventeen stone bloke. My plan was to raise my fitness levels and lose thirty pounds of weight by strict diet and hard training.

Prior to Lorenzo bringing my new Reeboks I had planned this new regime by writing down sets of abdominal exercises; various arm, leg and shoulder exercises using only bottles of water as the weights for weight training. My diet plan was simple. I merely excluded all meats except chicken and cut out bread and all the little treats from the economato like cakes and biscuits. Crikey! There was enough deprivation inside without denying myself treats. I knew it would be hard but bollocks to that. Time in prison had to be made best use of, and improving health and fitness was top of my list, besides writing my journal.

The sun was shining on April Fools' Day and spring was in the air as I speed walked around the yard. I was breaking in my new trainers with two hours of hard marching. The Russians were training hard today by piggyback riding around the yard. They took a turn each by jumping on each other's backs and racing around then swapping backs on each lap of the yard. There was no laughter - this was hard, serious training performed by hard, serious men. Six Russians galloping around had to be avoided so I changed direction to anti-clockwise so I could see them coming.

"Good morning, Eengleesh!" they gasped, each time they passed.

"Good morning comrades!" I replied each time.

Earlier I had prepared an area of the concrete floor under the awnings by washing it down with buckets of bleach and water. I brushed the water away leaving a clean patch of floor where I would put a blanket later when it dried. This small act of preparation attracted much attention from fellow inmates. After two hours of pounding the yard I spread my blanket on the ground to start my abdominal routine. I did my planned sets of leg raises and crunches then tore a strip off the edge of my blanket to use as a restraint for my feet to do sit-ups. I tied the length of cloth around a concrete pillar, adjusted my blanket so that the cloth held my feet and my backside was on the blanket, then I started my sit-ups.

On 1st April I started my day with half a lemon crushed into a cup of water. I ate nothing until I had completed my workout and then ate two apples for breakfast. My lunch and evening meal depended on what the cookhouse produced; so if it was fish or chicken I would eat some, if not I would eat a portion of bran flakes bought from the economato mixed with a handful of sultanas. I maintained this regime for one hundred and fifty seven days until my release on 5th September, and built up my routine to include two thousand abdominal exercises and lost fifty pounds in weight. I lost muscle as well as fat, but I felt great, vibrant and hard.

As I trained I would watch other men ruin their lives on heroin simply because they were in a dark place and could see no future. They fell into the hands of Satan's elves, the smack dealers of Daroca. The dealers were forever searching for the faces of likely mugs that had allowed the prison system to beat them down instead of staying morally strong and creative. It did not take long for a man to fall into the heroin trap once the rot set in. The dealers would join them in their rant against the system and slowly but surely fit them up for a free fix. They kept it cheap for a little while until their victim was hooked, thereafter they had a regular customer. There were many such men in Daroca.

All of the Arabs and many foreigners smoked hashish but they all shunned the heroin dealers. The media often state that hashish is the stepping-stone to heroin, but I think they are quite wrong. I am not advocating the use of hashish, but I think that millions of people use hashish daily and they never feel the need for heroin. Many heroin users have told me they have never used hashish in their lives and I have no reason to disbelieve them. However, I can only tell you about what happened in prison.

A Valium pill in Daroca is worth a packet of cigarettes, and tranquillisers vary in cost depending on how strong they are. Sleeping pills are also a currency, because the doctors tend not to hand them out like sweets like they do in other prisons, and many of the blokes have problems sleeping. Maybe it was their consciences keeping them awake, though I doubt it - most of these men had no conscience.

Thinking about my family was the major cause of insomnia in my case, but I did not take sleeping pills because they can be habit forming and I avoided putting chemicals into my body. When the problems occurred I solved them with martial arts breathing exercises and meditation - that always worked for me.

The heroin dealers in Daroca were no different than in other Spanish prisons. They were mainly gypsies serving sentences for murdering their clients. They were of an ilk, insomuch as they all wore an adornment of Christ somewhere on their bodies; either a tattoo of the Saviour wearing a crown of thorns, or a large flashy crucifix, polished bright so we could all see it. They often wore a tattoo of a dagger on their necks, the inmates' badge of pride - proud of what they have done, whether it be the killing of a man, woman or child. Why these creatures used the image of Christ on their person is beyond me, they cannot even write His name.

The heroin was brought in with their womenfolk on vis-à-vis visits. The usual pug was the vagina and rectum. The conjugal rights visit was held in a private room in the ingreso building, which was void of security cameras and screws. Before the gypsy made love with his wife he must first remove the contraband - gypsy foreplay. After lovemaking he must ease it up his own arse, with the help of his wife, mother or sister - after all it is a family business.

Miguel, the guitar playing schmuck from Barcelona, had just returned to the wing from his vis-à-vis. His tribal brethren were all over him like a smallpox rash. Happiness radiated from the group because the transit of heroin from wife to wing was successful. The screws were aware of the goings on and seemed not to care about the new load of smack on the wing. Miguel was waiting for the shower block to open at 7:00pm so he could retrieve the smack, undisturbed by the screws that never entered the showers. Miguel was typical of gypsy dealers. He bragged about the incoming smack to other tribal members who treated him to coffee and ciggies in the hope of a free fix when the shit came in.

I was in the shower when Miguel and his cronies entered and gathered around the shower stall, as Miguel fished for the smack up his arse. The screws knew something was going down because they knew that gypsies tended not to use the shower block, and right then there was a crowd of them in there. The steam clouded thickly, as the men showered in very hot water and Miguel pulled the smack from his hole. My clothes were piled on one of the wooden benches but the steam was obscuring my vision of them, so I left the shower stall to get dried and dressed quickly. Gypsies were taught from a very early age how to rummage bags and clothing in the blink of an eye. I thought it best to get out quickly in case a fight started and, besides I had an Omega gold watch in my clothing that I wanted to keep.

Suddenly there was a commotion across the room. The ruckus loomed out of the steam towards me as a naked Colombian throttled a gurgling gypsy. He let go with his right hand to punch his big fist into the muckworm's face. There was a distinct cracking sound as teeth were knocked out. The second blow splattered his nose like a squashed tomato to gush blood down his front. The third blow missed, as a pinchou punctured the Colombian's upper arm, as the other gypsies joined in. The Colombian was a giant and one of the few I had seen who could handle himself in a slugfest. He yanked out the pinchou and slammed it into the face of Jiminez, the headman of the gypsy tribe on modulo dos (wing No: 2). The bone pinchou entered the face just beneath the eye, plunged through the tongue, and out through the lower jaw. The scream alone was worth buying a ticket for. The Colombian drove his knuckles into the guts of Jiminez just beneath the sternum, which sent him into unconsciousness.

Suddenly there were too many to handle. Two gypsies jumped on his back. One of them got a chokehold on his neck as three more moved in from the sides. I positioned myself to pull the two men off his back, but was beaten to it by Rudi the Cuban. He punched into the kidneys of each gypsy so hard it sent the Colombian to his knees. The gypsy nearest me was about to thrust his pinchou into Rudi's back when I hit him with a hefty punch to the ribs beneath the stabbing arm, causing a loud crack as bones broke. My second punch slammed into his neck just under his ear. He dropped like a log to the wet floor. Removing the shitty bone from his hand I stabbed it hard into his buttock from where the doctor would remove it later.

Suddenly a stab of panic ran through my veins, as I realised that any chance of early release would be lost if I got caught up with this lot. I grabbed my bag and barged and shouldered my way out of there through fighting men and screaming gypsies. Entering the yard I closed the door behind me and strode off in the direction of the comedor. I put my bag down and got out my writing kit and started my journal, knowing the rumpus would begin at any moment.

It began with the arrival of cachero screws carrying truncheons. The duty screw closed the comedor gate locking us in. The prisoners in the sala were locked in, as the remainder on the pateo and the blokes in the shower block were subjected to a search and the wounded were removed to the enfermeria for treatment. There were shouts and screams as the walking wounded shuffled past the comedor gates on their way to the enfermeria. I was pleased to see that Rudi and the Colombian were not amongst them.

Later the gates were opened and everything was back to normal. Miguel's smack was on the wing so the gypsies were happy. Rudi the Cuban came to my table as I ate the last meal of the day, to thank me, as did the Colombiano. I did not feel the need for thanks, so it was a nice surprise.

The Lone Mexican

"Metadona!" was called over the tannoy, which prompted a rush of bodies to the main gate of the modulo where a nurse waited with her shiny chromium plated trolley laden with little plastic cups. Their behaviour was incredible. They knew they would get their methadone, but the barging, pulling and pushing, arguing and scuffling happened every day. The result was always the same. Everyone got their cup of methadone.

I witnessed the goings on from my table in the comedor. Three burly prison officers were corralling the noisy, scuffling crowd in the corridor into some semblance of a queue. When the scowling nurse was ready for her first patient she nodded at the baton wielding screw, who then shoved the emaciated gypsy he was holding back with his truncheon, forward toward the nurse. The noise ceased immediately as the gypsy swigged his methadone greedily and ran his tongue around the inside of the cup to get every drop. The nurse then told him to call out his name to the screw holding a list of the patients. The screw knew the name of the gypsy but the shouting of the name ensured the methadone had been swallowed. Each junkie had to call out his name after drinking the methadone, so that he could not spit it into another cup when he got back on the wing.

The screws knew about the brisk trade in spat out methadone. Junkies lurking nearby would offer their arses, or perform any perverted act, in return for the methadone in the mouths of the gypsies. I saw pathetic heroin addicts holding plastic cups that people had discarded after drinking their coffee. They hung around the gate waiting for returning junkies to barter for the spit. Because of the awareness of the prison officers usually every drop was swallowed. But for the really desperate junkies, some of the gypsies would regurgitate their methadone in the lavatory and the pathetic creature would drink it, phlegm and all. The diabolical heroin created addicts that would do almost anything for a fix, even kill for it. I remember the methadone queues in previous prisons, they were all alike, insomuch as they were predominantly Spanish gypsies and the trade in spat out methadone was always brisk.

The one exception to this was La Moraleja prison where there were not many Spaniards and very few Spanish gypsies. The few European addicts in La Moraleja had to go to the enfermeria for their methadone, so we never heard the cry 'Metadona!' The heroin addict would go with the normal crowd who needed medication or to see the prison doctor. A high percentage of the prison population of La Moraleja was South American and their drug of preference was cocaine. However smack was always available.

That thought took me back to La Moraleja to the time when Vito, the Mafioso hit man from Sicily and a member of the Mezclado (my gang of international villains) had a big problem. Vito had a job in the cookhouse, which was a bit unusual because all of the kitchen staff were South Americans and they thought it was something of a closed shop for them. They looked on Vito as a fly in the ointment and an interloper taking a job from a South American. They plotted to get rid of him. The plot was laid and a small bag containing five papelitos was planted in his clothing, inside his locker, in the changing room of the cookhouse - then he was grassed. A perplexed Vito was taken down the block and locked in a cell. The group of South Americans did not know about the Mezclado from the Carabanchel, they also did not know that Vito was a member. They would soon know all about the Mezclado and rue the day they fingered Vito.

Vito was locked in isolation for five days, one day for each papelito. During those five days Ali Safave, Abdullah Habibullah, David my cellmate and I questioned all the dealers of smack and the known mules, to discover who had bought five fixes of smack. It was easy to find the culprit because South Americans never buy heroin and the dealer remembered him well. The scum sucker who bought the smack was the gopher for Paco, the Mexican foreman of the cookhouse. Nacho, the lizard-faced Bolivian, had carried out Paco's orders without considering the consequences. These cunts thought they were fireproof - they were about to meet the Mezclado.

Vito had lost his job and had had five days to think about it. We welcomed him back with the news of his grass. He had already figured that out and was impatient for revenge. Fear of being killed or injured in prison was a terrible thing because there was nowhere to hide. The prison grapevine was most efficient in getting bad news quickly around a prison. A whisper here, another there and the targets were soon hit. Most of the South Americans were sent to La Moraleja from other prisons when it was first opened not so long before. Some of them, like me, had come from the Carabanchel so they knew about the Mezclado. When some of them were whispered to about Paco and Nacho being on the Mezclado shit list, they told Paco to ask for a change of prison as soon as possible. They knew the Mezclado was akin to a firing squad and there was no escape. When the message reached Paco he fobbed it off as just so much bullshit, but as more South Americans told him tales about the Mezclado it started to worry him. The stories grew and so did his anxiety. His cellmate started telling people about the onset of nightmares. Soon the word was getting to him in a big way and when someone told him that Vito was a professional hit man, a real Mafioso, his fear escalated. His every move was being watched and he knew it, because we wanted him to know it. It was leaked to him that Vito's favourite method of execution was garroting with piano wire, but cheese wire would do just as well.

As the days passed Paco looked quite ill with a pallid complexion and sunken eyes nesting in darkened sockets. Paranoia and fear were eating him alive. His tall figure began to droop from the shoulders. He kept himself surrounded by kitchen staff and was never alone, until one early evening when Nacho the gopher entered the pateo gymnasium.

The pateo gym was a room off the pateo containing weights and benches for blokes who wanted to lift a few weights - serious musclemen used the polideportivo where the weight room was fully equipped. The moment Nacho entered the pateo gym the Mezclado went into action. Abdullah Habibullah stationed himself near the screws' office as Ali Safave stood in the doorway to the pateo. Vito quickly wended his way through the few strolling inmates in the yard and entered the gym unnoticed. Nacho did not see the concussing blow that felled him. Vito pulled out his tongue and cut a deep crucifix into it and heaved him face down onto a bench so the blood dripped from his mouth to the floor, forming a red pool. Vito waited for the all clear from Abdullah Habibullah through the partially open door, then fell in step with a group of passing inmates.

One of Paco's compadres was told that Nacho wanted him in the gym, which was the main location for trading cocaine. Thinking the obvious Paco and his pals strolled across the yard to the gym. Coincidentally, a snivelling chivato was telling the screws that a fight was happening in the gym. The screws burst into the gym to find Paco and his pals trying to revive Nacho. The screws discovered a small bag of cocaine on the bench next to Nacho. So they were all taken down the block as Nacho was taken to hospital. Vito got his job back in the cookhouse and four Europeans joined him, breaking the closed shop grip of the South Americans.

This incident took a bit of planning and a lot of luck because it happened on the only afternoon of the week that Paco had off work. The snivelling grass was one of the few Spaniards prompted to tell the screws by giving him a packet of ciggies. The bag of cocaine was a mixture of crushed aspirin and a little cocaine, enough to stick if you know what I mean?

Paco was not let off the hook. Vito kept the evil eye on him when he came back from isolation. The pressure was still on. It was only a matter of time before Paco would be removed from the wing, because this was a workers' wing, so you were transferred to another wing within two weeks if you did not have a job.

It was the worst two weeks of Paco's life. He was now the lone Mexican because, without his position as foreman of the kitchen, he was of no further use to his hangers on. Prison was a cruel place and loyalty amongst Hispanics non-existent. Everyone was out at work during the day so the wing was quiet with just a few prisoners who worked shifts and the few that were sick. Paco positioned himself at a table in full view of the screws and did not move for two weeks. After that he was transferred to another wing and was found in the wing library with a crucifix sliced into his tongue on the first day. His injuries kept him in hospital for a while before he was transferred to another prison. No matter how new the prison the goings on was much the same as in the old prisons.

I was truly pleased that the Mezclado band of brothers had survived the transition from Carabanchel to La Moraleja. I felt safe in the company of men, of whom other men were frightened shitless. I wished that they were all there with me in Daroca.

Queer Jottings

Nutmeg was in a right state. He was ultra nervous and did not know what to do with himself. He was due to attend a magistrate's court in Zaragoza because he had made a denuncia[103] against three prison officers who stripped him naked in front of other prisoners then made fun of his sexuality.

I found this person annoying and stupid so I tended to ignore his presence, especially now that he had made enemies of his keepers. The screws hated him for changing his religion and now that hatred was compounded by this act of denuncia against their colleagues. He would live to regret that.

He approached me yet again to ask for coffee and cigarettes. I refused but he was persistent and demanding. I felt his mental state was deteriorating with paranoia and nervousness. Everyone was fed up with his demanding and ill-mannered begging so now he had no friends on the wing. I did not want to be his friend and I really did not want the screws to think I was his friend.

"Fuck off away from me!" I yelled at him, as he aggressively demanded coffee.

"You have money! Buy me a pack of smokes!" he yelled back at me.

"I can't afford to keep you in ciggies," I told him.

"You have money in your account, just buy me one packet!"

"Ask Willem the clog, he has money," I said, smirking.

"You know I can't ask him," he said, pouting.

"And now you know you can't ask me, so fuck off," I said quietly but meaningfully, so he stalked off looking for someone else to beg from.

Just a little while before he had started writing rough notes about the sequence of events since he was arrested at Barajas Airport in Madrid nearly eight years previously. He had asked me to help him to write a book about everything that had happened to him, including the death of his parents and how he had deserted his wife and two

---

[103] denuncia - report

children to run away with a young man. He told me about how he knew he was a homosexual when he was about fourteen years old. I told him to write it all down and maybe he could find a publisher that specialised in homosexual writing when he got out of prison. That was not such a good idea because he enthusiastically started writing on my table and instantly became a pest by asking how to spell this word and that.

"What do you think of this?" he would ask, thrusting his manuscript under my nose.

I agreed to look at his work every week if he would fuck off back to his own table to write. This he did, this but the time he spent writing at his table diminished with his enthusiasm. However, the content of his manuscript was an eye opener into the life of a queer in prison. He suggested his writing would become a bible for queers in prison. I thought it totally revolting and a stomach-churning effrontery to manhood.

The first few pages he brought me contained the events leading up to his arrest in Madrid. His words showed me just how stupid he was. Having cleared customs he should have left the airport but he decided it would be a good idea to sit in the airport restaurant and have a cup of coffee and a smoke. He ought to have been miles away when the police joined him for a smoke in the airport restaurant. 'Follow me,' said the policeman and he was in the bag. The subsequent shakedown produced two kilos of cocaine and a nine-year sentence.

He scribbled about how he first realised he was a queer. He was about fourteen years old when it happened. He was sunbathing on a beach near Cape Town in South Africa when a man emerged from the sea right near him. The man was well built and handsome and as he came out of the sea he exposed himself by pulling down his swimming trunks and masturbating, spurting his seed on Nutmeg's feet. Nutmeg was astounded and thrilled as the man returned to the sea and swam along the surf to where his family was sunbathing behind multicoloured windbreaks. The memory and vision of that man stayed with him throughout his young life. Even on his wedding night he visualised that man on the beach. The memory faded when he left his wife and children to live with a young rugby player of equal good looks.

His manuscript had page after page of sordid accounts of gross misconduct and homosexual incest with three gypsy brothers with whom he shared cells in a previous prison. The brothers were shagging each other as well as Nutmeg. He handed me page after page of explicit anal sex describing how he loved each of the brothers and what they did to each other and how wonderful the aroma in the cell was after the group had finished humping. The stink of semen, shit and sweat was like the best Omani frankincense to him.

I was truly sorry I had agreed to help him with his book. I had to renege on the deal because I found it too difficult to read. It was an affront to my manhood.

Niki And Sergey

Easter weekend in Daroca and the weather was still unkind with a blustery wind blowing rain across the yard. Nobody would be out in the yard until 09:00 am when the economato opened. The serving hatch opened onto the yard so the queue would have to brave the elements. I needed postage stamps and envelopes so I waited until the queue died down and then nipped around the puddles of rainwater nestling on the uneven concrete of the yard.

Standing in the sala doorway I watched the queue dwindle. A new arrival had joined the queue. He had arrived the day before with another man. They were big men and looked very hard. I somehow knew they were Eastern Europeans. The man in the queue was called Niki. He had introduced himself the evening before; thinking I may be from his neck of the woods he approached me just before lockdown. Disappointed I was not Ukrainian, but delighted I was not Spanish, we managed to communicate by speaking German. He told me his friend was Russian from the outskirts of Moscow.

Niki was tall and well built with a thick neck and slim waist, obviously an athlete of sorts. I suspected a boxer because his handsome face showed signs of having been battered sometime in the past. His hands were so big they made his body look somehow out of sync. My instincts told me this was a dangerous man. My instincts proved correct.

I waited for the queue to diminish to one man then dashed to the serving hatch to buy my bits. The gypsies seemed not to recognise a capable and probably very dangerous villain. Jesus Lopez approached Niki from the windward side as he had his back to the driving rain. I could not see the pinchou from where I stood but I knew he always carried one. Niki responded to the ambush with an elbow jab into Lopez's chest. As Lopez doubled over holding his guts Niki's big hands simultaneously boxed the gypsy's ears causing instant loss of consciousness. A powerful stomp to the head with his size twelve boot ensured a lengthy period of concussion. Luckily the security cameras were focused elsewhere and I had positioned myself in front of the screws' office window to block their view, but they were not looking anyway.

Niki walked toward me carrying two steaming cups of coffee, his hard eyes flashing left and right in case there were more gypsies to deck. He smirked and winked as he passed me in the doorway. I ran to the hatch to get my things as three gypsies quickly gathered up Jesus Lopez out of the puddle of water to carry him into the sala. A visit to the enfermeria was unavoidable - they could not wake him. The screws were perplexed because nobody had grassed Niki, so they guessed it was a tribal dispute. I bought my stamps and envelopes so I could write to my loved ones to tell them I was doing my time nice and peacefully and not to worry because I was in a nice place in the Spanish countryside. Hmm.

Niki later told me that Jesus Lopez had demanded a pack of smokes and four coffees. He felt the point of the pinchou in his right kidney. Lopez had lifted Niki's jacket with one hand and pushed the weapon through his shirt to prick his back with the other. Niki's instant reaction was unexpected and professionally executed. Jesus Lopez is lucky to be alive. The fact that Niki was never grassed meant only one thing, revenge gypsy-style. Had he been grassed he would have been sent to another wing out of harms way, thereby robbing the gypsies of their necessity to save face. Niki was a marked man and retribution would be swift. I warned Niki about the gypsy need to destroy him in order to save face. He said he knew all about the ways of the gypsy and would take the necessary precautions. I told him the shower block and lavatories were the favourite ambush sites. Looking me in the eye he thanked me for the information. I could see no fear in those cold, steel blue eyes. I knew this man was something special, a highly trained soviet soldier. Just my instinct, you know?

I was quietly writing my journal on Good Friday morning in the comedor. The tables furthest away were occupied by a group of chattering gypsies, as a lone gypsy sat behind me with his back against a warm radiator playing a guitar. Fortunately he was an accomplished guitar player and his music was enjoyable on this cold morning. Suddenly there was a discordant strum performed dramatically for effect. The noisy chatter ceased so the only noise came from the twittering sparrows in the eaves. The menacing silence was like an invisible shroud. Niki had entered the dining hall. A wordless hush descended and a hostile maliciousness spread through the silence, as Niki stood stock still near the central aisle. The granite face of the Ukrainian slowly turned through a ninety-degree arc on his thick muscular neck, his flinty gaze taking everything in as he exuded hard-fisted violence. His fists were bunched big and hard with white knuckles promising broken bones and scars to any would-be assassins.

His friend the big Russian entered wearing a black reefer jacket and on his great head was a woollen ski cap. The menacing atmosphere increased as he strode purposefully up the aisle toward the gypsies pointing his big sausage-like forefinger at Papa the elderly boss of the gypsies. Sixty-two year old Papa stood five feet tall in his stocking feet. He wore a flat cap and was wrapped in a fleece jacket against the cold. He was a sprightly man with white hair and beard clipped short, but those bright eyes in a wise face was a sham, he was thick as pig shit. Fear wiped the sneer off Papa's face as the big Russian singled him out and told him that should anything untoward happen to Niki he would personally break him in two and shove his head up his arse. The level tone and confident voice in which the Russian delivered his message chilled Papa to the bone.

Just then, the duty screw Don Angel, entered the dining hall and silently approached Niki from behind. Sensing a movement Niki spun around quickly making the screw jump in surprise. Don Angel flew into a terrible rage cursing the two extranjeros[104] to hell and back. The two big men simply stood there expressionless and towering over him as the screw spat obscenities. Craning his fat little neck to look up at them he suddenly stopped his tirade, abruptly about turned and marched off to the safety of his office as fast as his little legs could carry him. What he saw in those two faces was enough to put the fear of Satan through his guts. Don Angel was an experienced, long serving prison officer in Daroca and had seen the faces of murderers and bestial child killers so often, he must have instinctively known when he was in the presence of brutal killers. Yet he was in for a

---

[104] extranjeros - foreigners

shock when he looked into the ill-boding eyes of Spetznaz paratroopers, the Russian elite fighting unit that had slaughtered thousands in Afghanistan and Chechnya.

The two fierce faces softened as they joined me at my table.

"I get you coffee Eengleesk," said Niki, grinning from ear to ear. "Now, I learn speak Eengleesk," he added, chuckling as the guitarist scurried away from the warm radiator to join his tribe at the other end of the dining hall.

The chatter soon picked up again as calmness returned and the menacing atmosphere dissipated. The big Russian introduced himself as Sergey. Practically every Russian I have met has called himself Sergey - I wonder why? Maybe it was his real name, but who cares? They asked why I was in prison so I told them my story in Gerspanglish (a mixture of German, Spanish and English), which went down well with them. Then it was my turn to ask them. They were bank robbers but had killed people who tried to stop them. They were nailed with umpteen robbery with violence cases, but on their last job they were caught red-handed and shot their way out of the bank, killing two innocent bystanders and the policeman who tried to arrest them. Their sentences for various crimes totted up to thirty-nine years a piece. These two dangerous men would be seventy years old when they got out of there, so they really did not care a flying bollock about anything, screw or prisoner, but they did live in hope of getting a permiso.

One would think there was no possibility of men like that being allowed out for a six-day break. Wrong! Javier, an athletic Spanish bank robber and killer had just gone out on permiso for Semana Santa (Easter). He had committed over thirty bank robberies and shot dead a woman as he robbed a bank. He got a twenty-three stretch and he was out on permiso, so all was not lost for the Russians and it would be interesting to see if Javier returned after Easter.

I was amazed these two Russians had not been separated in different prisons. They even shared the same cell. They were also been told they could work and earn money in the prison workshop, but first they had to get jobs as a destino on the wing. They would be watched to make sure they worked well and then when a vacancy occurred in the kitchens or workshop, they would get the job when it was their turn. Looking at these two reckless hard men I knew they were not going to be around long enough to get jobs in this prison. My instincts proved correct, as you will see later.

Easter

Easter Sunday 2007 and I telephoned my wife to wish her Happy Easter and to tell her I loved her. With brave words she told me to hold my head high in that den of iniquity. She said remember Jerusalem.

I will not cease from mental fight;
Nor shall my sword sleep in my hand –
Til we have built Jerusalem –
In England's green and pleasant land.

I love my wife. Her words gave me strength.

The sun was shining that Easter Sunday so I took advantage of it and walked the yard. Other prisoners were walking alone rather than in their normal groups. They must have been thinking of families and home. I was no different as I marched around with visions of my wife and family flitting around my mind. The flow of images set in motion by the emotions of this holy day, another milestone in my life as I struggled to remember Easters past.

Childhood memories flickered on the screen of my mind as I quickened the pace of my march around the yard. I remembered as a young boy asking my mother if I could become a priest. She asked me why I wanted to be a priest. I told her the college where the priests learned their trade had a swimming pool. She laughed her head off.

My childhood thoughts dwindled as I thought about Daroca, no swimming pool there. No gymnasium, no hot water, nothing apart from that yard to walk around in, a table to eat from and a damp cell to sleep in. Fucking hell! What a dump!

I quickly changed my thoughts to better times as I remembered an Easter in Morocco. I was in Nador waiting for a cargo to come from Kartama to be loaded onto my RIB that was moored in Sebkha bou Areq (Mar Chica), the big lagoon east of Nador. A member of the Moroccan royal family was visiting the area so a massive security operation had held up the movement of hashish for a couple of weeks. I lived in luxury in an apartment on the outskirts of town, away from prying eyes. The local drug lords kept their sea captains and RIB jockeys hidden from rapacious rivals who would seek out skippers to deliver their mountains of hashish. I was jealously guarded and given anything I wanted, just to keep me hidden until the day my craft was loaded and I could sail away. Daoud, the drug lord, telephoned me to ask if I would like to join him for lunch in one of his favourite beach restaurants in Nador. I remembered the succulent fish dishes with beautiful salads and shellfish side orders - my mouth watered. Daoud was an enormous Moroccan, with many hectares of hashish. The restaurateurs fawned over him, ensuring he had the very best they could offer.

The duty screw ordering everyone inside for the 1:00 pm feeding suddenly disturbed my reverie. I quickly forgot my Easter in Morocco. I joined the queue of about one hundred and fifty men that started at the serving counters and snaked back out into the sala. I watched as the usual scuffles happened as the Arabs and gypsies tried to get fed first. It was soon my turn to be fed, so I held out my bandeja so the orderly could ladle two scoops of pig stew onto the metal tray. I moved along to the next orderly who dumped a dollop of cannelloni next to the pig stew. A bread roll and a bruised, maggoty pear were heaped on top by the third orderly as his cigarette ash fell down his dirty white apron. I went to my table and the Arabs flinched with horror as they clocked my food. The pig stew was made with chickpeas and lumps of pig fat. There was no meat, just fat and thick skin with layers of grey fat still attached. It stank slightly of putrefaction. The cannelloni also looked offensive. With the memory of Daoud's fish restaurant fresh in my mind and the looks of horror on the Arabs' faces, I quickly dumped my food in the swill bin. In so doing, I looked across at the gypsy tables to see them shovelling this shit down their gizzards like a bunch of starving Biafrans.

On rejoining my table the Arabs were grateful for my ditching the obscenity I had placed before them. They were truly ill at ease by being near to such shite. I told the Arabs about the years I spent in the jungles of Malaysia and that the food cooked by the British army cooks in harsh jungle conditions far exceeded the quality of shite the

Spanish produced here in modern ideal conditions. I used to laugh at the jokes about the Army Catering Corps (ACC) - Andy Capp's Commandos, the Aldershot Concrete Company, Any Cunt Cooks, and many more, but I wished some of them were there then, to show these useless uncaring wankers how to cook.

We were soon herded upstairs to our cells for afternoon lockdown. I was in for a treat because Ahmed and Nuradin produced three large bocadillas[105] filled with tuna fish, salad and olive oil. We sat on our beds relishing the tasty treat and swigging non-alcoholic beer, enjoying our own little Easter party. My Arab friends cared not about Easter but they knew it was a special day for me. I was truly grateful.

Afternoons were always the same in our cell. Ahmed and Nuradin would sleep while I read one of my books. At 4:45 pm I would awaken them in readiness for unlocking at 5:00 pm and then we would leave the cell and lock it as I went to the yard and they went to work. Today there was no work for either of them so we all went down to the yard for a stroll, then I went in to do some writing in the dining hall. There were twelve men quietly writing and two men playing chess. There was calmness around me, which I liked very much. Though the noise from the smoke-filled sala could not be blocked out, there was a rare sense of serenity that evening.

But this was Daroca, so serenity flew out of the window as Bartolome Vivancoz ambled into the dining hall to sit at the next table to me, about ten feet away. He was a fiend in human shape, the lowest dregs of vice and a lump of a man with a massive head. His grizzly face turned to look at me as he scratched his dirty beard with one hand and his crotch with the other. Before he was arrested he was a goatherd so maybe he was daydreaming about his favourite nanny goat. As I looked at him I wonder if his boots hid cloven hooves. He stood to scratch his belly and crotch. His genitals were alive with crabs as he scratched ferociously with both hands. He reached down the front of his trousers to grub about down there to detach a crab then placed it between his thumbnails to crack it. Not surprisingly, this beast had been threatened by his paisanos many

---

[105] bocadillo - bread roll

times to wash and clean himself because people had to sit next to him to eat. He stank like a damp goat.

I looked at the ugly bulk of him and wondered at the terror he ploughed into the minds of his child victims. This mindless pervert was a rapist and murderer of young boys. He would rot in hell forever when he got there, for what he did to those children. In Daroca he was a rampant poof, shagging any of the queers who would have him. The only time he appeared clean was when he had a boyfriend, but that never lasted more than a couple of days because sex made him violent. He tore the ear and part of the scalp off of his last boyfriend as he reached his climax. The screws thought it was great, to keep him alone in a two-man cell so he could entice a new queer every now and then - anything to break the monotony of their dull as ditchwater lives.

He looked at me with doleful eyes that suddenly changed to astonishment as he saw the daggers of hatred in my eyes. He looked away momentarily then looked back at me to see my hatred focussing on him making him uncomfortable and nervous. He knew about my enmity with nonces so he jerkily got to his feet to bashfully shuffle out of the dining hall and into the noisy sala. I felt better then, that that particular evil creature had got out of my space and left the room. The disturbing influence of Satan had gone, so now I could concentrate on my journal.

My mind wandered away from dirty Daroca to the newness of La Moraleja prison when I was there nearly nine years earlier and where I met ETA terrorists with ponytails.

The ETA Ladies

La Moraleja prison was still not fully occupied in the millennium year, there were two new wings lying empty, but the most recent wing to be occupied was the mujeres[106] wing. The women were segregated from the male population, but occasionally I saw them when they passed the polideportivo on their way to the enfermeria.

They were mostly South Americans imprisoned for smuggling cocaine, but there were several Euskadi Ta Askatasuna (ETA) terrorists and a few local prostitutes. There were also a few babies and I often saw them with their mothers on their way to the enfermeria.

One sunny day my pet screw Don Phillipe told me that as I was boss of the gymnasium staff and the prison martial arts instructor, I was required to supervise the training programme for the mujeres modulo that was planned for every Saturday afternoon. Female prison officers would be in attendance to prevent fraternisation between the mujeres and the gym staff. Don Phillipe smirked as he told me about the female screws.

Unfortunately my friend David, the American, had been replaced by Frank, an ex-professional footballer from Ecuador, as one of my gym orderlies. David had returned to the States having served his sentence. I was delighted that David was free but Frank was a pain in the arse at the best of times. He would prove to be the undoing of the Saturday afternoon fun day.

That first Saturday with the women's wing was well planned. With Ali Safave refereeing and instructing the basketball game, Frank was to supervise the squash courts, and I took charge of the weights room and martial arts class, if they wanted to learn martial arts. Don Phillipe unlocked the main gate to let them in and he immediately kissed the cheeks of the petite Spanish prison officer, which was the beginning of a torrid humping session in his little office, as we organised the various activities.

The women prisoners entered the gymnasium and immediately formed their tribal groups. The prostitutes gathered in the lavatories

---

[106] mujeres - women's

because that was the only place you could smoke. The few gypsy women looked around to see what was not nailed down. The ETA girls soon found the squash courts and claimed them as their own. The South Americans ambled into the main arena to play basketball, but some of them went upstairs to the weights room. One of them dashed back down the stairs to tell her friends about the weights room, then brought part of that group back upstairs to lark about with the weight lifting equipment. As they swarmed all over the various pieces of equipment, the female screws enforced the no-smoking rule as best they could, but were fighting a losing battle in such a big place with so many corners and two floors to supervise. They gave up the ghost after half an hour and joined Phillipe in his office for coffee and cakes.

I simply sat on the tatami mats watching them lark about waiting for them to ask for help or advice - but nothing. They were dressed in a variety of tracksuits and shell suits and the women were all shapes and sizes. Some of them were obviously pals and did things together, but mainly they were surly and gave the impression that this was child's play and would rather be smoking a joint or back on the game in a Colombian back street. Some of them posed and postured ridiculously as though they had some kind of standing in this world - inhaling cigarette smoke, opening their mouth allowing the smoke to billow out then inhaling it back up their nose as though that was really clever.

I was in a quandary because I did not allow smoking in the gymnasium and here was a group of women breaking the rules. I was about to lay down the law when a hard-faced woman entered the room and the atmosphere changed instantly. A foreboding silence enveloped the room. She stood there looking around taking it all in. She looked at me with a glint in her eye then looked scornfully at the other women.

"Fuerra! Get out!" She said harshly.

Members of ETA, be they male or female, have a built-in hatred of Spanish speaking people not from Pais Basquo[107] a bit like the

---

[107] Pais Basquo - Basque Country

catholic protestant bitterness and bigotry of Northern Ireland. She looked quite fit and aggressive dressed in her Nike outfit. I felt my jaw drop as she unzipped her white tracksuit top to reveal a skin-tight khaki coloured T-shirt covering perfect breasts, which jiggled ever so jauntily as she skipped over to the wall bars to hang up her top. Her long blonde ponytail swung from side to side as she strode toward me.

"You the karate teacher?" she asked in accented English, here eyes steely blue and hard.

"Yes, I am," I replied, slightly surprised.

"Can you teach me to kick effectively?" she asked, looking meaningfully into my eyes.

"Yes,"

"My three friends will be here in a moment, can you teach four of us?" she asked, frowning and placing her bunched fists on her slim waist.

I could see the slim waist was as hard as knotted steel wire rope with striated sinew and abdominals visible beneath the tight khaki shirt.

"Yes," I said, as she stepped onto the tatami. "Remove your shoes," I said, not unkindly, "shoes are not allowed on the mats."

"Why?" she snapped.

"Because your face impacts the mat nearly as often as your feet, and shoes dirty the mat," silence for a moment, "and because I said so. Take your trainers off."

This lady terrorist was obviously the leader of the pack but her three friends were just as hard faced as they entered the weights room. There was an instant exchange of eyeball daggers at the few remaining South American women riding the exercise bikes. Bloody hell I thought, as I pictured a female punch-up. The hatred was tangible.

"Take off your shoes," I said loudly, "and come over here."

They looked at the woman on the mat as though to confirm all was well. She gave a discernible nod and they took off their trainers and shucked off their tracksuit tops. It was as though they were in uniform; they each wore the same training kit. They were slim and hard looking, each with determined expressions on their attractive, un-made-up faces. Apart from the slightest trace of lipstick and the perfume of antiperspirant spray, they wore no obvious cosmetics. Their teeth were perfect and their hair, though differing in colour, was each worn in ponytails. These terrorists had become a close-knit fighting unit in order to survive in prison - much like the Mezclado and me.

Amazingly they each spoke English very well. Over the years I have spent in six Spanish prisons, the members of ETA that I met had all spoken English and, in many cases, they also spoke German, French and Arabic. They had all been articulate, kind and excellent company. These four women would prove to be much like the men, clever, determined and tough.

The four ETA ladies were a big presence and I realised nobody else would be joining the combat class. I gave them a brief talk on etiquette and pain then started my ju-jitsu warm-up exercises. Part way through the warm-up, I thought Christ, they're ETA! In a previous prison, the Carabanchel, I was reprimanded for teaching ETA terrorists the art of ju-jitsu and I nearly lost my job. Now here I am again teaching ETA terrorists.

After first telling them to repeat the warm-up exercises, I walked out of the room then dashed down the two flights of metal stairs to find Phillipe the screw chatting up the female screws. I knocked on the glass door and beckoned him to come out. Irritated, he got up and came out, closing the door on the thick smoke and smell of coffee and cheap perfume. The enquiring expression on his face cracked into a grin when I told him I had ETA women on the mat.

"Can't you handle them?" he chortled. "I'll get rid of these scrubbers and give you a hand."

"They're ETA!" I said, concerned.

"So what? If they want to play karate, let them," he said, more seriously.

"Okay, no problem."

Off I went back up the stairs to find them diligently stretching and warming up and ready for work. Keeping them in line abreast in the mid area of the mat, I could not help noticing four different but perfect pairs of breasts held firm in some kind of training bras as I taught them basic blocks.

I only taught four basic blocks because blocks came naturally and were a variation of the four basics: jodan uke[108], chudan soto uke[109], chudan uchi uke[110] and gedan barai[111]. I instructed them to practise in time with each other and introduced them to the kiai. They were not self-conscious in any way and the sniggers from the South American women ceased the instant I turned to face them. I thought it was my authoritative figure, but no - it was the ancient throat-cutting gesture performed by all four terrorists as my back was turned. I watched them doing it in their reflection in the big glass and steel door.

There was time to teach these women at least one ju-jitsu technique. I told them to put their jackets back on because I wanted to teach them a sliding collar choke from a frontal attack. I ordered each of them in turn to punch me hard with a roundhouse punch to my face, this being the usual punch one receives during a slugfest or start of a fight. The first woman attacked me as the other three knelt on the edge of the mat to observe. The punch was thrown and I blocked it with a double-handed block. I had her repeat the attack so they could all see the block again. This time as I blocked the punch, my right fist travelled along her striking arm to smash into her neck. I pulled the punch to avoid hurting her. I then grabbed the punching hand and applied kota geishi[112] forcing her body to turn away from me so that I could step on the back of her knee to force her into a kneeling position. With my left hand I reached around to the front of her neck to grab a fistful of tracksuit collar to pull across her throat in order to choke her as I folded the punching arm behind her back to control her in a back-hammer hold.

In real terms the first strike into her carotid artery would have dropped her, so the remainder of the technique served as training in control and choke techniques. The woman, who I will call Ruiz, was

---

[108] jodan uke - upper block
[109] chudan soto uke - middle outer block
[110] chudan uchi uke - middle inner block
[111] gedan barai - lower block
[112] kota geishi - wrist lock

as hard as nails. She got up and knelt with the others quite expressionless on the edge of the mat, but I knew she was all fired up inside and raring to go. I was a Sensei of many years experience and I could read my students just like any other experienced teacher. All four women went through the procedure quickly then I paired them off to practise the technique.

These ETA women learned quickly but their mindset was somewhat different to other women. They were young women serving very long sentences for various acts of terrorism. Each of them found guilty of murder. They were proud, attractive and tough and between twenty and thirty years of age, with icy glints in each of their eyes. They exuded discipline and loyalty to each other as though they were an elite military unit, which I suppose they could be termed, seeing as how ETA was at war with Spain - much the same as the IRA behaved in the Maze Prison (Long Kesh) in Northern Ireland.

I barely had enough time to teach them another technique, so to dangle a carrot I demonstrated how to defeat a frontal attack with a devastating crotch blow. Again they knelt on the edge of the mat as I selected Ruiz for the first attack. Using the same roundhouse punch she attacked me. This time I ducked beneath the punch by stepping into a fighting stance with my left foot forward as I ducked. I then slammed a haito[113] into her crotch, but instead of impacting that sensitive spot, I jammed my hand against the inside of her thigh, avoiding great pain but letting her know she had been hit. This naturally made her double over to expose her back and neck to my uraken[114] to the vertebrae. My right knee impacted her heart to slam her upright exposing her throat to an empi[115], which could possibly have killed her if I had applied it properly. I pulled all my strikes to avoid unnecessary pain. I stood her still for a moment, holding her elbow to steady her. The three onlookers' eyes glittered with excitement. This is why they had come. This was the kind of stuff they were eager to learn. Bringing them all onto the mat I told them that the crotch blow would be learned during the next lesson.

---

[113] haito - inner knife hand
[114] uraken - back-fist strike
[115] empi - elbow strike

I made them kneel in mokusu[116] to calm them with breathing exercises, as the few South American women quietly moved out of the room. I knelt with the girls and told them quickly about not using these techniques on other prisoners unless absolutely necessary. I taught them how to bow, then I dismissed them and the security camera watched us leave. The security camera had seen everything so I guessed that combat classes for the ETA women would cease.

You may think dear reader that maybe I should have taught them techniques of a milder nature, not so violent or dangerous, but this was prison and prisoners, be they male or female, would not like being taught anything that was not effective in prison. The ETA women had already had some form of military training and would have lost interest very quickly if I tried to teach them kids' stuff. So we started as we meant to go on, more and more bone-crunching combat training. I would soon discover how tough they really were and then I would temper the training to suit them.

On my way down the stairs something caught my eye. I saw that the boiler room door was slightly open when it should have been closed and locked shut. It was always locked until I opened it to turn on or off the califaccion. I pulled the big steel door open and there was Frank the Ecuadorian thrusting himself into the backside of a South American woman who was bent over touching her toes making impassioned grunts and groans, or maybe it was Frank making all the noise. I quickly closed the door with a bang and Frank momentarily lost his rhythm, but heroically battered on to the hastened finish, or so he told me later. He was relieved to hear it was me that had banged the door and not the screw. Apparently Frank was not the only one to score this day. Phillipe the screw entertained the petite screw in his little office as the other screws kept smoking to a minimum in the main arena. Screwing screws. Hmm. Frank, being a typical Hispanic, could not keep his trap shut, so the whole prison soon found out about his back-scuttling session in the boiler room. He wondered why he was sacked. His envious paisanos had grassed him.

---

[116] mokusu – mediation

Frank preceded Captain Peter Smith, an ex-Royal Marine Commando officer who was my choice for the job in the gym. Peter was very fit and made life much easier for me by taking control of everything downstairs. He was the obvious choice to succeed me when I got my Libertad. Peter was very competitive and won practically every event he organised, especially squash. He never came upstairs to the weights room or to do martial arts, his love of ball games kept him too busy to lift weights or spend time on the judo mats. He was tall and slim without an ounce of fat on his body, and well spoken, a real gent. Men who mistook his good manners for weakness usually felt great pain; he was ruthless in attack and a skilled scrapper.

His sporting enthusiasm was contagious, even with the mujeres. He persuaded them to enter all kinds of contests like table tennis, badminton, squash and volleyball. There was probably more, but I was too busy with my combat classes, especially the ETA ladies class, the nicest terrorists I have ever met and I have met many terrorists over the years. They took everything seriously, there was no fun or larking about; with them it was a matter of discipline and training just like professional soldiers. They had obviously been training in their cells because their kicks, blocks and punches were performed as a drill and their timing was perfect. It was pleasing to see and showed they were enthusiastic.

The crotch strike technique in response to a frontal attack was received well by the ETA girls, but striking into the upper thigh instead of the groin took a lot of careful practice because groin guards are not available in prison. They must have suffered much bruising to their inner thighs because the practice was hard, fast and effective. They had a point to prove. They were warriors, ETA warriors.

One day Ruiz asked if I could teach them defence against knives and the dreaded, shit-smeared pinchou. I asked if there were weapons on their wing. Not surprisingly there were.

"Most of the gypsy girls have one and several Colombian girls have them. We need to know how to fight them because we don't carry them," looking at me with a glint in her eye. "We are ETA, so we are constantly searched. If one of us is caught with a weapon we would be separated and we do not want that to happen," she added angrily.

I knew better than anyone how she felt because that was why I had formed the Mezclado. Ruiz had done just what I had done to protect one another against dangerous jealous gypsies and primitives from South America. I hoped I would have the time to teach these girls many self-defence techniques of the most savage nature. I loathed people who used dirty weapons like the pinchou with its contaminated point.

After a hard warm-up session, which included a kicks, blocks and punches routine performed as a drill, I ordered them to pair off and practise each of the techniques they were taught. Positioning them around the edge of the mat I explained about the use of the knife. I told them that a downward thrust, as seen in many movies, was not used much in real life incidents, because the knife would be raised above the head to commence its downward stroke, thereby exposing it to any possible witnesses that may be nearby. Also the downward thrust required the attacker to be quite near his victim, so his midriff and chest was open to counter attack. Nevertheless later on I would teach them techniques to defeat this type of attack.

On that day we concentrated on the forward thrust into the guts or chest, which was the most used by men with knives. Women tended to slash, but a pinchou did not have a cutting edge, so it was reasonable to assume a thrust with that particular weapon would happen, so we worked on that assumption.

I handed Ruiz an empty plastic water bottle to use as a knife. It mattered not what they used as a weapon, just so long as they did not cause injury when they plunged it into their training partner's guts. Standing in the centre of the mats I ordered her to stab with the bottle. She first adopted a fighting stance and started moving around me as though stalking me. I noticed her ice blue eyes were flat and cold as she lunged and the bottle squashed against my sternum. I had not moved. I wanted her to experience the strike without defence or retaliation from me.

"Good!" I said. "Now do it again."

She stepped back, puzzled that I had allowed her to stab me.

"Don't worry," I said grimly, "I wanted to see you stab me properly because some students aim to miss. You didn't, so come on, stab me again."

She started circling me again, as though stalking me.

"Don't fuck around like that," I snapped, "I could kick the shit out of you before you could strike."

Moving quickly to face me she lunged with the bottle to my midriff. Stepping to my left I simultaneously parried, then grabbed the thrusting wrist with my right hand. Pulling her forward off balance I delivered a mae geri[117] into her heart, then pulled her face down onto the mat with my left hand against the elbow joint, I pushed my knee into her shoulder to apply ude hishigi[118] completely immobilising her face down on the mat. With my knee on her shoulder, pulling the arm to the left would have dislocated her shoulder, so I pulled slightly to the left so she knew what it felt like, and to realise not to fuck around with her training partner in this position. I did not want to extract a cry of pain that would embarrass her.

"Tap out when it hurts," I snapped.

Her left hand slapped the mat urgently as she tapped out. I raised my knee but kept her arm in tension as I massaged her shoulder.

"That should feel good," I said, as I gently released the pressure and placed her arm by her side. Stepping back from her I noticed the smile of fortitude - she could not wait to practise that one. I repeated the technique with each of the girls then paired them off for training. Women's breasts must not receive blows for obvious reasons, so I instructed the girls to kick lightly into the guts instead of the chest. They understood fully but still kicked hard into each other's guts. The memory of their discipline and enthusiasm would live with me forever and I felt sad when I thought about how they would spend the rest of their lives behind the bars of a cruel Spanish prison.

The mujere's visits to the gym soon ceased because of the jealousy of other prisoners. Seething after Frank's leapfrog act in the boiler room, sex-starved South Americans complained bitterly to their

---

[117] mae geri - front kick
[118] ude hishigi - straight arm lock

respective modulo prison officers. The bitterness was so great that Frank was sent to another prison and the gym sessions ceased. It was not Frank's dick that got him into trouble it was his big mouth. I was not bothered because my time in La Moraleja was coming to an end and the prison authorities had awarded me a six day permiso, so I was too busy making travel arrangements to worry about the goings on in the gymnasium.

The time for my six days at home soon arrived. Don Phillipe, my pet screw, met me outside the prison to take me to the railway station at Venta de Bano, a town twenty kilometres from the prison, where I would first get the train to Madrid then another one to Malaga on the Costa del Sol. There was a restaurant opposite the railway station in Venta de Bano and as I purchased my ticket Phillipe went into the restaurant and ordered coffee and brandy. This happened at 08:00 am so a liquid breakfast did not really suit me - but Phillipe thought it was a treat so I accepted it merrily. I prevented him ordering more. Nothing was going to ruin this day. I had a slice of tortilla instead.

Apart from the scenery the journey to Malaga was uneventful, though the service on board the train was far superior to any I have had elsewhere in the world. White coated hostesses pushed trolleys of food and drink up and down the aisles just like on an aircraft and the train was clean and graffiti free.

My mind was swimming with emotions as I sped south. I was a free man sitting in a railway carriage surrounded by happy, normal people who did not know I was a prisoner. The strange feeling of being an alien amongst ordinary people, as though I had something to hide and could they see I was different from them? Did it show? Could they see the butterflies in my stomach that had escaped and were fluttering around me? Emotions built as I neared my destination.

My heart skipped a beat as the train entered the station and I saw the crowds waiting to meet friends and relatives from the north. A thousand heads blurred my field of vision as I scanned them looking for the one I loved. Emotions washed over me as I shook in my shoes with apprehension. Where was she? A thunderbolt struck my heart the moment I saw the blonde hair amongst the darker shades of the throng. At last! I was whole again.

The head-spinning time I spent with my wife was soon over and I was on my way back to La Moraleja to finish the last few months of my sentence. Emotions on the return journey were simply various depths of sadness. Don Phillipe met me at the Venta de Bano railway station. I put a case of vodka in his car and gave him a bottle of Glenmorangie Scotch whisky, which he accepted gratefully. Phillipe would bring the case of vodka into the prison in plastic water bottles over the next few days. It was sold within a week because my regular customers had had nothing for six days. In a previous journal I described the business of selling booze in the polideportivo, so enough said. Phillipe dropped me at the prison car park and drove away. He would be on duty the following day and bring in the goodies I had left in his car. Stuff like smoked salmon and various cheeses and shopping I had bought for my friends, Peter Smith and Ali Safave.

On entering the prison I was given a rigorous shakedown by Don Manuel, better known as Mad Jack; a black belt Shotokan karateka, famous in his previous prison, Alhurin de la Torre (Malaga prison), for his brutality. He was sent to La Moraleja because of his cruelty in Malaga prison. He would return when things in Malaga had cooled down and I would meet him again in Malaga the following year. He rummaged my sports bag thoroughly, then x-rayed the bag and its contents individually, as another screw frisked me first then ordered me to strip naked and looked up my arse for drugs. I was then made to pull back my foreskin to check nothing was hidden there. I knew someone had spooked the screws into thinking I was bringing drugs back from my permiso. I wondered who would grass me up like that. Who wanted my job? I could not blame the Spanish because there were not many in that prison and I had nothing to do with them anyway. It had to be a European, an Arab or a South American. Hmm.

I was escorted to the enfermeria where I gave a urine sample to test to see if I had used drugs during my permiso - of course I had not. Had the urine test proved positive my Libertad Condicional would be cancelled and I would be kept there for a further year. I needed to find the grass and give him a lesson he would never forget.

As I was a model prisoner and had earned lots of brownie points for working in the gymnasium, and because I had friends in high places, I was granted Libertad Condicional in Malaga to start in the following month of May. This meant I would live at home in Malaga and sign on every month at Malaga prison for one year. Then I would be a free man having finished my sentence.

After a further naked body search I was escorted to the modulo and locked in my cell until breakfast the next morning. My friends welcomed me when I appeared for breakfast and all the Europeans were smiling and happy to see me, all except for the kraut table. The Germans seemed ill at ease as they picked at their breakfast and looked cautiously at my friends and me. I knew my grass was on that table.

I told Ali and Peter about the shakedown and as one their heads turned to look at the kraut table. Three krauts were talking to each other as one sat silently slouching in his chair. It looked like the others were purposely ignoring him. His name was Rolf, a big ginger headed oaf who had pestered me for a job umpteen times. He worked as a destino because he was as thick as pig shit. His first job was in the cookhouse but he nearly poisoned everyone so he was a cleaner.

We three eyeballed him as he squirmed on his seat and picked up a newspaper to hide his face. Later that day during feeding time, Vito the hit man caught Rolf's eye and gave him the old throat cutting gesture by drawing his forefinger across his throat. Rolf knew what that meant. He had to leave the wing quickly before he got injured or killed. Vito was the worst enemy he could possibly have. The Mezclado reputation was fearsome for anyone that fell under its shadow and Vito was a professional Mafioso assassin, so to get the finger from him was enough for most men to change their skids. The following morning Rolf was seen taking his shit to another modulo in an effort to escape the Mezclado, but he needed to change prisons because he would not escape otherwise.

During the next few days Don Phillipe brought in the vodka and other items my friends needed. I bought Ali Safave a pair of bag gloves for punch bag training, and for Vito special medicated toothpaste and mouthwash. Peter was delighted with his round of Stilton cheese and cans of Guinness that I bought in Dunnes Store in Fuengirola. That evening at feeding time we had a beano on our table with smoked salmon, cheese, whole-wheat bread and real butter, all washed down with vodka and orange. That was also my farewell party because the following week I was classified grade three, which meant I was ready for Libertad. It also meant I must be segregated from other grades, so I handed my job over to Peter and moved out of the wing to live in ingreso until I left.

Ingreso was the wing where people were processed in and out of the prison. It was a shithole of a place where I was lonely and miserable until the day I left. I was taken upstairs to the third floor and locked in a single (one bed) cell that overlooked the screws' car park and the bleak countryside. There were five men living on that landing and I had nothing to do with any of them. They were Colombians waiting for freedom. They had fuck all when they came and they had got fuck all then, so I was pestered for ciggies all the time. Even though they knew I did not smoke they still asked each time they saw me. I suffered in ingreso because I was locked on that landing for twenty-four hours a day with no exercise or fresh air. The food was abominable and thieves with fuck all to sell ran the economato. Fortunately I had my books and writing kit so my time was spent reading and writing notes that I used for this journal.

The day of my release slowly crept up on me, and one fine sunny morning I walked out of La Moraleja prison. Just prior to leaving I was allowed to give unwanted items to my Mezclado friends who gave me addresses and contact numbers for later years. In one of the envelopes given to me by Vito was a dried piece of meat like a skinless sausage, a German skinless sausage. I knew whose tongue it was.

Toe The Line

The wind and rain lashed Daroca prison as Nutmeg the queer was escorted out to attend court in Zaragoza for another hearing regarding the cachero screws stripping him naked in front of other prisoners and making fun of his sexuality.

It was the 11th April 2007 and the prison authorities decided to settle out of court because there was a lot of media attention attracted to this case. What a shame. Nutmeg could have been famous and journalists would have been fighting to write his book, rather than him pestering me to write it. That was the first thing he asked when he arrived back from Zaragoza.

"Will you write my story? You must write it now, lots of people are interested in me!"

"Fuck off!"

He went on to say that he would get five hundred thousand euros compensation from the Spanish prison authorities.

"Fuck off!"

Two days later the screws decided it was payback time. Time for revenge, screw-style. A young gypsy appeared on the morning of Friday 13th April. He sat on his bags at the bottom of the stairs as we all passed by him to go for breakfast. He was waiting to be allocated a cell. He was very dark skinned with black greasy hair and eyes that sparkled with madness. As I sipped my coffee and watched him the duty screw appeared.

"Numero cincuenta sies, Number 56," I heard him say.

Nutmeg's cell! Great! This was going to be funny. Nutmeg was alone at a table in the sala drinking coffee when the duty screw called him on the tannoy. Puzzled, he went to the office to be told he had a new cellmate. His face turned purple with rage as he flew into a tantrum, demanding that as a homosexual he must be allowed to live alone or at least have the person of his own choosing, Lhaktar, in his cell. He was actually dancing with rage and pique but when the screw pointed to the mad gypsy he nearly choked on wrath. He threatened the screw with his lawyer but that only served to fuel the screw's fire and had him reaching for his truncheon. Two screws escorted

Nutmeg and Jiminez Moreno, the young gypsy, to cell No 56. That name Jiminez Moreno would be heard many times over the tannoy to hand back items he had stolen from other prisoners; even the gypsies hated him.

Once the screws had supervised the stowing of Moreno's kit they locked the cell and escorted them both back downstairs. Everyone knew that items of Nutmeg's kit would soon be on sale and a constant war would rage until these two were separated. The screws were enjoying themselves. The screaming rows from cell No: 56 could be heard at least twice a day and I often heard giggling screws along the corridor. They really enjoyed the rumpus, just a few days later, when Moreno accused Nutmeg of trying to kiss him. Nutmeg immediately retaliated by grassing Moreno for storing heroin in the cell and for chasing the dragon every night. In a tit for tat rage Moreno planted heroin in Nutmeg's shoe but was discredited when Nutmeg proved that the shoe was not his, but a smaller-sized one stolen from a neighbour. The screws were hoping for a fight to happen because then they could spike Nutmeg's imminent parole, thereby keeping him locked up until the end of his sentence. However, in a subsequent fit of temper, Nutmeg screamed at the duty screw to move him to another cell. The screw immediately grabbed the opportunity and moved him instantly to cell No: 70, the home of Bartolo el Bruto (Bartolo the Brute).

El Bruto was another raving lunatic who had battered his wife and mother-in-law to death by banging their heads together until there was nothing left to bang. Bartolo was a big heavy man of enormous strength and fragile temperament. Towering rages would cause him to wreck his cell or batter the person he held responsible, be they prisoner or guard. Having served many years in Daroca, Bartolo was then a raging queer and looked on Nutmeg as his new shag bag. The screws were delighted. The South African queer was so angry and frustrated he was like a powder keg on legs, as he stormed around the yard with his hands thrust into his pockets. His face and neck were blood red and looked fit to burst as he strode around talking to himself and shaking his head negatively. A normal person would have accepted things and waited the few weeks for release; just sat tight and kept out of trouble, but there was no accounting for the behaviour of queers, especially that one.

Friday 13th April 2007 was the day I changed cells and moved in with Mike Sherman the American. That was the very last time I would ever change cells and, although I did not know at the time, that cell would be the last one I ever lived in. Rudi, the Cuban, was caught trading hashish in the yard. The security camera clocked him dealing and smoking so he was sent to a punishment modulo. That left Mike alone in cell No: 50. The duty screw wanted to put a Russian in with him. So Mike caught up with me as I marched around the yard, explained the situation and asked me to join him in his cell rather than have the Russian move in. I was quite happy with the Moroccans but Mike was such a nice bloke I decided to move in with him. Everything happened very quickly. The duty screw said to grab my shit and move at 5:00 pm when they unlocked us. Ahmed and Nuradin helped lug my kit and bedding along the corridor to Mike's cell. We heaved everything into the cell and Mike said he would help sort it out later when we got locked up for the night. Ahmed and Nuradin were sad to see me leave their cell, we had become good pals and now the screws might put a lunatic in with them. The duty screw ordered us downstairs so we left my kit in a heap on the bed and went down to the yard. Later, when we were in lockdown, I stowed my gear and made my bed. Mike very kindly let me have Rudi's bunk, which was the lower one, the best one. Mike had some great books so, on that first night, I settled down with Homer's *Odyssey*. Cell No: 50 is a two-man cell so there was no fear of anyone else joining us so we made ourselves as comfortable as possible and shared the limited space equally.

The next day I received bad news from England. My favourite niece Jacquie was having open-heart surgery that day. Over the following days I received news that she was in intensive care and terribly ill, but He answered my prayers and she was soon on the mend. This may seem not worth a mention about my niece but incidents like that affected prisoners greatly. The prison mentality magnified and amplified a family crisis into a catastrophe and threw a heavy blanket of depression over the person who could do the least in any crisis because he was locked up. All I could do was pray and boy did I pray!

Things with Nutmeg went from bad to worse as he became abusive with everyone. I thought he would soon give the screws what they wanted by getting into a fight at any minute. His antagonist, Jiminez Moreno the gypsy, was removed from the wing because he was too much trouble. Everyone had to guard their bags and kit because this brazen creature rummaged every unattended bag. Just prior to his removal he approached me and demanded cigarettes. I told him I did not smoke but that mattered not. He wanted me to buy him a pack of two hundred! I looked into his mad eyes and thought about William Blake's poem from 1794.

TIGER, TIGER
When the stars threw down their spears,
And water'd heaven with their tears,
Did He smile His work to see?
Did He who made the lamb make thee?

My being the lone Brit in that prison he thought I was easy meat, him being a tiger and all. The thoughts behind his eyes, that cast an evil spell with a fiendish delight in intimidation, rapidly evaporated as I crushed his bollocks in my iron grip left hand and choked him into silence with my right hand clamped around his windpipe. I held him in agony for just a few seconds, then pushed him backwards out of the dining hall into the corridor where I gave him a final memorable squeeze and released him to collapse in a heap never to approach me again.

The days and nights passed quietly as I settled down in cell No: 50 with Mike Sherman. Mike was a considerate man and, though he smoked, he never smoked in the cell. He was quite health conscious and was careful about what he ate. He was a clean-living man and our cell was spotlessly clean and smelled slightly of bleach and disinfectant. He was a wonderful companion and we swapped stories continually in the solitude of our cell and as we marched around the yard.

On St. George's Day the sun shone brightly and a football match was organised for the afternoon. I told Mike it would be good to watch because they all thought they were professionals and the slightest foul always caused a scuffle. On this day we were given a treat. Directly from the kick-off there was an incident off the ball that mushroomed into a violent slugfest. Acid Fran, the half-breed French Moroccan took a punch to his face, which was already badly damaged by an acid attack before he came to prison. The scar tissue was still livid and grisly looking. The flesh around his right eye was melted by the acid and looked like his eye would fall out if he bent over. The nearby right ear was burned off and looked like red wattle on a hen's head. His opponent, Juan Garcia, was punching wildly as Acid Fran lunged into him to sink his big teeth into Garcia's nose. The teeth closed over the nose and it looked like Acid Fran had taken most of Garcia's face into his mouth. The screams were profoundly gut wrenching as the nose was being torn from his face. The screws were quickly on the scene and they separated the heads with flailing truncheons. Acid Fran nearly choked to death on a piece of Garcia's nose lodged in his throat. The pair were dragged to the enfermeria where Garcia's nose was stitched back onto his face and Acid Fran's scar tissue was treated before he was sent down the block.

The game was restarted and play continued noisily with screws on standby ready to quell further rioting. Barging, shin kicking, and tripping continued blatantly but retaliation was by way of a return kick a minute or so later. No more fisticuffs today, at least not on the football pitch, but it would be interesting in the showers after the match. Many disputes were settled in the shower block because the screws never entered the place until they thought it was empty when they went in to check it before locking the doors.

The next day was my wedding anniversary so I lay on my bed remembering that happy day in Gibraltar eleven years before. I read the anniversary card from my wife again and again and each time there was a lump in my throat. How fortunate I was to have a wonderful loyal wife who wrote great letters to me every day. I knew in my heart that she was thinking of me now as midnight drew near. My vision provided me with the sight, sound, touch, smell and taste of my heroine. Susan my rock, my Excalibur, and in this evil place I saw her face in my mind each day. She was my goal. She was my priceless reward when I left this terrible place. In her daily letters she told me to pray to Jesus every day and I know in my heart she helped me defeat the nightmare of Satan.

The power of prayer was marvellous and could clear my mind of invading negativity, which caused stress and weakness in others who turned to heroin and other such false crutches in that evil place. I saw gypsies with tattoos of Jesus on the cross, or wearing His crown of thorns with blood trickling down His lamentable face, adorning their backs. I saw Christ's face tattooed on the calf muscles and biceps of lowbred greasy bastards who could not even spell His name. They would sell their arses and offer blowjobs to pay for a fix. They were like monkeys, always looking for something to steal. They would do anything to chase the dragon.

There was a gypsy there who I called Mr Bean because he looked just like him. The Crucifixion of Christ, etched in great detail and colour, covered the whole of his back from neck to buttocks. I wondered what the queers who plundered his backside thought as they looked at that colourful scene. He should be drenched in sulphuric acid to erase it and a new tattoo to replace it should read: *Leviticus 18: 22 and 20: 13 you detestable bastards.*

Coincidentally, it was that day when Nutmeg approached me again to write his book for him. He had written more filth into his journal and insisted that I produce his book. To humour him and because I was curious I agreed to read it and offer advice. It was difficult for me to read because of the explicit portrayal of homosexual bedroom behaviour. He named his many boyfriends and casual sexual partners and how he had fallen in love with each of them. Vividly describing the resultant oral and anal rutting was a portrayal of normality in his eyes. It was difficult for me to read that because it was an affront to my manhood and sense of decency. Thinking that maybe I was being a bit prudish I showed the journal to Mike Sherman and was relieved to see that he was equally uncomfortable and scandalised. Like myself Mike was an experienced world traveller and likely more broad-minded than the average man in the street. However, we were aghast at the revelations in Nutmeg's writing pad. We both knew what queers did but, when it was written in a blow by blow (pun) account by someone we knew, it offended our primal instincts and Christian morality, and after reading it the repulsion I felt for that person increased tenfold. Rather than taking it seriously Mike and I made fun of Nutmeg's adventures and I was sorely tempted to disclose some of his antics in a humorous way, notwithstanding the feeling that I should water down the actual sex scenes because they made me inwardly cringe. Also, I did not want my reader to think it was disgusting pornography. That actually happened in prison so maybe I should not attempt to dilute it - I would put some thought into that and decide later.

The jefe del modulo on that day was Don Raul, a small man barely five feet tall. He was a little man hiding inside his blue serge uniform. He shouted a lot and locked all doors behind him; so we quiet ones writing in the dining hall were locked in as he left with his coffee to walk back to his office. Each time someone needed to use the lavatory there was a lot of shouting and rattling of iron doors before he came to unlock our big iron gate. Then he had to return to allow the prisoner back into the dining hall. This guard spent much of his time on his feet. He was a puny man and looked like a swarthy Harry Potter and his spectacles were those thick ones that magnified his eyes; so he could not hide his nervousness as he controlled the queue to see the doctor. His eyes were wide as he shouted at the gypsies and Arabs trying to barge in at the front of the queue. He could see there was going to be a problem. So could I.

The Russians, Niki and Sergey, were first in line to see the doctor, so the inevitable happened as Wolfman, a large hairy Moroccan, tried to elbow his way to the front. I never knew Wolfman's real name but Mike and I named him Wolfman because of his uncanny resemblance to Lon Chaney Jnr, made-up as Wolfman in the old movies of that name. Wolfman's front teeth tinkled across the dining room table towards Raul the screw, who blanched instantly and stepped back mouthing into his walkie-talkie to call for help, then a few seconds later the pounding hooves of the cavalry were heard approaching from the screws' office. Too late! The doctor was about to do some real work for a change as Sergey battered every face within reach. His big fists became a blur as noses were flattened and eyes blackened by his fury. Niki kept Sergey's back protected from shitty sharpened bones.

The screws approached and warily surrounded him with truncheons raised. Suddenly he stopped and pointed at Raul the screw and loudly blamed him for not controlling the queue. Niki joined his pal and accused Raul of being cowardly and ineffective. This outburst did not save Sergey from going down the block, but it did stop the shiny truncheons from pounding his skull; and as he was removed the queue reformed with the wounded at the front supervised by two screws. Just another day in Satan's arena.

On Sunday 29th April 2007 my Moroccan friend Ahmed had a visit from his eighty-nine year old father. Ahmed had not seen his father for over three years so was delighted with his visit. On Thursday 3rd May 2007 Ahmed received news that his father had died - a very sad day. Nuradin explained that Ahmed's father got himself a visa and travelled from Tangier to Spain and all the way to Daroca because he knew he was dying and wanted to say goodbye to his son. Nuradin said that according to the Holy Koran a soul took forty days to leave the body and some men like Ahmed's father knew when the forty days had begun because they experienced a difficulty in breathing. As the days passed the soul made its way down the right side of the body and down the right leg to exit the big toe of the right foot at the moment of death. These men believed that actually happened, and the reason for the soul taking forty days to exit is because a man is normally frightened of death so he mentally resists the passage of the soul, hence forty days. I never disputed such a belief because of the problems it would cause for me on the dining table. I was their guest, the lone Brit, why should I doubt their beliefs? They said nothing about the crucified Jesus rising from the dead on the third day to ascend to heaven. So I put that snippet of information in the library of my mind. Whoa! Nuradin just amended his statement by telling me it was not in the Holy Koran. Nevertheless all Arabs believed in the forty days for the soul to exit the big toe.

At feeding time the Arabs on my table confirmed Nuradin's statement, nodding sagely at me as he gave me his 'told you so' expression. I looked for smirks among the grizzly faces and found none. Ishmael pushed food into his big hairy face then tore a piece of bread off his loaf and shoved it around his metal tray to soak up gravy and meat before shoving it into his cavernous mouth. His lantern jaw stopped chewing as he caught my gaze.

"Que pasa Kreestoffer?" he said, through a mouthful of food, his oily brown eyes full of guile as everyone stopped in mid chew to look at my smirking face.

Looking at them all in turn, I smiled.

"Lo no dijo nada - I said nothing," I uttered.

Puzzled, they all exchanged glances, then the penny dropped as Nuradin spluttered.

"We are not joking about the big toe!"

With his eyes wide and his face twitching, he blurted it out in Arabic and they all fell about laughing and shouting.

"Seguro, seguro! For sure, for sure!"

Dear reader, believe what you will about the big toe exit for the soul, but I was convinced they really did believe this to be so. What I believed mattered not to them but over those past three months these Arabs had accepted me as one of their own, so I toed the line. Hmm. I knew better than anyone that if I were not a skipper there would be no room for me on that table, but I was a skipper and I accepted gifts of fruit and other nice things. I never asked anything of them, nor they of me, but I did have their addresses and telephone numbers in Morocco and Spain. Each in turn had approached me to work with them when I got out. They had each plotted to use me to transport their hashish across the Mediterranean Sea. Consequently, I was offered more holidays in Morocco than Thomas Cooks could supply. I believed their plans were genuine, as they all had access to mountains of hashish that needed exporting.

Nuradin's plan was for me to haul hashish and illegal immigrants to the Canary Isles from his home port of Safi on the west coast of Morocco. Ishmael's plan was much the same, but he operated out of Tangier. Abdellatik's plan was to sail from Saidia near the Algerian border on the north coast and take the cargo to France. I already told you about Abdelmalik's plan out of Algeciras and I could tell you twenty more plans, but that would merely confirm the prison jobcentre was desperate for yacht skippers and RIB jockeys. I understood their needs because I had seen many failures and losses of cargo in my time.

One time, when I was resting between jobs, I witnessed four failed attempts in one week! I was staying in Nador in an apartment owned by Colonel Amer, a drug baron of considerable wealth and influence. I was due to sail out of Sebkha bou Areq (Mar Chica) with two tonnes of happy herb, so I had ten days to kill waiting in his apartment for a new boat. During this time four different skippers were briefed in that apartment and stayed with me until their departures. The first skipper was a Spaniard with two paisanos as crew. They left the apartment at midnight and went to Mar Chica where their loaded RIB lay ready to sail. They returned the next day having dumped their cargo over the side at the sight of a blip on the horizon. This was a common trait with spick skippers and the main reason nobody wanted to employ them. They would ditch two tonnes of hashish in as many seconds when they got the wind up. The three subsequent cargoes landed in the laps of the Spanish police because the Moroccan skippers were so slow and lacking navigational skills that they arrived in Spanish waters in broad daylight and were easily captured and imprisoned. Colonel Amer lost eight tonnes of hashish that week, which at that time was worth two thousand five hundred pounds per kilo in England - twenty million pounds! Had it gone to Finland you would double that figure.

When a Moroccan inmate met an English RIB jockey or yacht skipper in prison he thought he had won the lottery and immediately laid claim to him and slotted him into his operation as quickly as possible. Plans were laid with all the time in the world to plot everything to the nth degree. That was how millionaires were made in prison. The Moroccans on my table were no different than all previous Arabs I had met in prison over the years. They thought they had found the answer to all their dreams if they could strike a deal with me to sail their cargoes to Spain, France or elsewhere. So I played along with them and listened to their wonderful get-rich-quick plans because life inside was much more interesting if you did not let on that you were retired and would never sail again.

    I made my act of contrition to my maker six years previously and I had come to terms with my punishment and the heartache I had caused my family. Then I knew in my heart that I would never do a wrong thing again in what was left of my life. No matter how much money I did not have my sailing days were over.

Intimidators

Angel was a grizzly-faced Spaniard with a forty-seven stretch for murder and armed robbery. He looked nothing like his name suggested. A tattoo of a scorpion was on his right forearm and on the left was the Grim Reaper complete with scythe and sinister hood over his scary skull. He was possibly forty-five years old, six feet tall and heavily built.

He was a seasoned intimidator and was high in the gypsy hierarchy. But to me he was just another lowbred creep missing the warmth of the open fire in the earth packed floor of his lair on the outskirts of Madrid. His friend, Juan Carlos Espeleta, was also a bank robber and was doing a five stretch for his troubles. He was over six feet tall, owned the meanest of faces and was built like a brick shithouse. He frightened people. Juan Carlos was possibly thirty years of age and he was the principal intimidator on the wing. He never bought ciggies or coffee, he persuaded weaker men to buy them for him and his horrible pal Angel. They were a formidable duo and were headed my way.

It happened on Friday 11th May 2007 when they approached me to ask if I would teach them martial arts. At that time I was training with Sergey the Russian and Giorgio the Sicilian doing physical jerks and jogging. During a break in training I showed them a defence technique against a knife. Suddenly we had an audience so we went back to physical jerks and jogging, but the word was out - the Brit is teaching martial arts, hence the approach by Angel and Juan Carlos. I explained that I was not teaching martial arts because I had not got permission to teach in that prison; besides that I had no desire to teach anyone in there. Angel strolled away but Juan Carlos gave me a withering stare that could only mean trouble. Blokes like him tended to get their own way, normally by bullying. Looking deep into his mad eyes I winked and jogged away to catch up with Sergey and Giorgio.

The next day the sun shone brightly in the yard as I started my ten-lap jog, with triceps dips and press-ups performed on one of the benches at the completion of each lap. This was just to get loose and warmed up for my more intense ju-jitsu warm-up that I did each morning in the yard. Sergey and Giorgio had been running hard around the yard and each had a good sweat on. They joined me to start neck exercises, then we went through the gamut of physical jerks that I had used for years in my ju-jitsu routine. After thirty minutes or so of military style exercises I taught them basic kicks, blocks and punches. But first I taught them basic stances like sanchin and zenkutsu dachi[119], well-balanced postures from which to practise kicks, blocks and punches. The morning was spent doing just that, but vigorously focussing on form and power.

At midday we were drenched with sweat and went for a well-earned shower. I had told Sergey and Giorgio about Angel and Juan Carlos' attempt at joining us and they thought nothing of it, apart from being pleased I had refused them. I was on my guard as I showered, but Juan Carlos did not appear, at least not on this day, but I was always cautious each time I entered the shower block. The days drifted by with the strengthening sunshine and I stripped my bed of blankets as the cell became hotter and stifling. Mike bought a small electric fan from Willem the clog, so that made life easier in the cell, but the morning training continued with no let up in effort and more requests to join my small group for ju-jitsu training.

Sergey and Giorgio were a mismatch because Sergey was head and shoulders over Giorgio so when the Terrible Turk, who is the same height and build as Giorgio, and Alexandrov, another huge Russian, asked to join I accepted them. Now I had four students who were very tough and dangerous men. The Terrible Turk was the name Mike and I gave to Zeuzay, a powerful man from Ankara in Turkey. He had served nine years of a twelve year sentence for heroin trafficking and was due to leave shortly on Libertad Condicional. He gave me his contact addresses in London, Zagreb and Ankara because he would have liked to have me in his organisation. I wondered what kind of set-up he had if he was locked up in here for nine years while everything was running smoothly on the out. During the time he spent inside he had wanted for nothing. He had his own

---

[119] sanchin and zenkutsu dachi - fighting stances

single cell with a television and curtains. He was the only inmate here with electric appliances in his cell, like an electric kettle, hair drier, PlayStation and DVD player. Each week he had food brought in from the village shop and he was fixed up with a job, a fiancée, and a house in Spain; all the criteria required to qualify for parole in this country. Money talks. The day he got out of there would be the last day anyone in Spain would see of him. He would be away like a long dog with a new identity and back to work hauling heroin across Europe. This determined and dangerous man would never again set foot in Spain - but right then he was there training with me in the yard.

I increased the pace of the warm-up session and added extra exercises to lengthen the time spent on physical jerks. We then did twenty minutes of kicks, blocks and punches as a drill before moving on to learn choking and joint wrecking techniques. My own personal fitness level was increasing nicely and I was getting sharper day by day. My little squad of international villains reminded me of the band of brothers I created in the Carabanchel prison in Madrid in 1998. We were called the Mezclado and they have featured in previous chapters so I will say no more about them. Though Daroca was an evil place it did not have the same meanness as the Carabanchel - but the danger was still there in abundance and the same attitude of awareness was required to survive in that dreadful place.

The prison officers had noticed my group of training martial artists and had begun to take an interest, as had the security cameras mounted on the prison walls. So had Angel and Juan Carlos, the intimidators who were sitting with their gypsy friends and glared at us from across the yard. I knew in my heart that an ambush would be laid in the very near future, I also knew it would happen in the shower block. I told my group about the refusals to Juan Carlos and Angel regarding joining us and that an attempt at loss of face for me was imminent and I thought it would happen in the shower block, so watch my fucking back!

"But we all shower together," said Zenzay the Turk, "every day," he added, in his gruff accented English.

"Yes, but Juan Carlos will choose his moment carefully, so be aware when the place is full of steam," I said.

Scanning their hard faces I thought it prudent to teach and practise knife defence techniques during the next few days. So I concentrated on that aspect and made the training hard and violent - so violent that I hurt each of them with my demonstrations. So what? They were hard men and I did not get paid. This was prison and knife attacks were the real deal in here. Besides, they would not want it any other way. These men were like gladiators and they thought like gladiators, only too pleased to have another weapon in their armoury. Each ju-jitsu technique was another weapon to them because the defence coin, when flipped, became a terrible nerve and bone wrecking attack that could cause prolonged agony or instant death to their attacker. I was a purveyor of violence. That is what I taught. Not to attack but to defend in the most effective way, so my attacker was neutralised and given a lesson he would not forget for a long time.

I was in the furthest away shower cubicle from the exit and I noticed a gypsy furtively trying to see who was in which shower cubicle. He could only look at a few at a time then go back out because naked men do not like being looked at. I knew he was looking for me. At last he found me and quickly went to report to Juan Carlos. Knowing what was about to happen, I quickly changed places with Sergey, as the thick clouds of steam got thicker. The others had clocked the gypsy and guessed what was going down and they waited. The steam was so thick you could barely see your hand in front of you when they came in. Juan Carlos carried a long brush handle sharpened at the end and smeared with shit from the filthy lavatories. He was creeping toward the furthest away cubicle to stab me with it. Through the clouds of steam, I watched him slink past me toward Sergey who lay in wait for him. Five gypsies followed him as the noise of splashing water and shouting men calling across the fog of steam to each other distorted the warning shout from Rafa, his lieutenant gypsy, as I stepped out behind Juan Carlos and punched him very hard in the nape of his neck. I grabbed his thick black hair with my right hand as my left hand snaked around his throat. Yanking him backwards, so he sat on his arse in the wet. I applied a violent hadake jimi[120] and he was unconscious in seconds. The five gypsies screamed in terror as their exit was blocked by a group of naked men - very big naked men! Buster, one of my Moroccan friends, bit the face off one of them as Giorgio, Sergey, Alexandrov and the Turk punched and gouged the eyes of the others. Some of the men blocking the exit joined in just for the fun of it, or maybe they had scores to settle and here was their opportunity. While this was happening Juan Carlos lay on his back unconscious as I gave him two tremendous punches, one to each eyebrow, so that each time he looked in a mirror he would remember not to take a shitty stick to the lone Brit. I picked up his shitty lance and wiped the tip inside his mouth so he could taste it when he awoke. I then stabbed it into his buttock so he would have a problem sitting for a week or so. Then I stuffed it down his trouser leg for the screws to find later. The shower block fell silent as the water stopped running and everyone quickly dried, dressed and departed leaving six fully clothed very sore muckworms lying unconscious in the wet.

Extra guards came to the wing to escort the sorry bunch of gypsies to the enfermeria. Two gurneys were brought to take Juan Carlos and Rafa away because they were deeply concussed. I expected all kinds of things to happen like shakedowns and questioning, but nothing happened. Life just went on as usual. Juan Carlos and two of his tribe were sent to another wing because they were found with weapons on their persons.

This incident served two purposes; firstly, it was a deterrent to other would-be assassins and, secondly, it made my international friends aware of the need for a united front against the gypsy tribes prominent in all Spanish prisons. As a foreigner in several Spanish prisons I had many experiences with Spanish gypsies, all of them bad. They were mostly illiterate and incredibly selfish. If a gypsy offered you something you had best beware, it was a sprat to catch a mackerel. They are sly and bereft of conscience no matter how many tattoos of Christ they wear. I hated to think of the face of Jesus as the badge of low cunning, but when I see it on the skin of murdering nonces it

---

[120] hadake jimi - naked strangle from the rear

makes me truly cringe inside. In the evolution stakes they are way behind the rest of the populace, but in their macho mentality, they place themselves above all other species on the planet. Loss of face could be as trivial as refusing to give one of them a cigarette in front of other tribal members, or complaining if one of them queue-jumped. Once you had incurred what they perceived to be loss of face you had better watch out. As you innocently went about your business thinking nothing was wrong, the low cunning bastards would be plotting something nasty for you. Any act of friendship toward you, a foreigner, was a complete sham. You were not one of their tribe and you never would be.

Giorgio was the lone wop. He was a hard and dangerous man, a Mafioso. He was the first to comment on his singularity. His granite features showed no concern, but he made a suggestion.

"We should stick together after this. Let them know we are a gang," he said.

"That's right," said the Terrible Turk, crinkling the brow of his pugnacious face, "those street turds will gang up on any one of us now."

We sat quietly on our rustic table in the yard as the sun shone brightly on that lovely day.

"Yes, we will look to each other's backs from now on," said Alexandrov.

The dialogue was my interpretation of men speaking a mixture of Spanish, English, Russian and German, which I have no problem with. But for you, dear reader, the gobbledygook of international prisoners would be just a jumble of unintelligible words, so I humbly translated for easy reading.

There was a lot of heroin on the wing, which made it difficult to assess the aftermath of the gypsy bashing. Nevertheless, we would all be on red alert for a long time, especially as Angel was brooding alone with murder in his eyes.

Ambush

Prisoners came and went every week in Daroca. Thursday was the usual day for new arrivals because of the way the transport system worked between prisons. Every Thursday a Guardia Civil bus came from Valdemoro prison in Madrid, which was the main distribution point for prisoners. Prisoners were sent all over the country from there. I use the term bus loosely because it looked to be a bus outwardly, but inwardly it most certainly was not a bus. It was a cruel contraption on wheels manned by cruel uniformed Spaniards.

Three new prisoners arrived that week - one Austrian and two gypsies. I did not say a word to the Austrian but doubtless in the very near future he would approach me. The two gypsies would also approach me to beg for ciggies or coffee or any bloody thing.

Abdelmalik also returned from his extended permiso. He told me that during his six-day break he had to report to his local police station and, when he did, they promptly arrested him because the original arrest warrant was still live. How fucking stupid and incompetent were those fucking Spaniards? Later, when I was released, I was to discover just how incompetent they were. When I arrived at Heathrow Airport the British police promptly arrested me because the European Arrest Warrant was still live. The fucking spicks had not deleted it from their computers! I wonder why I hated them? Abdelmalik was released at the end of May and was waiting for me in Girona. He would get fed up waiting and sooner or later go ahead without me. Good luck Malik, take care and do not get caught.

Nuradin came to me with a letter he had received from Zukzuk, an Algerian who was released about two months previously. Zukzuk was the Arabic word for breaking wind, so you can guess how he got his name. He could play his national anthem through his arse! Nuradin brought the letter because I was mentioned in dispatches. He showed me the letter but I could not make head or tail of the Arabic script. It looked as though Zukzuk had dipped a spider in some ink and let it run around the page. I asked Nuradin if he was going to reply.

"Fuck him,' he said, "he no fuckin' good."

Such was life amongst the Arabs, so I assumed I would also be spoken about in the same vein - after all, I was an infidel. Nevertheless, Nuradin insisted I take my wife for a holiday to his hometown of Safi on the west coast of Morocco.

"Come, come my friend, you are welcome. Welcome you are to my house. Not big house, but clean house. She like! She stay one week, she want stay one month more! She buy house in Safi. You wait see my friend, you and she be much happy," he enthused.

Nuradin bin Sahara lived on rue Hamria near the harbour. No doubt my wife and I would be treated like lords and we would have had a wonderful time. But I knew Nuradin wanted me to sail happy herb and illegal immigrants to the Canary Islands. Just a few years ago it was fairly easy to sail hashish across to Tenerife, but these days there are hundreds of illegal immigrants arriving each week in ramshackle craft of all shapes and sizes. Consequently the chances of getting through the dragnet of patrol boats had diminished dramatically, so it was truly a kamikaze job. I expected never to see Nuradin bin Sahara ever again once I left that pisshole.

Another Moroccan with a French passport was expelled to France that week having served two thirds of his sentence. He was a big man of about sixty-five years and wore traditional robes and a fez. The Spanish police escorts arrived to take him to the French frontier and were shocked to find his luggage piled high in ingreso. They could not fit him and his luggage in the little car so there was a question about his luggage. The screws decided to give him a final shakedown and emptied his two big holdalls and two plastic refuse bags. They found two dozen prison issue bed sheets, six blankets, several pairs of prison issue shoes and an assortment of prison issue garments, a large block of cheese and tins of tuna stolen from the kitchens. The bed sheets and blankets had the prison logo imprinted in the cloth, so not sure what the hell he intended to do with them. His few remaining personal bits were thrown into the car and he was taken to the French border, leaving behind a forlorn heap of stolen goods at the prison gates. He could not carry it all anyway, so he would have needed help all the way home. Maybe he thought he could take the prison trolley with him. Such was the Arab brain - he jeopardised his freedom for a sack of crap!

The soul-destroying days and nights of inward emptiness and despair inexorably continued to sap the souls of the feeble-minded who fell prey to the ever-present smack dealers. One such victim committed suicide the previous day. He was out on permiso and with his family in Zaragoza. He should have enjoyed six days of freedom with his family, but he was very much in debt to the gypsy smack dealer Jesus Lozano and was desperately trying to get heroin to smuggle back into prison, as instructed by the gypsy, in order to repay his debt. Failure to do so would result in serious injury. As I wrote my journal, I could see Jesus Lozano holding court just a few tables away from me. He had long black hair and if he wore a feather in it he would have made a good Geronimo. His swarthy arms were ugly with self-inflicted scars and tattoos of Christ on each bicep. I could see another on his chest with Christ looking skywards with a gold halo around His head. He laughed and joked with his compadres and had forgotten about the death and debt of his victim. He thought about his victim's family like he thought about the North Pole – not once!

Lozano was constantly on the lookout for signs of depression on the faces of men, especially new prisoners lost and bewildered in the strange new world of prison. He kept the new ones under observation seeking signs of depression. This was second nature to him. As depression increased on the faces of potential clients he would strike and offer a free fix. He would teach his victims how to chase the dragon and after a few days of cheap fixes they were hooked.

Many times I tried to dissuade men from losing their souls to Satan, but my persuasive Spanish was just not strong enough. Jesus Lozano the tattooed heroin dealer hated my guts. He hated me more than he hated the screws and with good reason. He bore the scars of my knuckles on his eyebrows and his front teeth were missing. He stupidly stalked me for two days after I persuaded Lorenzo La torre de Francia, a German speaking Spaniard who was educated enough to heed my warning, to refuse further coaching from Satan's gypsy troll. When Lorenzo refused further fixes Jesus Lozano knew that I was responsible for rescuing Lorenzo from his covetous grasp. He immediately set about trying to kill me, or at least inflict serious injury with the bone pinchou I knew he always carried, which I must assume was smeared with rat shit or AIDS shit. His compadres informed him of my every move. Each time I went for a piss he knew about it. They watched me training and even watched me enter my cell each night. I knew I was being set up for an ambush and so did my friends.

He made his move on a sunny morning as I queued for coffee in the economato queue. There were thirty or forty prisoners milling around the serving hatch so conditions were ideal for a stabbing with so many inmates blocking the view from the screws' office. I observed him in my peripheral vision as he left one of the rustic tables to walk across the yard and join the queue. I turned to my left and then to my right to check the security cameras. They were scanning various groups of men around the yard. They were not focussing on the economato queue. I knew this was going to be it. Wang, my Chinese friend was sipping coffee just off to one side of the queue and observing the assassin who was fast approaching my back.

"Ahora! Now!" he shouted.

I sidestepped, about turned and parried the thrusting pinchou. Grasping his right wrist I pulled him forwards and down onto a front kick that knocked out his front teeth. He collapsed face down on the concrete yard as I stomped his head onto the unyielding surface of the pateo. I quickly flipped him over and gave him two titanic punches to each of his eyes. Suddenly there was a shrill whistle from the screws' office as they realised from the movement of the queue that a fight was in progress. I had no time to deal with the pinchou, that I was about to stab into his arse, because the queue dispersed in an instant. Leaving Satan's troll unconscious and bleeding, with his pinchou firmly grasped in his sleeping right hand, I made off with the dispersing crowd to do a lap of the yard. I strolled with Wang and some of my friends who had been with me in the queue as part of my ambush, as the screws stood, hands on hips looking down at the shitty pinchou in the hand of Jesus Lozano. The queue reformed after

Lozano was removed to the enfermeria. The pinchou was confiscated and the screws seemed not to care who had laid him out. There would be no sympathy from them, especially because of the dreaded shit smeared weapon. Besides, they loathed the gypsies more than we did.

Lozano was back from the enfermeria in time for feeding, but he could not eat much as his gums were shredded a wee bit where his teeth used to be. Each of his eyes sported staple stitches and had turned black and blue with a pretty jaundiced border surrounding the top part of his face and meeting on the bridge of his nose. Dried blood could be seen in his nostrils due to his kissing the concrete and breaking his nose. He now hated me even more, but like others in his tribe, he now knew just how deadly the lone Brit could be.

Gazing at the face of Christ tattooed on his unctuous skin I could not stem the tide of hatred I felt for that particular specimen of the sub-species gitano Espanol[121] who was one of Satan's henchmen.

---

[121] gitano Espanol – Spanish gypsy

The Suicidal Yogi

Nutmeg, the South African queer, had just returned from another permiso. He spent six days with his bum boy friends in Zaragoza. One of them, who he said was a doctor, helped him to decorate his apartment.

I found his stories unbelievable because he had been locked up for eight years and one needed money to rent an apartment in Zaragoza. I did not believe his story about receiving compensation from the prison authorities regarding the incident with the screws when he returned from a previous permiso. He told me that the old man who rented him the apartment said he did not need to pay the rent until after he left prison at the end of July. I did not believe him. I also did not believe his doctor friend, who was the son of a prominent politician, was helping him to find a corrupt judge who would somehow release Nutmeg's Algerian boyfriend Lhaktar so they could live happily ever after in Zaragoza. Hmm. I heard on the grapevine that Nutmeg's bride to be, Lhaktar, was bent over touching his toes most of the time. Acid Fran had a pal over there who said Lhaktar gave blow-jobs in the showers at midday and was available for rogering at 7:00 pm until the shower block closed for recuento at 7:45 pm. Nutmeg wrote love letters each day to his beloved sand boy, but there appeared not to be much return mail. The queer fool was like one of Disney's lovesick rabbits, kissing letters and loudly proclaiming his love for a raghead poofta who lifted his djellaba[122] for all and sundry over on modulo cuatro (wing No: 4). Nutmeg proudly showed Mike and me a photo of Lhaktar. Not surprisingly, he looked like an AIDS victim and was a ringer for Muhatma Gandhi, a veritable bag of bones. Mike and I agreed that it was highly likely he had the AIDS virus squiggling up his arse because that place was rife with it.

The last weekend in May was very wet and quite cold. Nevertheless, I did a two-hour workout in the blustery yard alone - everybody else stayed indoors out of the rain. I finished my workout

---

[122] djellaba – loose garment worn by Arabs

at 11:30 am and strolled across to the entrance corridor leading to the dining hall where I could relax until shower time at twelve noon.

The duty screw was the five feet tall insect, Don Raul, wearing Cosmo Smallpiece spectacles on his ugly face. I asked politely for him to open the gate so I could enter the dining hall. He flew into a tantrum saying he was not my doorman and I must stay in the yard or go into the sala. I explained that I was a non-smoker and the sala is too smoky for me.

"Mala suerte! Bad luck!" he sneered, as he opened the gate for a Spanish inmate.

I tried to enter with the spick but he raised his podgy hand like a traffic cop, indicating that I stay out. A minute later he opened the gate for another Spanish inmate and again refused me entry. I muttered loud enough for him to hear.

"Racista, Racist."

He looked at me as though I had pissed on his boots. His cheeks turned rosy as his eyes widened behind the thick lenses of his spectacles. My accusation had touched a nerve, so the runt of the litter flew into a rage and spluttered incoherent Spanish as he turned the key and tried to fling the big Iron Gate open, but it was too heavy for him to do it well. I strode through without saying a word. My one word had sufficed. The gate crashed closed behind me with a terrific clang. I did not look back. I was not impressed by the noise created by an arsehole in blue serge.

The team of screws on duty were all short arses full of their own self-importance grumpy and mean to everyone except their paisanos. A foreigner must have upset them. Their attention was taken away from me by a shout from the yard and much hilarity. A Spaniard lay naked on the wet floor in the centre of the yard. He had an enormous erection pointing skywards, which was surprising considering the cold wind and rain. His dick looked gigantic because it was the biggest part of him. He was spindly thin like a Belsen inmate and his face was virtually a skull sheathed in pallid skin, like he had a condom pulled over his head. His sunken Spanish eyes glittered with madness as the screws dashed across the yard to lift him bodily off the wet concrete and take him to the enfermeria. His erection was waving around like a palm tree in a hurricane as short arse Raul's face glowed red with embarrassment and howls of laughter erupted from the spectators.

Wilfrido Moreno, the skeleton with the big dick, had served four years of a twenty-three stretch for murdering his Spanish girlfriend whilst on holiday in Morocco. The story was they were both stoned on high-grade pollen and the girlfriend got too friendly with the Moroccan who sold them the dope. Wilfrido awoke to find his girlfriend kissing him passionately, as the Moroccan was happily rogering her from behind while she knelt on the bed. Wilfrido wondered why she was rocking to and fro as she kissed him, so turned on the light to see a befezzed Arab with his dishdasha[123] tucked under his chin as he back-scuttled the girlfriend. The melee that followed produced a dead girlfriend, a badly injured Moroccan and a murder charge for Wilfrido. He was sentenced and imprisoned in Morocco but applied for transfer back to Spain. Luck ran out for Wilfrido because just a few days after his transfer to Spain, all foreign prisoners in Morocco were released with an amnesty to celebrate the birth of a new member of the Moroccan royal family. Had Wilfrido stayed in Morocco a few more days, he would be a free man now. No wonder he was out of his mind.

The next day Wilfrido returned to the wing battered and bruised. The little men in blue serge had worked him over with their big sticks. Raul the freak screw had struck again. I was training in the yard when Wilfrido approached me. I was doing abdominal crunches when he loomed over me. There was a look of madness in his eyes and besides looking up his cavernous nostrils I could see two livid scars across his throat hiding beneath his scraggly beard. In trying English he asked if he could borrow a pen. I got up off the floor and rummaged my bag for my ballpoint pen.

"I didn't know you could speak English,' I said, as I fumbled for the pen.

"Not very well," he said nervously. "I need to practise, but you are the only Englishman in the prison and you are always busy writing or exercising."

---

[123] dishdasha - loose, long-sleeved garment

"If you want to practise your English you can always come over for a chat when I am writing, but not when I am training," I said, grinning.

"Oh, I'm sorry I disturbed your training," he said honestly.

"Not at all," I lied, "I've just finished, so sit down and tell me your story."

He sat opposite me across the rustic table and smoothed his grey hair, which was very long and worn in a ponytail. His massive aquiline nose suited the shape of his face and made him serene looking and not at all like a crazed killer.

"I do yoga to keep calm," he said, his grey-bluish eyes looking right through me.

He looked to be about forty years old, even though his hair was grey and he was very thin. A typical Hare Krishna type.

"You ever been to India?" I asked.

"Oh yes, a long time ago," his eyes seemed to glass over as he remembered better times. "Have you been to India?" he asked.

"Yes," I replied, "also a long time ago."

"Where were you?" he asked enthusiastically.

"Bombay," I answered, remembering the abysmal squalor and the continuous smell of shit and the sound of slapping sandals adding to the clamour of heaving humanity.

"Oh, a lovely place,'" he announced, underlining the fact he was quite mad.

I remembered Bombay as being the place I wanted to leave most in my life before I came to Daroca.

"It is only a lovely place if you like the smell of shit," I said, looking at his great schnozzle, wondering if such a magnificent proboscis was nerveless.

"I think you are not happy and content with life," he said, staring into my eyes.

"I can't think of any reason to be happy in Daroca," I said, "but I will be happy when I get out."

"Do you meditate on past lives?" he asked.

"No," I said, wondering what was coming next.

"Oh, I do," he said, with a faraway look in his eyes. "I go back thousands of years. I smell the people and taste their energy. That is why I am content. I go back in time every day."

I witnessed this man lying on his back on a blanket every day with his fingers in his mouth and a rag or a sock over his eyes. He often stood on his head chanting the 'Om' word of Tibetan mantras and was reminiscent of a yogi (not the bear).

"I like the wide nose Indians best, they are so happy with life," he said, closing his eyes.

"Who are they?" I asked, as I gathered my kit in readiness for a shower.

"I am not sure about their country, but I think they are Incas."

"Maybe next time you see them you should ask instead of smelling them," I said facetiously.

"Oh, they cannot see me. I have tried that and they don't know I am amongst them. This is a very spiritual skill that we all have, so we cannot appear as a life form."

"How did you learn to do this?" I asked.

"Many years ago when I first studied yoga, I experimented with LSD and what I thought to be drug induced visions during my meditations turned out to be real life visions because I was able to recall the visions without the use of LSD."

"So LSD opened the gates if you like?" I asked.

I was interested then as I noticed he was speaking perfect accentless English.

"Exactly, I haven't had any drugs since I was in Morocco and I don't need them."

"That is very interesting," I said, "but how do you feel about killing your woman?"

"I feel sad about that and regret doing it," he replied.

"So why did you do it if you think you are so enlightened?"

"It was a moment of insanity because I awoke as she was kissing me. She was ecstatic because she was kissing me and being fucked by another man at the same time. My love for that woman was very deep. She was the only virgin I have ever known and I cherished her."

"Were you stoned at the time?" I asked.

"No, I wish I had been. It wouldn't have happened if I had been stoned, but she was. The Arab had given her some burbuja and taken advantage of her confusion in the dark bedroom. I don't know which is worse," he said sadly, "the sense of loss of the love I killed, or the crushing shame in my heart."

He paused for a moment as though weighing up which part of the guilt hurt most.

"Do you think about this all the time?' I asked.

"No, I lose myself in meditation to escape the stress and depression," he answered. "The visions distress me very much."

"So how do you deal with the distress when it does get through to you?"

"I try to kill myself," he said.

His face was deadpan as though someone had told him a joke he already knew. Raising his chin he poked his forefinger into one of the livid scars hiding under his beard.

"See this scar?" he said, riding his fingernail along its length. "I nearly succeeded with that one."

"Oh yeah, what happened?" I asked.

"I crushed one of the prison issue razors to get the blade out of its housing."

His eyes seemed to glaze as he relived the act. With his right hand he pinched the skin of his neck and tugged it downwards, stretching the skin and started making a cutting motion with an imaginary razor blade in his other hand.

"As you can see, I made a deep cut and kept going deeper like when filleting a fish."

"Why did you cut there?" I asked.

"Because I wanted to hook out the carotid artery to cut a piece out of it and swallow the piece so there was no chance of repairing it."

"What happened?"

"I got as far as the artery but I couldn't get my fingers around it to pull it out."

"Why was that?" I asked, as I wondered about pain thresholds.

"Because there was too much blood, it was too slippery to grip," he said, looking at me as though we were discussing the removal of a fishhook from a trout's mouth.

"So what did you do?"

Touching two fingers to the outline of the vein beneath his ear.

"I was just about to shred it like this,' he said, slicing a finger across his neck, "when a prison officer struck me down with his truncheon, knocking me out."

"Where did this happen?" I asked.

"In there," he said, pointing to the shower block. "I was standing in front of the shaving mirror just by the door and the funcionario strolling by saw me through the open door. I woke up in the enfermeria."

"So you didn't bother doing that again."

"Oh, but I did," turning his head, he poked his finger into the identical scar on the other side of his neck. "I started this one in the servicios over there," he said, pointing across the yard to the stinking shit pit. "A chivato told the funcionarios what I was doing, so they knocked me out again before I finished."

"Did the act of trying to kill yourself not dispel the depression?" I asked.

"It did actually, but not the feeling of shame and utter loneliness and sense of loss."

I thought that was the end of the conversation, but suddenly he pulled open his shirt to reveal a mangled nipple which looked like a fried egg with the yoke broke.

"I did this with a plastic knife. One of the red ones we eat our food with."

"Christ! How did you manage that?" I said, amazed at the mess of his chest.

"It took me a while to get it sharp," he said. "I sharpened the cutting edge and the point on the yard wall, but it wasn't strong enough to get through my ribs."

"What happened this time?" I calmly asked, as I looked at the scarred pectoral muscle and the remaining bit of nipple.

"Again, a chivato told the funcionarios what I was doing."

"Where?"

"In the servicios again," he said, pressing his fingers into the mangled skin. "I had cut back the skin and flesh to expose my ribs and the knife broke as I tried to push it between my ribs to puncture my heart."

There was an expression of sadness on his face, a sorrowful look in his eyes, the frustration of failing to kill himself showed like a lost opportunity, like paradise had shunned him. I knew in my heart this man would die in Satan's arena.

"Why didn't you do it in your cell?" I asked.

"Because my cellmate is aware of my intentions and would prevent it," he said, with a sneer. "That is why I am in one of the first cells near the night shift funcionario's office."

There are several cells on the first floor reserved for kamikazes, the men who want to end it all. They are housed near the screws' office for obvious reasons.

"Has anyone offered counselling or treatment of some kind?" I asked.

"Oh yes, that strip of a girl who is the shrink tried to lecture me, but she is bereft of life experience, compassion and knowledge. She's a fucking pest."

I had to agree with him as I remembered the vacant face of the young blonde girl who wore the same old black overcoat and brown boots each time she visited the wing. She once asked me if I loved my wife and did my mother beat me as a child, and did I beat my own children. She asked these questions as she scribbled gobbledygook in her notebook. She was like all the other spick shrinks I have met – young, scruffy, full of her own shit and as useful as a chocolate fireguard. I imagine that an EU ruling ordered that all EU prisons would have a shrink, so the spicks employed a local girl from a nearby village to give her something to do. In fact, our prison shrink was from Daroca village and amazingly this strip of a girl interviewed sociopaths and international brutes who did not speak her lingo, yet she was instrumental in what happened to those men in there.

As I wrote these words she interviewed a man who cut off his uncle's head with a Japanese sword. This was a local man from

Daroca and I could see them chatting like old pals. They were laughing heartily together, possibly about someone in the village. He was young, with his hair worn in a ponytail, and a baseball cap perched jauntily on his head with sunglasses jammed on top of the large peak. He never wore the sunglasses - they were there as an item of cool, or so he thought. He was a small bloke about five feet three and quite slim. He was of a nervous disposition and spent most of his time prowling up and down the northern end of the yard talking to himself, as his Walkman radio hissed techno shite into his already jangled brain. I did not know much about this young nutter, simply because I wanted nothing to do with him. However, he did get out on permiso and, because he was local, he did not suffer abuse from the screws. He was quite privileged and lived alone in a cell with a view of the village and countryside. I heard people say they heard the screws letting him out after recuento late at night and then letting him back inside at 06:00 am after spending the night at home in the village.

From my point of view being the lone Brit and, knowing how the racist bastards treated me, I find it hard to believe that they were so soft-hearted - but he was one of their own and Daroca was in the arsehole of Aragon, which itself was a wilderness, and he probably had relatives in uniform in there, so why should I doubt it?

Mad Ramon

The village of Daroca held its annual fiesta celebrating the day of Corpus Christi on Thursday 7th June 2007 and all civilian staff had Thursday and the rest of the week off. My Spanish lingo teacher decided not to come back at all, so that was the end of my Spanish lessons. I never did get to know his name, but my cellmate Mike and I called him Boston because his ugly face was just like that of a bug-eyed Boston terrier. His teaching ability was zilch and the smartest thing he ever did was to give me a Spanish dictionary. I was pleased he did not return after the village fiesta because that gave me more time to spend training and writing.

I decided to dedicate mornings to physical training and evenings to writing. I assigned myself to write daily from 5:00 pm to 7:30 pm in the dining hall where I could peacefully write to my loved ones and work on my journal. I wrote letters each day to my wife and family and a day did not go by without my posting at least one letter. I received letters every day except Sundays; there was no mail on Sundays. Letters arrived for me and I often saw them on the pile on the duty screw's desk. He would eventually hand out the mail to his paisanos but accidentally drop mine behind his desk and tell me I had none. This happened often and the racist prick would give me my mail the following morning with a smirk on his waxy face - loathsome bastards.

I devised a training routine to enable me to do two hours of physical jerks and one hour of martial arts training. I threw myself into this training regime with so much gusto that I gave myself aches and pains I had not had since playing rugby as a teenager. I persevered and worked through the pain, which went away after just a few days. I piled on extra press-ups and abdominal exercises to improve my endurance and enhance my waistline with a bristling six-pack. I used bottles of water in lieu of weights to do exercises to improve punching power and sustain a long barrage of punching. This hard training was watched by prisoners and screws with much interest and enhanced my standing as the deadly Brit.

The Spanish do not like the idea of retaliation when they attack someone; hence the reason why Spanish bullfighters never play with bulls that have not already been wounded and weakened before they face them.

I held my head up in that place and intimidators and liberty takers avoided me because I retaliated mercilessly. I enjoyed my status as the lone Brit who taught martial arts - the lunatic Brit, the deadly Brit, who never backed down no matter the odds. If pride was a sin then I was a sinner because the inhuman treatment that robbed one of one's pride in prison did not work on me. In fact my individualism, like my serious training and aggressive martial arts teaching, my mass of fair hair, my 'good morning' instead of 'buenos dias', my table manners, and my military bearing made me stick out from the crowd. My pugnacious and assertive attitude was my outer defence that deterred would-be intimidators. My formidable skills in violence together with an ability to inflict harrowing nerve-shattering pain were my outer defences, which gave me my jodido loco Inglese, fucking lunatic Englishman, reputation in six Spanish prisons. Yes, I was a sinner and proud to have been the deadly Brit in that Spanish pisshole.

Ramon was my nextdoor neighbour in cell No: 51. He was tall and slim with broad shoulders and muscular arms. His handsome face was framed by masses of black curly hair and his dark eyes were chillingly flat and evil. He was fit and exercised daily. I reckoned he was about thirty-five years of age and if I was the jodido loco Inglese, he was the jodido loco Espanol. He was always cheerful and well mannered with me, but with his paisanos and Arabs he was vigorously hostile.

"Good morning, good morning. Berry good, berry good!" he said, every time he met me regardless the time of day.

He often sat with me as I wrote and I must admit I enjoyed the distraction as he told me stories about himself. His crimes were kidnapping and bank robbery. He kidnapped the bank manager of the bank he robbed and received a twelve stretch for his troubles. His twelve-year sentence was subsequently reduced and so he had only two years to serve. The reason for the sentence reduction was because he was certified insane. I thought he was play acting, just like another prisoner was play acting in there, but when I saw him sink his teeth into Lucien's throat and try to eat his Adam's apple, I knew he was for real.

Lucien was a Moroccan who had lived in Paris most of his life. He stupidly tried to cheat Ramon at dominoes. From where I was writing in the dining hall I could see the domino game through the barred gate of the sala. I was busy writing when the rumpus of dominoes clattering across the floor of the sala distracted me. I quickly looked up to see Ramon yank Lucien out of his chair by his ears. Lucien's eyes were wide with fear. Ramon's eyes glittered with madness as he head butted him on the nose, which burst like a tomato, then spun him around and smashed him down backwards on top of the heavy domino table. Ramon pulled Lucien across the table so his head lolled over the edge. He pushed a thumb into Lucien's eye forcing his head down over the edge of the table making his Adam's apple protrude from his stretched throat and attacked it with gnashing teeth as furious animal sounds came from his throat. A chilling scream roared out of Lucien as his blood ran down his neck.

Moroccans would not stand idly by while an infidel was killing one of their own. Jean Pierre Amhouti, another French Moroccan, crashed a chair across Ramon's head as another Moroccan by the name of Daoud grabbed handfuls of Ramon's hair to pull him off Lucien's throat. Blood poured from Lucien's nose and throat as the two were separated and several Arabs closed in on Ramon to start kicking and punching him. Ramon pulled an Arab to him and chomped into his ear, biting clear through it in a trice. Blows rained on him as he grabbed another and bit into his face, taking a mouthful of cheek and tried tearing it from the screaming face. Three screws were quickly on the scene swinging black truncheons. A xylophonic melody rang out as big sticks collided with Arab heads. Ramon went down under a flurry of flailing truncheons. Reinforcements arrived in the form of panting screws carrying big sticks and everyone involved, including a few spectators were herded out of the room and taken down the block where they spent the night. Lucien was treated at the enfermeria before being taken to solitary.

The next day at 5:00 pm the cells were unlocked as usual and as I came out, I received the usual greeting.
"Good morning, good morning. Berry good, berry good!"

Libertad

There was a Moroccan prisoner who had to be assisted everywhere he went. His name was Tariq and he was caught driving a van with two hundred kilos of Morocco's best herb. He was fine until he was sentenced and sent to Daroca, where he suddenly developed a shuffling gait and a stoop. Apparently he had undergone all the relevant tests and the experts could find nothing wrong with him.

I watched him day after day and he was a bloody good actor. It took him and his assistant one minute to walk thirty feet; they never changed pace even when it was pissing down. His assistant was a fellow inmate who was paid one hundred euros per month to share his cell and help him do the things people did to get through each day. He was a pathetic sight to see but nobody there showed pity for him. Not even his countrymen helped him; they all knew he was acting. He showered every other day and his assistant set a chair under a water tap in the shower block. He sat under the tap as his assistant poured shampoo and shower gel on him. The wet tiles were quite slippery and many able-bodied men slipped and fell in there, but I never saw him slip or stumble. Hmm.

The sun shone brightly and glistened on the beads of sweat running down our faces. We crunched the final set of fifty sit-ups before a two-minute deep breathing exercise. The warm up physical jerks were over so we practised kicks, blocks and punches before practising attack techniques. Tough workouts are Zen to violent prisoners. Hard men thrive on the ability to focus on exercise that takes them to their endurance threshold. I often took an exercise to failure - to collapse unable to perform another repetition, to lie gasping on the floor unable to do another press-up or sit-up. I did this each day and though my midriff was like a sheet of steel, I still challenged the previous day's effort. I started the abs routine with leg raises and worked through several variations of stomach exercises so that the final sit-ups amounted to over a thousand reps of abdominal stress. I did this each day of the week, hail, rain or shine. Other prisoners joined in the workouts but only the true hard men stayed the course and I told you who they were. The Spanish could not hack it and those that tried fell by the wayside. Besides, I did not teach martial arts to Spaniards because they were all wife beaters or nonces, apart from Ramon.

We were practising chokes when my name was called on the tannoy. I wiped my sweaty face with my towel and shrugged on a dry vest. The duty screw was beckoning me to hurry. I took my towel to dab the oozing sweat from my brow and entered the screws' office to see Marivi the social worker. Dressed in an ankle length white chiffon dress, she looked quite cool and reminded me of Madonna the singer. She smiled sweetly as three screws stood nearby with sour faces. Handing me a ballpoint pen she asked me to sign some papers she had brought. My cellmate Mike Sherman was standing nearby and as his Spanish was far superior to mine I called Mike over to translate. It was my freedom paper and I was to be expelled from Spain on 4th September 2007. It was 28th June so that left me just two months to serve in Satan's arena. I gleefully signed the papers and shook the hand of the grinning Marivi.

I returned to my combat class in the yard and told the questioning faces about my Libertad. Backslapping and handshakes all round and then I told them I needed to sit alone and think for a while. They continued training while I looked on from a shaded bench. The relief of pending liberty was a profound feeling of joy that only a prisoner can feel, but a similar response to the news must be felt by prisoners' wives and families who suffered the loss of their loved one over long periods of time. Thoughts crowded my brain. How would it happen? Would they fly me to the UK or take me to the French border? Thoughts were piling up. I knew sleep would be difficult that night.

Another prisoner sat down next to me on the bench and interrupted my thoughts.

"Dame cigaro amigo," he said, in a demanding tone.

I looked into the cold grey eyes of a Spanish nonce. He could be a child's grandfather with his white hair, moustache and beard. His name was Jesus and he was so badly thought of in there other prisoners referred to him as the Maricon de mierda (homosexual turd) which is a term of intense vituperation reserved for the most depraved homosexuals. Sitting next to me was the reason to bring back the noose. This creature had maimed young boys during frenzied sexual assaults. He was in there sharing a cell with another nonce, a fellow homosexual who also preferred children. These two monsters received three meals a day, did no work, and achieved sexual gratification each night in their cell. To achieve sexual gratification they shagged or performed oral sex on each other while visualising the debauchery they had performed on the children. This thing sitting next to me should have been put down like a mad dog. Instead, he would one day be released and, like many others, he would strike again.

The politicians of Europe do nothing to protect the children. They know that sex offenders and child killers are not frightened of the consequences of getting caught. There is no deterrent. So make one and do something right in your feeble political careers! I will help you. I hereby volunteer to execute all child sex offenders. I would not need ropes or fancy injections, just give me a pistol, one bullet, a refuse sack and a couple of bin men. I sometimes think about the evil Roy White and Ian Huntley, the infamous child sex killers. What do they do for sexual gratification? Of course, they visualise their crimes and masturbate or shag their cellmates then go for a game of pool or watch the telly. The victims' families suffer because they know this happens with these creatures, this is why they should be put to death, and besides it's cheaper. I often wonder why people in Parliament and other high office such as judges and ministers find excuses not to execute these demons? They know it is the only deterrent.

As I looked into the evil face of the Spick nonce, his shaggy eyebrows and scruffy beard reminded me of a sheep's arse. His breath smelled like the inside of a bin man's glove and my urge to commit murder was overwhelming. The evil head suddenly lurched away from me under the impact of Sergey's monstrous fist colliding with his ear, converting it into a cauliflower and rattling the brain inside the skull so violently it caused a concussion. Checking the security cameras were not looking our way, we quickly scooped him up and rushed him into the nearby shower block. We dumped him into the cubicle furthest away from the entrance and as I turned away I heard a loud crack as Sergey stomped the slumped nonce. I later heard he had a couple of cracked ribs. I hardly slept that night because I thought the nonce would implicate me in his injuries, but heroin was discovered in his blood and the medical orderlies loathed the Maricon de mierda so nothing came of it.

On Friday 13th July 2007 I received a letter from Andrew Cox the British pro-consul in Barcelona. He informed me that the prison authorities told him I would be taken from Daroca on or about the 4th September to the French border. This was good news because my wife was waiting for me at our house in Lezignan Corbieres in the south of France. All I needed to do was plod on with my fitness regime and keep out of trouble.

My days were now taken up with training all morning in the yard and then taking a shower before feeding time at 1:00 pm. After the pandemonium of feeding time the metal trays were counted and we were herded upstairs to our cells. Mike my cellmate was always ten minutes later coming up because he was a destino and mopped the sala floor after feeding time, but he was destined for better things. He was chosen to take charge of the economato, the best job in the prison. I was pleased for Mike, he deserved a break, especially as I was leaving shortly. The new job would be good for his morale.

My other friend Sergey the Russian fell foul of the screws. He thought he was fireproof after demolishing the Maricon de mierda and went on to batter a few gypsies. He was under observation when he had a problem with Alf the mad Algerian. Alf was so called because he looked like Alf the creature from Mars in the American comedy series. Alf was a six-footer with ginger hair and milky white skin; an albino Arab with a peanut brain and a hidden pinchou, but his weapon did not have shit smeared on the tip. I was doing my abdominal routine when I heard a shout. Sergey and Misha, a fellow Russian, were jogging around the yard when Alf lumbered into them accidentally. Sergey pushed him out of the way and Alf sprawled on the concrete floor of the yard. Alf responded by pulling out his pinchou from his sock and lunged at Sergey whilst still on all fours. The cruel spike sliced into Sergey's heel, causing an inch long gash just above the leather of his running shoe. The wound was deep but did not prevent the tremendous downward punch from Sergey's big, hard fist opening Alf's eyebrow like a letterbox - this terrible punch was followed by three more heavy blows as his face came apart around his left eye. The open flesh of the eyebrow hung down over the eye pouring blood into the second open wound beneath the eye where the flesh had broken on the cheekbone ridge of the eye socket.

The spick grasses were on their way to the screws' office but the screws had been watching anyway and were quickly on the scene with big sticks. Sergey and Alf were taken to the enfermeria before being taken to islamiento.[124] From there they were probably moved to different wings. I never saw Sergey again.

On Thursday 26th July 2007 Jose Louis the king of the gypsies died at 5:00 am in his cell. His eldest son, Louis, shared the cell with his father and was now tearfully mourning his father. Apparently he had had a heart attack. His wife told him the day before that she was fed up with everything and was leaving the family home to start again with the new man in her life. Jose Louis had no knowledge of the new man and everyone said the shock killed him. Jose Louis and his son had spent thirteen years in prison for killing his son-in-law who was a wife beater. He regularly battered Jose Louis' daughter until one day he broke her jaw and knocked her front teeth out. Jose Louis and his son went round to his house and killed him. Father and son were due for release on parole that year. Tough shit Jose Louis.

I had just finished my workout and was relaxing in the sunshine in the yard when Oswaldo, a hard-case Venezuelan joined me at my table. He knew I was leaving in September and wanted to keep in touch with me. He had family in London and wanted me to have dealings with them. Oswaldo was a bit of a lad. He was caught with three tonnes of cocaine in the Atlantic Ocean one thousand miles south of the Canary Islands. He was skippering a thirty-metre trawler named *Poseidon 1*, when the famous Spanish Customs ship the *Petrel* captured him and his eight-man crew in rough seas. It happened on 4th July 2003 at 3:00 am when two Zodiac RIBS manned by armed

---

[124] islamiento - solitary confinement

commandos overtook and boarded *Poseidon 1*. The *Petrel* took them to the Spanish port of Vigo in Galicea. At their trial they each received a nine-year sentence. And now Oswaldo wanted me to meet his relatives in London with a view to setting up another cocaine operation. I went along with his wishes because, being a big softie at heart, I liked to give men something to look forward to for when they got out. Besides, I liked Oswaldo. He was a brave mariner and he took no shit from the gypsies.

A man called Arturo was Oswaldo's big pal. He was a gentle giant and possibly the biggest man in the prison. He spoke a bit of English having lived in Hammersmith in London. He was also doing a nine stretch for hauling cocaine from Colombia to Spain. He joined me on my table in the dining hall on the day Nutmeg got his Libertad. It was Saturday 28th July 2007.

"I am glad the maricon has gone," he said, in his heavily accented voice.

"So am I," I said, looking into his smiling face.

For a big man he was softly spoken and had a very kind nature, which belied his incredible power and ferocious skills at tearing apart people who mistook his kind nature for weakness, more often than not a gypsy. Arturo often sat with me for a chat and to practise his English. As usual he brought me a coffee and a biscuit.

"Am I in your book?" he asked, grinning.

"You are now!' I chuckled, as I scribbled the word Arturo at the top of the page.

It was at that moment a wounded bird hit Arturo's face and fell wriggling onto the table between his massive hands. He quickly but gently closed his hands around the bird as another hand tried to grab it. It was the hand of Prudencio Sotoca, better known as the Inuit because he looked just like an Eskimo. He was a big man with a tiny brain and was a mindless bully. Reaching for the bird he plucked it easily from Arturo's grasp because Arturo knew the bird would die if he held on to it. A cry of triumph echoed in the dining hall as the Inuit hurled the injured bird at his gypsy pals, who in turn started kicking it around the floor between the tables of the comedor. A trickle of blood ran down Arturo's cheek from where the bird's beak had nicked it, but that was not the reason for Arturo's bloodlust, as he launched himself from the bench to slam his monstrous knuckles into the Inuit's throat. Sotoca dropped like a corpse in the aisle between the tables and lay there like a sleeping Eskimo as Arturo tore into the gypsies. I moved quickly to join Arturo and watch his back, but I could only look on redundantly as he floored three gypsies with his flailing sledgehammer fists. Their faces were battered and bleeding and someone's tooth was embedded in Arturo's knuckles. Arturo picked up the nearly dead bird and gently put it in the large pouch pocket of his fleece top, he then stooped over the Inuit and battered his face with a flurry of very hard punches. The Inuit would remember this day for a very long time. Arturo kept the bird in his cell and to my knowledge it was still there in Daroca in very safe hands.

August arrived and Spain went to sleep for a month. I increased my workload regarding physical training and built up my abdominal routine to two thousand repetitions of mixed sit-ups, crunches, leg raises and martial arts exercises to improve my core and endurance. My workouts were now taking over three hours to perform, but I was thriving on the effort and feeling really pleased with the results of my diet and exercise regime. I took to reading more books instead of writing and, as my time to leave drew near I found I could no longer concentrate on my journal and my attention span decreased so much, I found that I had to spend my time exercising to pass the time.

September arrived and I was informed that I would not be going to France. I would be expelled from Spain directly to the UK and escorted to Madrid to be put on a flight to Heathrow. I had sent my final letters to my wife and family so the last few days were spent training during the day and reading at night. I had my sports bag packed in readiness for my exit and Mike knew who to give my surplus kit to. Oswaldo was to get my trainers and the rest of my clothing was for my Moroccan friends. Mike had my books.

The 4th September arrived and nothing happened. The cruel bastards had me believing that I was to be free that day. I felt more and more nervous as the day wore on. I expected to be called to ingreso for processing out but nothing happened. My wife and family expected me to arrive in England. My wife had travelled from France to meet me. She was waiting for me in London. Oh, you fucking lousy Spanish bastards, I should have known better than to tell my family when to expect me.

That night Mike consoled me as best he could. He knew I was distraught though I tried not to show it. We talked into the night and I must have fallen asleep because at 5:00 am the cell door was pulled open and the duty screw woke me up to tell me I had ten minutes to get out of my cell and downstairs to meet my escorts to Madrid. I quickly washed and shaved, gave Mike a big hug and quietly left the cell. Creeping silently along the corridor as everyone slept I was pleasantly surprised to hear a chorus of goodbyes from behind the closed cell doors of my Moroccan friends. How the hell did they know it was I creeping past their doors? Suddenly, everyone was shouting, "Fuck off!" because that was the only English I had taught them - one of the few times in my life that I enjoyed being told to fuck off.

The duty screw escorted me to ingreso to be processed out and to meet my police escorts. The duty screw simply said, "Adios," and disappeared back to his lair. I was quickly fingerprinted and had my photo taken. A female screw appeared with the money that was in my peculio. She gave me my money and my passport, looked at the policeman and policewoman escorts and said, "Buenas dias. Adios!" then waddled away along the corridor without another word.

A big iron gate opened electronically and there was my chariot to freedom, a small police car. My bag was thrown in the boot and I was locked in the rear seat for the ride to Barajas airport in Madrid. The car moved forward to negotiate further gates before we actually burst out into the glorious sunshine of early morning Spain. Clear of the final prison gate the car sped off toward the village of Daroca. Looking back at the prison, it seemed to disappear underground as the car drove along the ascending road to freedom. I had survived in Satan's arena and I was going home.

I was escorted onto Iberia Flight 3164 to Heathrow and was first on the aircraft. I left Spain at 1:15 pm on 5th September 2007. On arrival at Heathrow three plain-clothes officers promptly arrested me because the Spanish had not deleted the International Arrest Warrant. It was still live on European computers. Realising the eternal incompetence of the Spanish, the British police cleared me within twenty minutes. The Home Office terminated the arrest warrant and had my name removed from European computers.

I walked out of Heathrow after first telephoning my wife and family to tell them I was on home ground. I caught a bus to St. Albans in Hertfordshire where I met my wife at the railway station and held her in my arms for a very long time. At last a free man.

About The Author

I decided to write my bio in a more personal form because my previous books all have my biography in much the same format but obviously this changes with the addition of another book. So here is a bit more of me and, this time I have got loads more to tell you.

My writing career started in prison where I kept a daily journal, which I continued throughout my prison life. I wrote as events unfolded. So hopefully you will understand the anti-French and anti-Spanish sentiment that was created due to the often brutal and racist treatment I received from prison officers and inmates alike. Fortunately, I have put all that behind me now and discovered that my writing proved to be therapeutic and saved me from probable mental health issues.

I had to re-live all of my horrifying experiences and found that documenting them was like getting it off my chest, which through much re-writing from my journals and needing to make for easy reading and the tide of bile and hatred receding, brought about the therapeutic normality I needed to keep my sanity. I must also add that being a martial artist provided me with the spiritual and physical strength to survive many unpleasant situations.

Another positive aspect of my experiences is being asked by people with family members held in French or Spanish prisons how to survive, or even recover when they come home. Soldiers ask much the same questions of me. I explain that I am not a shrink and totally unqualified to offer assistance other than writing their experiences in book form, which hopefully provides them with the therapeutic effect it had on me. Oh, and you never know your luck, you may get published just like I did. Maybe I have lessened the affects of PTSD in some of them, who knows?

Education: SS John Fisher and Thomas More School, Widnes, Cheshire.
Corp of Royal Engrs: EPC (Adv) English; Maths, Unit admin, Communication skills, RAEC German language,
RAEC Instructional technology.
Combat Engr grade 1.
Driver RE grade 1.
SASC Weapons Instructor.
Joint Services Intelligence Wing: Resistance to Interrogation Instructor.

I am a 4th dan (black belt) karate and ju-jitsu instructor.
I was the World Combat Federation Representative for Spain and Portugal.
Member of International Budo Association: 4th dan ju-jitsu.
Member of FALMA *Departamento Nacional Buguei* Spain. (Black belt)

2002: returned to UK and started my writing career.

I have two books published by Penguin/ Random House Group (Mainstream).
Titles: THE LONE BRIT ON 13 and CARABANCHEL.

My third book, THE ASSASSINS CODE 1, published by Strand Publishing UK. (I retained the Film Rights for this work). The screenplay is ready for pitching and is available from my agent or directly from me, as are all of my screenplays.

My fourth book BENEATH THE POPPY FIELDS published by Strand Publishing UK. (I retained the Film Rights for this work.)

My fifth book SATAN'S ARENA published by Strand Publishing UK. (I retained the Film Rights for this work because I intend writing a docu-series, which includes all of the twelve piss-holes in which I was incarcerated, one where I was manacled in irons.)

I have eight completed screenplays and a four-part TV series ready for pitching. One of my screenplays is "optioned." Also, I have a two-part TV series of one hour each part ready for pitching.

I was a guest on several national radio shows and appeared on various TV shows.

RAW TV produced THE DAREDEVIL DRUG RUNNER for National Geographic, which is currently being screened worldwide. I am the subject and narrator of this one-hour show. The actor Mark Wingett plays me.

My current project is to complete the Arrowsmith trilogy:
THE ASSASSINS CODE1, MOTHERLAND, BLOWN
This is the adaptation from screenplays to books, which is a hell of a challenge that I am about to enjoy. I know because THE ASSASSINS CODE 1 was one such challenge - one book down and two to go! I am eternally grateful to Strand Publishing UK who have agreed to publish MOTHERLAND and BLOWN to complete the trilogy.

Chris Chance - Contact Info, Agent, Manager | IMDbPro
My website is: www.chrischance.co.uk
My work and trailers can be viewed on my website.

AVAILABLE FROM STRAND PUBLISHING UK LTD

The Strand Book Of Memorable Maxims - ISBN 9781907340000
The First Casualty by J Adam & MA Akbar - ISBN 9781907340031
The Challenge of Reality by Bashir Mahmood - ISBN 9781907340048
The Path Of The Gods by Joseph Geraci - ISBN 9781907340055
The Strand Book of International Poets 2010 – ISBN 9781907340062
The Assassins Code 1 by Christopher Chance -ISBN 9781907340123
Tragedy Of Deception by Humayun Niaz – ISBN 9781907340130
Marie Antoinette, Diana & Alexandra: The Third I by Alexandra Levin – ISBN 9781907340161
The Box by Clive Parker-Sharp – ISBN 9781907340154
Storm Over Kabul by Imran Hanif – ISBN 9781907340208
Rhubarb And Aliens by Paul Hutchens – ISBN 9781907340215
The Deceit Syndrome by Dr Paul Hobday – ISBN 9781907340222
The Curse Of Beckett's Wood by R.E. Witham – ISBN 9781907340246
Beneath The Poppy Fields by Christopher Chance – ISBN 9781907340253
Satan's Arena by Christopher Chance – ISBN 0781907340260

For more information about our books and services visit the Strand Publishing UK website - https://strandpublishing.co.uk
Follow our Blog page - https://strandpublishing.co.uk/blog
Watch editorial and authors' videos via the Youtube channel: https://www.youtube.com/channel/UC41tg7SqMwPQGcS7aLDkUDw/videos

All our books are available to order online direct from the publisher Strand Publishing UK via the website – https://strandpublishing.co.uk/shop
Also Amazon.co.uk and Amazon.com, Kalahari.com, WH Smiths, Waterstones, Blackwells, Ingrams, Gardeners, and from all good booksellers and libraries
Follow #strandpublishuk on Facebook; and Twitter @strandpublishuk; and Strand Publishing UK on Instagram and LinkedIn

Visit the Lightning Source website or read the link below for further information on our Environmental Responsibilities.
https://help.lightningsource.com/hc/en-us/articles/115001410043-Environmental-Responsibility

www.ingramcontent.com/pod-product-compliance
Lightning Source LLC
Chambersburg PA
CBHW071146160426
43196CB00011B/2022